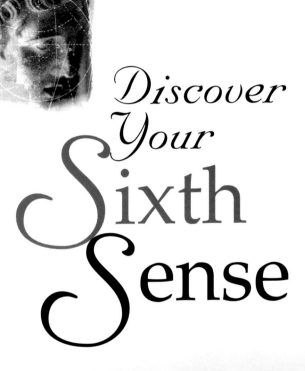

Discover
Your
Sixth
Sense

Discover Your Sixth Sense

Julie Soskin

CARROLL & BROWN PUBLISHERS LIMITED

*The practical guide
to developing your
psychic skills*

Contents

Intuition explored 8

Chapter 1 10
Background to spiritual self-development

Chapter 2 26
Where science and spirit meet

Chapter 3 42
Stage one: foundation for spiritual self-development

Chapter 4 72
Stage two: unfoldment of the spirit

Chapter 5 96
Stage three: psychic sensitivity

Chapter 6 118
Stage four: integration of self

Chapter 7 138
The self and tarot revealed

Psychic powers revealed 162

Introduction   164

Chapter 1   170
Discover your psychic potential

Chapter 2   206
Extra-sensory perception

Chapter 3   234
Psychic tools

Chapter 4   262
Psychic healing

Chapter 5   296
Encountering spirits

Chapter 6   312
Psychic protection

Chapter 7   320
Higher consciousness

Index   330
Acknowledgments and references   335

Intuition explored

Chapter 1

Background to spiritual self-development

In this chapter there are some current theories about

spiritual self-awareness and the various definitions of

terms and processes most commonly linked with it.

Important concepts include attunement to subtle healing

energies and communication with spirit both within and

outside the self.

The journey to self

Spiritual development can be seen as an adventure, one where the individual is the hero or heroine of his or her own life. Like most adventures, it takes courage to embark on it, as it requires honesty and an exploration of self and, like any gripping story, it will have its good and bad times. Often the process may feel as though you are opening a "Pandora's box" with no idea of what you may find inside. Yet many students of spiritual development express that they feel an inner pull, a vital need to explore, wherever it may lead. In a sense, spiritual discovery is about the very meaning of life, not just the roles we play – such as being a mother or father, the work we do or the status we hold in society – but who we truly are. It encompasses deep questions about the meaning of life and living and as such could be described as the greatest and most important journey of all. The spiritual pathway is not for the faint hearted but it is not just hard work; it is also fun, exciting and joyful. The value of this voyage of discovery is also the adventure itself. What will happen? What will I find? Who will I become? It can be a challenging and a deeply rewarding task.

Because by its nature it revolves around the self, any true development has to be experiential. In other words, we have to live it; not in our head, mind, or even our heart, but in the reality of every hour of every day. Like any relationship, getting to know a person is enthralling and exciting and what better person to get to know than oneself? The journey is a process of unfoldment of self, uncovering the extraneous aspects of the individual so he or she is taken deeper into his or her real core, essence or spirit.

In the first part of this book, I look at the meaning of the associated concepts and background to spirituality. I explore constructs and theories that are currently being propounded in spiritual literature and science. Contemporary methods of spiritual development recognize the needs of the individual and how he or she understands his or her own truth, so the book is interspersed with authentic experiences from students of their own spiritual processing.

This book does not set out to convert anyone to any set of beliefs; contemporary spirituality is cross-culture and religion. It does, however, ask us to look at our beliefs, mind-sets and any patterns that may no longer serve. It is important to question everything. What might work for another person may not work for you, and that does not mean something is right or wrong. In one sense there is no right and wrong, only the truth of who you are. We are all different, with different perspectives on life. These have been brought about by our upbringing, education, the society in which we live and our individual experiences, which are unlikely to tally completely with those of any other living soul. Therefore, the spiritual journey is completely individual. Written on the ancient Greek Oracle at Delphi were the words "Know thyself". To do this requires integrity of one's truth and yet many people do not even know what their real truth is, but go blindly through life. This book can be taken on many different levels but its aim is to promote thought and explore spiritual perspectives; where that leads is up to you.

Spirituality

Spiritual generally relates to the non-physical, and can be thought of as a state that lies beyond physical reality. Spirituality can also refer to an awareness of one's inner self, and a sense of connection to a higher energy or power. It might be perceived to be associated with religion, but need not be connected to any. It has been described as the way we orient ourselves towards the divine, and is also described as a personal connection to the universe. Conversely, religion could be described as a doctrinal framework that guides sacred beliefs and practices, helping to structure the way people worship. Being spiritual does not necessitate having any set faith or model; indeed, the ambiguous nature of the concept is often taken to mean something outside religious context, referring to ultimate meanings and values in life.

There are various differing opinions on the meaning of spirituality but one of the commonalities in recent literature is that there is a difference between religion and spirituality. Religion means to tie together and is therefore seen as the organization of spirituality and facilitates making meaning of our world. Religion usually has a set structure that teaches people about God ("universal light force energy" or "all that is") and the way in which to live their lives. Therefore, it need not be a personal lived experience but a set of values to underpin society, life and living.

In the context used within this work, spiritual is not confined to any particular religion or dogma, but rather it is used according to its dictionary definition, from the Latin word spiritus; spirit, the essential or core part of the person. Every individual, regardless of his or her culture, is thought to have a core part of self, which is considered to be the highest aspect of self. Spirituality is thought to be realized through personal encounters and experiences of a sacred or divine presence. This concept is integral to psycho-spiritual practices and in this sense learning is achieved, not just in the head or even the heart, but in the reality of the lived world of the individual.

Spirit might be thought of as the vital life force, which motivates people and influences life, health, behaviour and relationships. However, spirituality is not just thought to be an inner quality. It also can be a way of understanding your relationship and connection to something outside of your self that provides meaning.

Although individuals may identify the spiritual sense as something that could be either an external or internal experience, these do not have to be mutually exclusive. In spiritual development, the individual is usually thought to link to a higher power, which is generally accessed through the deepest core of self; however, there also can be a connection with a higher power outside the self.

Acclaimed biologist Alister Hardy, drawing from the fields of psychology, animal behaviour, psychic research and anthropology, propounds the hypothesis that: "Spirituality is natural to the human species and has evolved because it has biological survival value." Evolving might suggest some form of purpose in the process, but Hardy seems to imply that there is a direct intuitive awareness that is ever-present or innate. This is a contentious issue, which is similar to the thorny question of whether "nature or nurture" makes the difference. Are the building blocks of spirituality within us at birth or do they develop? If the definition of spirituality is that we all have a "core" or essential part of self, it follows that spirituality is present in everyone and, like all our faculties, it therefore has the potential to be developed. In recent years, the notion of spirituality has begun to emerge outside any set structures and refers to profound inner experiences that could be characterized by such traits as awareness, energy, depth, understanding of self, a holistic outlook, intuition, courage, acceptance and love. It also could be described as that which implements the growth of positive and creative values in the human existence.

In the past 10 years we have seen an explosion of interest in diverse disciplines including education, religion, psychology, health, healing and the arts. It seems there is personal desire to get in touch with something more, something beyond the personal self, and this has spilled over into the media. It is now common to see these subjects covered in lifestyle articles and magazines. Some of these are un-authenticated and somewhat superficial; however, in the last few years there has been increased intelligent debate and discussion about the whole area and this is encouraging the emergence of spirituality as part of the mainstream agenda.

Although this book defines spirituality as the core and essence of a person, it seems likely that any common definitive meaning will continue to be elusive because of the personal nature of spirituality.

EXPERIENCE

" I had many years of addiction and although I was able to hold down a very demanding job it was eating into me. I was in a dark, fearful void and I was not living a life that was real or true to myself. Through spiritual practices in therapy I came to look at the deeper areas of self. For me, spirituality is being at one, with me and the rest of the world. It's looking at life from my authentic self, from my soul. The way that I look at life is from a much richer perspective today because before I would look at life just from the personality and now I don't look at life quite the same, I look at life from the deeper level of my soul and that's what I feel to be my spirituality. I have shifted, it's just a different way that I look at life. I see people at a much more deeper level — at a soul level.

I remember looking yesterday at a friend as a human being with so much richness and joy. My job as a crime officer took me into areas of meeting people who were very dark, but now I can look at people differently and my vision is only out of goodness and not looking for what they may or may not do or who they are or what they have done. I see them and I go right to the core of them. I also see much deeper into many things: pictures, nature and trees. You can actually see them in a different way, you can hear the music of a tree, you can hear the music in water dripping, you can hear sounds that you never thought you could hear, just in the silence. You can hear the world can't you? It's good isn't it? "

Contemporary spirituality

Spiritual concepts relate to qualities of life that go beyond the ordinary physical and material states – the feeling that there is something more to life. Religions have social structures and officials such as priests and elders to ensure the purity and propriety of practice. Contemporary spirituality, on the other hand, depends on the experiential journey of encounter and relationship with others – powers and forces beyond the scope of everyday life. To be spiritual is to be open to more than just the material in life, and to expect to encounter and nurture a relationship with it.

Many orthodox believers feel that finding your own spiritual truth outside a religious context is not desirable, for where is the comfort of the society, the followers and practices that have been built up over hundreds and thousands of years? Religions offer support to the community, often holding society together, and the people involved have grown and progressed as a result of their shared culture. Nonetheless, although religions and religious leaders may give support to their own "tribes" and advise moral ethics, unfortunately they also have used their ideals and teachings as excuses to carry out awful things in the name of religion. Due to the global media these incidents have become evident and have led to an increasing suspicion that religions have not always got things right. Many religious people who claim they may be ready to die for their cause may not be prepared to live in peace and harmony with their neighbours. Contemporary spirituality, however, demands authenticity, a need to "live" your beliefs, not be told what they should be.

Generally, contemporary spiritual self-development practices do not stipulate that the student has to follow any particular belief system. Rather they are sympathetic and tolerant towards any tradition, faith or religion that aids the individual in his or her spiritual progress. These practices do, however, encourage the mystical notion of the transcendence of human understanding and the ability of the individual to communicate directly with a higher force. They also propound that spiritual unfoldment is possible for everyone.

If the whole area of spirituality is not necessarily within a set model or structure, we no longer have to be nuns, monks or priests to access greater spiritual truths. We can become our own priest or priestess. In some ways, this makes the task harder. If you are cloistered from society it may be easier to concentrate on the spiritual aspects of self than if you have to bring your truth into the material world, your work place, and relations with family, friends and lovers. Without any set models, who is going to tell us what is right? We are now being asked to come of age spiritually, to make our own decisions and to take responsibility for them.

Spiritual psychology

Roberto Assagioli developed a form of spiritual or "transpersonal" psychology, which he labelled "Psychosynthesis". He maintained that we all possess a super-consciousness described as the "psyche", which contains our deepest potential, the source of the unfolding pattern of our unique human path of development. This super-consciousness or deeper aspect of self continually invites us to levels of healing and wholeness, hence the prefix "trans", which means beyond or above, in this case, the personal state of an individual. Transpersonal psychology can be applied to the entire spectrum of human experience; it honours the spiritual dimension of self and the deep human need for transcendental experiences.

The psychological and the spiritual might be interwoven and often cannot be separated; therefore individuals need to be seen as "psycho-spiritual units". Indeed, the words "psycho-spiritual" can be used as an alternative to "transpersonal". Psycho-spiritual and transpersonal work takes account of the fact that individuals may have aspects of self that mask deep spiritual connection and that they need to unfold, and possibly dissolve, unhelpful aspects of self to allow greater contact with the spirit within. Some of this work, therefore, necessitates looking at more psychological aspects of who we are or who we think we are. We can then loosen negative patterns so they melt away and allow us contact with the divine within.

EXPERIENCE

"At the beginning, spirituality was quite a flaky word for me because you know, it's kind of trendy. But I learnt about the shadow and the light side of me, about accepting both sides of me, about neither being good or bad, about integrating the whole part of me, looking at both sides of who I am instead of saying that's the bit I present to the world but these are my other little bits that I don't want anybody else to know about or to see, and I don't have to suppress them anymore because it is all part of me. I used to look at life, good or bad, right or wrong, black or white, in many ways, well I don't do that now."

The main focus of psycho-spirituality in this book is the development of spiritual self-awareness, and in common with transpersonal psychology it deals with aspects of the individual beyond the personal state. However, although there are many similarities between transpersonal and psycho-spiritual practices, not every transpersonalist openly embraces the worth of subtle energies, intuition and the psychic, nor do they always utilize them as an integral part of their learning. Psycho-spirituality can draw on and acknowledge practices outside the psychology remit, such as ancient rituals, meditation, chanting and yoga.

If spirituality is innate within us how can we access it? We may need different means to look at this form of learning. People often speak of a feeling of being called or pushed with some sense of knowing. But how do we connect with this deeper sense of knowing and of what quality is this knowing? Because it is unseen and often unexplainable, it therefore requires something other than our normal means of learning.

The "sense of knowing" can be described as an unseen or intuitive sense. Developing and trusting the intuition can, therefore, be a positive advantage in the unfoldment of the spiritual self. Real intuitive spiritual work is not so much concerned with accumulating information as understanding one's own spirituality experientially. There has to be a real experience, the student has to be observant and then, by recognizing difficulties and how they manifest in his or her life, the individual is able to make changes. This is unfoldment. Later on, I will be demonstrating some useful transpersonal exercises to assist spiritual growth.

EXPERIENCE

"You spoke about what will was and it was suddenly my turning point. I started to think about what my true intentions really were and some of them were quite shocking but I remember thinking this is exactly how to get the balance between my will and my emotions, integration of the heart and the mind, which previously was all 'gobbley gook' to me because I was too emotionally based. My emotions were overwhelming and powerful and I was 'out of sync'. So what I learnt was, clarification and the act of will, that was a revelation and I now have a much better understanding of who I am."

Spiritual self-awareness

The English dictionary has a long list of definitions related to the self, which describe emotional, mental, physical or spiritual aspects. In the last 20 years, the vast growth in self-help groups and therapies has turned self into jargon. In psycho-spiritual studies, the spiritual aspect of self is regarded as the higher aspect of self. However, the term "higher self" is itself confusing because "higher self" also can be seen as the innate, core and soul aspect of self, which is also referred to as the inner self, nature or being. Conversely, the lower layers of self include the more mundane or known aspects, i.e. the social, emotional, mental, psychological, ego or personality selves and, in contrast with the higher self, they do not necessarily make contact with the essence, spirit or soul of the person. The concept of the self in many Western cultures is generally that of the outer layers of personality and not the true inner layers. However, psychologists such as Jung, Assagioli, Rogers and Maslow have sought to incorporate this "higher" aspect of self within their work. Jung's definition of the higher self is "The God within and the individual in seeking self-realization and unity becomes the means through which God seeks his goal." Jung wrote extensively about the spiritual, seeing it as "infinite spaceless, formless, imageless".

Orthodox faiths are generally uncomfortable with what they see as self-serving spirituality. The word "self" is often regarded negatively and thought to mean selfish. The word "self" might be deemed contrary to the Christian exhortation to "love thy neighbour", but this ignores the next part of the phrase, which is, "as thyself". The emphasis on compassion for the weak often ignores the positive aspects within us, and can produce dislike for strength. But in spiritual development a strong inner self that comes with maturity is vital. In contemporary spiritual

EXPERIENCE

About 28 years ago, after going through a lot of changes, including dark night of the soul, I felt complete awareness of who I was, complete and total healing and complete love. Up until then I had been experiencing a lot of difficulty, psychic attacks and a lot of confusion, in a sense life was blowing through me and I seemed unable to do anything about it. I was blown around like a leaf in the winds. Up until then I hadn't any experiences, but I was looking for truth, exploring all kinds of interesting avenues. I had no real certainty of anything, until the experience of spiritual development and although things didn't shift over night, it actually gave me a place to work from, to balance everything.

practice, self-respect and self-love are not thought to remove the person from God or higher states of being but rather become the very means by which first-hand communication with a higher power is reached, and from that it is believed that the emancipation of the true inner spirit can occur.

The negative aspects of self are like veils obscuring the true inner nature or highest self, and need to be parted or drawn away as the individual journeys deeper and deeper towards the core of his or her spirit. In this book we will aim to assist this unfoldment process through experiential learning to actualize the reality of yourself as a spiritual being.

Intuition

Intuitive information can be seen as eccentric in nature, as it rarely follows any set pattern. So given the uncertainty of this subject, why choose intuition as a navigator for a spiritual self-development programme? Is it a reliable source of truth? It could be argued there are many better ways to find one's spirituality; following a religious practice, or finding an authentic spiritual teacher, for instance, and these are often part of the spiritual process. However, because of the individual aspect of spirituality, your in(ner) tuition might assist the journey of self. That being the case, this faculty needs to be developed, for like any quality – mental, physical or intellectual – it must be possible for it to be trained.

Many indigenous peoples, prior to Western conquest, worked with what "felt" right. Tribes often existed with an intuitive rapport between their people. Their communication was spontaneous, open and honest. They spoke with truth and it worked because personal feelings were above board and accurately expressed. This, of course, requires transparency in aspiration, interest and desire. Our culture rarely promotes such transparency.

Authentic spiritual self-awareness is thought to require openness. We need therefore to ask what stands between our truths? The educationalist Peters tells us, "Our wishes and fears limit how we see the world ... (they) can lead to windowless tunnel vision, to a peep-hole on the world determined by our own preoccupations".

If fear limits our world, could it cloak our truth, and if so might it affect our communications with our inner being or self? If we throw light on our fears, negative patterns and assumptions, could it bring us closer to our inner selves and enable contact with our inner beings? Accessing intuition is thought to provide a readily accessible decision-making tool which might aid the process of unveiling aspects of our lower self, which cloak the core or true spiritual self. In accessing intuition we get closer to our true inner self.

Paraphrasing Abraham Maslow, Peters suggests our inner nature is cloaked and weak, it persists underground, unconsciously, even though denied and repressed. It speaks softly but it will be heard, even if in a distorted form. It has a dynamic force of its own, always pressing for open uninhibited expression. This force is one main aspect of the will to health, the urge to identity. It is this that makes psychotherapy, education and self improvement possible in principle.

So how can we hear this soft inner voice that is often obscured? Can religious notions guide us through? Can logic discern its elusive nature? Intuition may not be all that is needed for this task but it might give us another valuable tool to access our deeper nature.

Therapy as part of spiritual development

Recently, integrating spirituality and psychotherapy has become a significant area of interest. It is thought that the spiritual path and the therapeutic path do not need to contradict each other, in fact they can complement each other. In this situation the therapist has two roles. One is the role of psychotherapist, the other of spiritual teacher.

One could argue that combining the roles of psychotherapist and priest can present all sorts of problems, not least being that however good the

EXPERIENCE

"This week I had to make a decision on a house move and I was so scared and the fear of it has been far more overwhelming than anything else. As soon as I actually exchanged contracts I had committed, and do you know, the fear went. Because the fear blocked me from getting in touch with my inner self and I couldn't access what my intuition was because it was just fear upon fear upon fear. Actually when I exchanged it was relief and I thought 'well you're committed now so get on with it' and it's the same about embracing intuition. Once you commit, all sorts of miraculous things start to happen to you. I feel as if I have a diamond inside of me now, whereas before I had a gaping hole that was raw and I don't have that anymore."

"My son had a breakdown, which was a form of psychosis through being involved in drugs and working and living abroad and the stresses that can create. The psycho-spiritual work I did had a therapeutic effect as it helped me through my son's breakdown. I'm almost absolutely certain that I would've gone mad if I hadn't had that other life to come away to. I was then able to balance myself and create balance within the structure of the home that I'm sure I wouldn't have been able to do. Previously, I hadn't had that discipline to create light and energy to counteract the chaos that mental illness can produce."

training of the therapist, it might not provide him or her with the disposition to take on the role of priest or spiritual director. Previously, "being spiritual", has been part of both organized religion and contemporary spirituality's concept of learning to be your own teacher. It might lend itself to being used as a therapy. However, it has been suggested that therapists may take the place of communities and relationships that have been lost, and thus better suit the circumstances of the modern world.

Over the last 50 years the upsurge of interest in psychotherapy, together with a much greater awareness of other cultural religious practices, has led to the importance of the person being acknowledged. It is increasingly thought that a more healthy concentration on the self, far from removing the individual from God or spirit, becomes the very means of allowing a first-hand communication with a higher power. The self therefore takes centre stage in our observation and inquiry, and that is why some aspect of psychology may not just be an advantage; it might be a necessity.

Arguably the personality part of yourself is not the core, real or authentic self, and it might mask or confuse our deeper connections, which need careful teasing out with the help of an expert. Psychological inquiry looks at personal meaning, and spiritual practice looks beyond our ordinary human concerns towards the realization of the ultimate. It has been suggested that some form of psychology might assist spiritual practice by helping to shine the light of awareness into all the hidden aspects of our conditioning. This describes some form of loosening effect on the whole psyche, possibly in line with the classic notion of the dissolution of the "veils of illusion" or "unfoldment". In the process of unfoldment there often needs to be a letting go of negativity, which can be psychologically very messy and uncomfortable. This being the case, someone not trained in the psychological process may either be unable to assist or may even exacerbate the problem. I have found that in certain cases some form of therapy alongside spiritual development can be advantageous.

The new age

The New Age Movement gained momentum soon after the Second World War and accelerated into the 1960s. The educationalist Sir George Trevelyan, who had an influential effect in the UK promoting New Age beliefs from the late 1940s up to his death in 1996, stated, "Try to change society without the inner change in man and confusion will be the sole result".

"New age" describes a broad group of contemporary movements, therapies and quasi-religious groups who are seeking personal self-realization. The title "new age" is, however, technically incorrect as most of the practices are not new, but derived from age-old practices. Nonetheless, the movement is generally seen to promote the concept of the importance of self as a way to higher knowledge. Autonomy and freedom are highly valued, and it is felt that authority lies with the experience of the self.

Although some new-age individuals join cults, others also go to church or are interested in Buddhism and other religions. This movement has undoubtedly had a social and cultural effect; and, in the media, it is still common to find references to the new age alongside the 1960s' "anything goes" attitude.

One might therefore question who does the teaching in new age practices. There seems to be an array of candidates, which include those within the Eastern tradition of guru or master, to anyone who wants to set him- or herself up in a workshop.

Criticism of strong guru-type leaders, which have seen some resurgence in new age circles, is that they can set up dependency with ingrained spiritual projection. Facilitator and writer John Heron says, "This can be seen as dubious in the way it is used to legitimate spiritual power over people, by telling them what an impossible, unregenerate mess they are in without direction from those who claim to know the road to liberation". Heron is also critical of Eastern practices and may well be correct that some strict systems are male-dominated. My experience over the last 20 years, however, is that the revival of

ancient practices has been subdued to accommodate Western minds and also, far from being led, or indeed exclusively filled, by males, these systems attract a large percentage of female leaders and many new age writers even actively propound the "Rebirth of the Goddess".

The argument for new age practices is that there is value in the multi-variant spontaneous coming together of different faiths and practices, which puts power in the hands of the individual to find what suits him or her best. However, some new age practices are diverse and unstructured, with little real desire to intelligently examine themselves. Therefore, I share some sympathy with the scepticism towards the more dubious new age practices and I would urge the genuine spiritual seeker to be discerning. Nonetheless, some of the more reputable therapies involved in the new age movement – including homeopathy, naturopathy and spiritual healing – have gone a long way in the last few years to bring themselves in line with professional standards.

EXPERIENCE

I treated the whole new age thing with a lack of respect. I was going to a different workshop every week. All sorts of things like angels, energy healing, past lives, spirit release and all sorts. It wasn't as though they were bad or anything but doing it this way I got no depth. It became like a form of entertainment, and there's nothing wrong with that, but they must have taken loads of money from me. In the end I had to find something with integrity, but more than that I had to commit to really working on myself and that process does not take a weekend, it's a lifetime's work.

Spiritual education

In an increasingly multi-cultural society the question of spiritual development and learning is a pertinent one. There is, however, some difficulty in giving content to the idea of spiritual education without identifying it with either religious or moral education. Nonetheless, there is a growing idea that spiritual education needs to include personal experience and to be open to discussion on what are described as the "big questions", i.e. the meaning of life, etc.

Recent literature says spirituality is considered a "hot topic"; there is increasing professional interest in spiritual matters paralleling that of the general public. Far from denying its presence, there has been an explosion in the number of focus groups of theological experts from diverse faiths exploring the subject. So what form can spiritual development take in a multi-cultural world? There is an argument that to have a better understanding of all faiths it is preferable to have in-depth knowledge of one. I have some sympathy with this notion as I have noticed that students who have had little or no religious education often have no frame of reference in which to evaluate their own experiences. This, however, could be perceived as a good thing as no prescriptive elements will have been indoctrinated. The students have to decipher the experiences for themselves. Perhaps we need to look into different methods and begin to teach spirituality from an open perspective accommodating and facilitating the emergence of the individual's own beliefs.

There is, however, growing recognition of the value of mystical or transcendent knowing, including some altered states of consciousness. This allows in another way of knowing – one that perhaps supersedes sensory perceptions and analysis as an effective means of knowledge. The trouble with this is that mystical experiences can be misdiagnosed and, that being the case, they could take one down very difficult paths of illusion. Nonetheless, whole new models are opening up as we look to re-engage with the spiritual nature of self.

If we accept that people see their worlds in unique ways, does it not follow they will also experience their own spiritual development in unique ways? The need to follow one's own truth seems to be gaining momentum through the desire for the genuine, and the expansion of the spiritual notion of unlimited knowledge and love. This being the case, educationalists may need to make a shift of paradigm from being exclusively rational and intellectual to experiential and intuitive. Later on in the book we investigate this through one's own experiences.

EXPERIENCE

"I made changes through acknowledging my experiences and commitment to the knowing. I had to do something different to what I was doing because I was repeating the same mistakes each time expecting a different result but getting the same result, so something had to change, which was probably caused by an avoidance of the pain at any price. I turned to alcohol and I would try to drink away the pain. You drink it and it would numb the pain, just like a paracetamol it takes your headache away but the pain was still there the next day. It was an avoidance technique and not a very good one. Now I have to embrace that pain, sit with out and open thoughts, you know, learn from the pain. I've sat there and worked through the pain and when you are in the pain when it's been an absolutely total agony but when I've come out of it, I've come out, you know, a stronger person. I've got my depth inside of me, I've got more richness and more grounded and I can say to you that was horrible but it was the best lesson I could've learnt."

Chapter 2

Where science and spirit meet

This chapter includes some interesting theories

that connect current scientific thought to spiritual and

psychic perceptions.

Can there be science behind spirituality?

Can there really be a scientific explanation for a psychic "connecting with the light", or a genuine basis for the third eye? Is it possible to communicate without words and can a healer really sense another person's illness or pain? One of the key aspects that makes psychic phenomena seem so unacceptable to science is that while people talk about different types of "energy", whether it be "healing energy", "psychic energy", "spirit energy" or "angelic forces", no psychic has ever been able to explain scientifically what sort of energy it is that he or she experiences. To scientists, energy comes in clearly defined types – heat, light, sound, electrical, chemical, nuclear – but none of them seem to apply to the descriptions of psychic experience.

The problem possibly lies in underestimating just how sensitive we really are, and how even when experiencing something tiny, it can sometimes cause us to react in a very big way. For instance, many people experience strong emotions when they hear a few bars of a piece of music, or have vivid childhood recollections when they smell something familiar, yet these strong reactions and vivid pictures are triggered by only a few sound waves or tiny molecules in the air, which cause a cascade effect in the brain, allowing many connections to be lit up almost simultaneously with the relevant spark. It is like a crowd of people waiting outside a department store on the day of its big sale: it only takes one person to open the door and in seconds a thousand people have poured through, all looking for things within the store, essentially "doing" the same thing while all looking for something different.

Despite many experiments under laboratory conditions, science finds it hard to accept any psychic phenomena as being valid. However, the more our scientific knowledge grows, the more we find the unlikeliest things occurring in nature and the universe – from particles like the *neutrino*, which stream through space, passing right through everything in their way, including our bodies, to particles that seem to be in two places at the same time. There is also the mysterious "dark matter" that accounts for 85 per cent of the universe. Although physicists can measure it, no one has a clue what it is. It seems the limitations lie far more in our ability to comprehend, than in any restrictions within the universe itself.

"Energy" means "a capacity for movement or change", so when we experience anything that moves us or makes us feel different, whether or not we know what it is, what we are experiencing is caused by one or more forms of energy. Whether we touch, taste, see, hear or smell, we bring all that information up to the brain in order to make sense of our environment and so everything we ever experience in our lives and the world around us is being processed internally. Our senses are the windows through which the brain sees outside our bodies, and this means that our whole world is probably shaped by the extent of our experiences and understanding. When we come into contact with something completely new, we might struggle to make any sense of it in the same way that primitive cultures with no concept of electricity, seeing our technology for the first time, might regard a torch as something magical. As it is, they only know that the torch can make light, but understanding electricity opens up a whole new world of possibilities.

We know of nothing more complex than the human brain and we have still only scratched the surface of its full potential. However, the brain, like every cell in the human body, functions by two processes that make the whole mind-body system work: chemical and electrical processes. So no matter what form of energy we interact with outside of our bodies, our understanding of it comes from the chemicals and electric currents buzzing around inside our brains. A good example of how our perceptions really are interpretations is to look at sparkling lights or moving colours. What you see is the picture your brain creates from the information sent to it by your eyes. Now if you squeeze your eyes tight shut, you may also see sparkling lights and moving colours, but these are created purely from the internal workings of the brain. These two very different kinds of stimulus result in very similar interpretations. So what is happening to our minds and bodies when we have psychic experiences and what are the triggers that are so difficult for science to measure?

In the natural world, many plants and animals have capabilities that often seem like some sixth sense. Turtles who find their way through millions of square miles of open ocean to return to the beach where they were born, birds that can see the magnetic field of the earth and animals who seem to predict coming earthquakes are some examples. Even sensitivities that we understand can still seem way beyond our own, like a dog's phenomenal sense of smell or a bird of prey's eyesight. Because we tend to regard ourselves as so different from other animals, we usually

think our apparently limited human senses are incomparable to their greater abilities. Mother Nature, however, is rarely wasteful and if something works she will use it over and over again. Often the only difference is whether or not the stimulus is strong enough for us to be consciously aware of what is happening inside and outside our bodies, so perhaps we need to look more closely at how our bodies could be using subtle senses to do extraordinary things.

Our sense of well-being is strongly affected by our comfort and the quality of our surroundings. For instance, the reduced levels of light in winter can cause Seasonal Affective Disorder (SAD), resulting in loss of motivation and depression. We also know that changing the chemicals in the air around us – through the use of incense or perfumes – can make us calm or excited, and that different types of sound can induce every emotion – from stress and irritation with the disruptive noise of building works, to exhilaration or calm with the appropriate piece of music. If we become too hot or too cold, the body puts more effort into regulating our temperature, which in turn can cause irritability and loss of concentration.

Is it possible, therefore, that psychic ability is equally affected by the comfort of the individual, and that any outside influences that increase stress levels will in turn reduce a person's sensitivity?

Light, colour and the chakras

Of all our senses, we use and depend on our eyesight more than any other. We "see" because information is sent to the brain by our eyes, but vision is not the only way we experience light. What we see as visible light is only a narrow band of energy in the middle of the electromagnetic spectrum, which ranges from very high frequency waves known as gamma rays to very low frequency radio waves.

Very high frequency energy has tiny wavelengths far smaller than a billionth of a metre; as the energy slows down, the waves stretch out so that the longer radio waves are many kilometres long. Regarding the wavelengths that we recognize, we know that ultraviolet rays from the sun burn our skin and that some cookers use infrared energy. So, if energy at both ends of the visible spectrum can burn us, what can be happening with the colours in between? And just because we can't "see" the faster and slower wavelengths, does that mean they don't affect us? In the natural world there are many examples of light affecting behaviour; we wouldn't be alive if plant cells didn't open and close with red and blue light to create the photosynthesis that gives us oxygen.

It is quite reasonable to describe radio waves as "slow light": after all, the only difference between the waves that burn our skin and the ones that carry our music is the speed at which they travel. When we turn on a car radio, we can drive wherever we want and continue to listen to a programme. We can start our journey next to the transmitter and drive for miles in any direction and still hear it. How? Because energy is everywhere, and we are simply driving through a sea of it while tuning in to a single point on the waves. We tune the waves through a radio set to bring them to a vibration that we can actually hear but the waves themselves surround us all the time.

Light is the same, just faster. If you stand under a clear starry sky and pick out a single star, you are looking at light that has been pouring through space for billions of miles. You can lie on the ground, go up in a plane or get in a space ship and fly towards it; the point being that you can see it anywhere because its energy is everywhere. The same applies to anything you can see. If you sit on a hillside you can look at things such as a blade of grass by your feet or a tree on the distant horizon and, while your eyes may only be able to focus on one thing at a time, the energy bouncing off all those things is bathing your body all at the same time.

It is known that some blind people can distinguish colour by touch. Much less common but just as real are people who have been blind from birth and yet can paint pictures as realistic as any sighted person. Despite having no visual experience of colour or perspective, they still perceive the world lying beyond their physical reach. It is only through viewing distant objects that we have the visual impression of things seeming to get smaller as they get closer to the horizon, so is this an example of the mind and body translating the electromagnetic information in a completely different sensory way?

Can we see and focus the wavelengths of light without the use of our eyes and is this another way the psychic feels able to connect or tune in to things?

The chakras

The Eastern chakra system (see Chapter 3) traditionally comprises seven energy centres that run in a line from the crown of the head to the base of the spine and resonate with the colours of the spectrum. In essence, the base or red centre is associated with our primal animal instincts and the centres then rise up in consciousness until the highest spiritual connection is at the violet crown. Each centre has positive and negative attributes depending on the individual's state of balance.

Colour is used extensively in marketing and manipulation because we respond to it in predictable ways. (You wouldn't want your toothpaste to come in a brown tube would you?) But apart from obvious likes and dislikes, colours actually make us feel different. Many fast food restaurants use vibrant red in their decor because, as with rich foods, we can't help being attracted to it. Surrounded by it we feel energized and alive, but like rich food, we can only take so much of it. In a relatively short space of time our senses are satisfied and we are ready to move on, ensuring a steady turnaround for the restaurant. Another example of colour being used to influence moods is painting hospital walls and prison cells in pastel shades to relax patients and calm violent prisoners. Think how different you feel when you walk in a field of bluebells as opposed to one of poppies or sunflowers.

Our spoken language intuitively associates states of mind with colour (see box right) and if we compare these with the chakra system we can see some interesting correlations (see Chapter 3).

At the centre of the chakra system lies the heart centre which resonates with green light. It is here that the individual is said to feel a sense of balance and harmony, where a sense of peace can be found. It is noteworthy that if we go back to the visible properties of the electromagnetic spectrum, the energy above the crown centre and below the base centre can be physically damaging to us. In exactly the same way that we will die if we become hypothermic with cold or from heat exhaustion if too hot, and we feel just right on a warm spring day, the green balance point of the chakra system and electromagnetic spectrum is also the optimum survival point for us as physical animals.

Electro-sensing

Electricity is generated by the movement of the electrons orbiting around the nuclei of atoms and different types of atom have varying amounts of electrons, which makes some easier to move about than others. We use metal wires, especially copper, in all our electric appliances basically because it is the easiest substance through which to drive the movement of electrons. In our everyday lives we are only really aware of electricity as an energy when we turn our domestic appliances on and off, but it flows through our bodies every second of every day and is an essential force in every living organism. All our activity creates electricity, every movement of muscle and beat of the heart, even your brain will maintain a steady electrical current of around 10 microvolts simply by reading these pages.

It may be hard to detect but every electrical flow generates an energy field. Is it, therefore, something that we can feel consciously and does this play a part in psychic experiences?

We hear performers saying that they thrive on the energy coming from an audience, that it gives them a rush of adrenaline. We sometimes describe angry people as "prickly", and often say that we can feel someone's sadness or empathize with other peoples' stress levels. Is it possible that those emotions are somehow affecting the electrical fields being generated by the body and could the differences in the electrical fields be what a psychic or healer is sensing when he or she describes a person's aura?

Sometimes we try to find answers to mysteries when the answers might be closer to hand. Every illness we ever experience is, at its basic level, a chemical imbalance. This chemical upset can be caused by the electrical functions of our cells being

RED with anger

WHITE with fear

in the PINK

got the BLUES

GREEN with envy

BROWNED off

BLACK moods

ANIMAL "magic"

Many animals have eyesight sensitive to wavelengths that are invisible to us. For example, birds and insects can see ultraviolet light. If you have a fish tank over your television set, every time you use the remote control, your fish can see the beam of red light flashing across the room.

disturbed so the wrong balance of molecules is created. Whether it is physical or mental, the problem still manifests by the body not being able to maintain its natural state of balance. It has been shown that people, especially children, living close to power lines, can suffer disorders such as leukaemia because the strength of surrounding electrical activity disturbs the natural structure of the body's blood cells. In other situations there are increases in the occurrence of tumours. However, not all effects are detrimental and even today we still use electric shock treatment for certain psychological and brain disorders.

It could be argued that when we are comfortable we don't actually feel anything. Not too hot, not too cold, not too wet, not too dry; we are only consciously aware of outside influences when they upset our equilibrium and then we begin to feel uncomfortable.

If we keep in mind that everything we do generates electricity in our minds and bodies, is it possible that the psychic will sense things much more easily in other people when they are calm and relaxed themselves, when their own buzzing electricity is quieter?

Chemical sensing and communication

Of all the methods of sending and receiving information in the natural world, chemical exchange is more commonplace than any other. Scent is so important that many mammals can reject their own offspring if they don't smell right. This is often observed when well-meaning people stroke young wild animals only for the animal to be rejected when the parent returns because it smells like a human. The entire cat family – from Siberian tigers to the family feline – marks its territory with scent, as do dogs, bears and many other species.

The main chemical triggers are compounds called pheromones, which, even though most animals detect them by breathing, don't actually smell very much, if at all. Pheromones can affect behaviour dramatically and science has shown that we are likely to choose a mate by subconsciously analysing his or her body chemistry.

ANIMAL "magic"

Sharks have one of the most sophisticated electro-sensing abilities in the natural world. They are so sensitive that they can hunt by detecting the electrical field of prey hiding under the seabed. Other fish have been found to be able to detect currents as tiny as 0.01 microvolts, and the ability is also found in reptiles and primitive mammals like the duck-billed platypus. which has electro sensors all round its bill, allowing it to detect the tiny energy fields of worms and other food below a muddy river bed.

Experiments demonstrate that human scents vary according to the balance of our genes and the smells we find most pleasant are those that chemically differ most from our own. It appears that we can smell the partner who can provide us with the healthiest offspring.

The ability of certain animals to detect tiny chemical changes may give us a clue to some forms of psychic sensitivity. Sharks can detect certain chemicals in solutions as low as one part per million, a male moth can detect a female from miles away on the strength of a single molecule of pheromone and many animals use similar pheromones to send out warnings of potential danger. It has long been said that animals can smell our fear, but dogs are increasingly being used medically to detect illnesses such as epilepsy, schizophrenia, diabetes and cancer through smell.

So, knowing that our state of health gives off a distinct odour that is influenced by chemical changes within the body, isn't it possible that a healer can detect another person's ill health by sense of smell?

The connection between body chemistry and light could be significant in understanding some psychic faculties, especially in relation to the chakra system. Light levels are important to our natural cycles and the patterns of waking and sleeping are obvious examples of this. The pineal gland sits within the brain and has long been associated with clairvoyance and the mystical third eye. Despite it being tucked away inside the skull, it reacts to changing light levels and is responsible for regulating many of the body's cycles. Over a 24-hour cycle, as the light changes, the pineal gland secretes varying amounts of a hormone called melatonin, which peaks at night, influencing the desire for sleep. The pineal gland is also responsible for triggering the hibernation and breeding cycles in animals.

Is the pineal gland really the mystical "third eye" and is this another way for the psychic "to see the light" by tuning in to higher frequencies?

As with plants and all animals active during the day, our activity increases with exposure to the violet end of the spectrum arising from increased sunlight and reduces as light moves into the redder frequencies. Since we know how varying light levels affect our body chemistry, can this also explain the link between the chakras and how they relate to our state of health?

ANIMAL "magic"

The tuatara is a nocturnal lizard-like reptile found on various islands off New Zealand and is rare in having an external "third eye", which connects directly to the pineal gland. This is only clearly seen in the young of the species and becomes covered over with scales at around four to six months old. This well-developed organ helps the young reptile to absorb ultraviolet light, which creates vitamin D in the body.

Body language

Throughout the whole of the animal kingdom, body language is an area rich in both conscious and subconscious signals. There are many obvious examples of aggressive and defensive displays such as animals baring their teeth, pinning back their ears or raising their eyebrows in alarm. Equally, a wagging tail or relaxed posture can immediately convey a non-threatening attitude.

With humans, a frown and a tapping foot are clear indicators of impatience, while a fisherman's arms held wide convey the size of "the one that got away". Humans constantly use subtle signals to convey specific thoughts to a friend or partner, particularly in situations where words are impossible or inappropriate; the tiniest movement of the head or a discreet wink can communicate a private thought. But how much information do we exchange through subconscious changes of expression or posture?

On another level, the autonomic nervous system that drives all the essential processes that we do not consciously control, such as breathing, heartbeat and digestion, is regulated by complex chemical changes in the body. This powerful system is responsible for many of our involuntary actions – like blushing and dilation of the pupils – which often display emotions we would far rather be keeping to ourselves.

Does the psychic unconsciously derive information by reading the subtle signals of unconscious and autonomic body language?

Our unconscious body language is often a clear indicator of our state of mind

and can sometimes give away more than we would like. We tend to have an unconscious but nonetheless clearly defined area of "personal space", which is usually around an arm's length from the body. When talking with strangers we will comfortably maintain this distance during a conversation but if someone moves within that boundary we will usually adopt protective postures such as folding our arms, which can be both a signal of defence and a genuine safety precaution. Even in seated conversation we might close ourselves off by crossing our arms and legs.

Is it also possible that we are shielding the chakras most sensitive to emotional and mental vulnerability, namely the sacral and solar plexus chakras?

Displays of emotion can seem to fall somewhere between conscious and subconscious actions. For example, it is fair to say that whilst crying is not necessarily deliberate or consciously driven, it is certainly not something that passes unnoticed by the person shedding the tears. As is the case with most other forms of communication, we have a scale of subtlety that ranges from the subliminal signal to the greatest display aimed at the widest audience, and the more sensitive or aware an individual is, the more signals he or she will detect. Tension is a good example; the clenched teeth or tight shoulders of someone under stress can be obvious to one person and pass completely unnoticed by another.

Are psychics more sensitive to the subtle variations and meaning of tension and muscle movement?

ANIMAL "magic"

Eyes open wide in alarm is a universally recognized reaction. From apes to birds and cats to humans, there is no mistaking the emotion behind the expression. Equally, creases in the brow of many animals can display a wide variety of thoughts and emotions. In humans, the flexibility of the muscles of the forehead enables us to communicate our thoughts in intricate and expressive ways.

Astronomical influences

Astrology has long been dismissed by science for several reasons, not least of all the fact that you only have to look at the night sky to see that when astrologers say that a planet is in a particular constellation, they are wrong by one complete zodiacal sign; so can there be any scientific basis for the concept of astrology influencing our lives?

As the earth is not a perfect sphere and has slightly flattened poles, it wobbles as it spins, which has the same effect as the handle of a spinning top moving in small circles opposite to the direction of spin. This effect is called precession and it takes the earth just under 26,000 years to complete one precessional cycle. If you imagine a line pointing out from the earth into space and drawing a circle in the sky, where the north pole now points towards Polaris in the constellation of Ursa Minor, it will gradually move through this circle and the north star will change as the cycle progresses. Half way round, in another 13,000 years or so, our north star will be Vega in the constellation of Lyra.

Although the origins of the zodiac as we know it are uncertain, it can be reliably traced back to Mesopotamia and certain cultural influences suggest it to be older than that, so the patterns that we know have been part of our culture for at least 5000 years. The gradual precessional shift in the orbit of the earth has meant that it has slipped away from the original alignment, which would explain the discrepancy between astronomical and astrological observations. The only important factor in astrology is the position of the planets in relation to the earth, with the zodiacal constellations forming no more than a background point of reference.

Many people are surprised to learn that the tidal influences of the sun and moon not only pull the oceans but physically distort the solid earth as well. It may seem astonishing but the surface of the earth

itself is constantly rising and falling beneath our feet. Even the gravitational effects of Jupiter on the earth's tides, though small, can be accurately measured and it is through the precise nature of gravity that science is able to detect planets around distant stars. If a star "wobbles" as it spins there must be something close by exerting a gravitational pull, so if whole solar systems and the solid earth can be affected, why not the more malleable creatures who populate its surface?

Another effect of the earth's distortion will be shifts of electrical flow through the earth, and, as the movements of all the planets are known to influence the movement of the sun itself, it follows that the magnetic field of the earth will also be affected. Scientists argue that the forces at work are too small to affect any individual, but as we have seen, tiny changes of electrical flow can and do influence the workings of the body. Could these also have an impact on our natural cycles? If our electrical energy is influenced it could, in turn, affect our chemical balance.

Could this explain why we will be more susceptible to certain influences at different times?

ANIMAL "magic"

There are numerous examples of animals influenced by the lunar cycle, from howling wolves to spawning coral, and the size of trawler catches is known to fluctuate with the phases of the moon. Research has shown that other characteristics are also affected, with one study revealing that the number of people reporting animal bites is double the average daily figure on the day of the full moon. Could the planets also cause these effects on a more subtle level?

The breath of life

For now, we can only surmise what processes may be involved in psychic phenomena and there is much to learn about the most subtle and sensitive processes within the body. The more we discover, the more things we find in the universe that at first seem to be completely implausible. It is interesting that science now regards time as an illusion; we and all other life on earth have evolved to use time in a particular linear way. If this concept is correct, is it also possible that, by returning to the quiet space of a meditative state, the psychic is able to step outside the confines of the illusion and access future information?

Along with the importance of quiet stillness, every spiritual background emphasizes the breath as a point of focus, whether it is chanting on the breath, yogic breathing or simply being aware of it flowing into our bodies. Other than the need for air, is there an aspect of breathing that we do not yet fully understand? We have seen that our chemical communications are sensed through our noses so is there more in the air than we know? Of the countless reports of hauntings, many people have described the experience as being accompanied by smells: someone's cigarette smoke, the aroma of cooking or perfume.

Is it possible that, like the sea of energy that surrounds us all the time, we can tune in to past smells or events that have existed in that space, or is it another aspect of seeing through the illusion of time?

There are many instances of people "intuitively" taking a different route while driving and then discovering that they have unconsciously avoided an accident or huge traffic jam.

Is it possible that along with other chemical signals we could, in our breathing, be picking up the increase of stress hormones or even pollution coming from a particular direction?

An astonishing discovery in recent years has been occasions when some transplant patients adopt certain characteristics of their deceased donors. This appears to show that the cells of the body retain more information than expected, which opens up yet more possibilities. It may be a little unpalatable, but, considering that 70 per cent of house dust is made up of human skin cells, is it possible that we are inhaling more information from each other in this way too?

At the deepest level of physical matter there exist only 92 different atomic elements and everything we know or have ever known is made up of a combination of those atoms. Atoms arrange and combine to form molecules, which range from the simplest substances to the most complex, making every rock, liquid, gas, plant and animal; but ultimately they return to their original state time and time again. We are all, quite literally, made of atoms that were once floating in space before the earth was formed. In every breath that we take, we inhale atoms that have been part of everything that has existed on the earth; so on a profound level, just as mystics have stated through the ages, we really are a part of the whole.

And if this is so, how might we get in touch with our individual part of the whole? We have discussed the need to be still and to be in touch with the deep part of the self that is within us. It seems likely therefore that we need to unfold or peel back the aspects of self that restrict this, and to do this it is thought that one needs to spend time on self discovery. In the next section we begin our journey of psychic and spiritual discovery with simple exercises that show how you too might be able to connect with the deep part of yourself, thereby attuning to the whole energy of life.

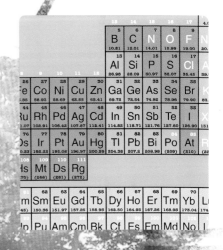

Chapter 3

Stage one: foundation for spiritual self-development

The first steps on the path to spiritual self-development
are those that enable individuals to be more open to
spiritual influences. Exercises in meditation,
visualization, accessing subtle energies and connecting
with your chakras will assist the process.

Meditation

Some form of meditation has been with us throughout history and, as we have seen in the previous chapters, there are positive reasons for its implementation. Meditation exists in many forms still in common use, including repetitive prayer, mantras and chant. Its purpose is to bring your whole energy into a state of stillness so you can be more in touch with what is real and right for you. It helps you to transcend the painful and negative aspects of everyday life and to live with a serenity, an inner peace, and a joy and love of life. It is the search for, and experience of, the relationship of the individual with him- or herself and the attunement to the whole universal energy. It is an alignment of awareness that draws us towards higher spiritual development.

Although many people believe prayer enables them to find solutions, many also advocate a form of "conscious" prayer, which means being aware of the connectedness to the divine. Prayer in its usual mode might be thought of as a request, a plea or a form of supplication to God or other deities, whereas meditation is seen as "attunement" or "at-one-ment" to a higher force or God. The terms "prayer" and "meditation" can cause confusion. As the transpersonalist and parapsychologist Charles Tart has written: "Meditation properly refers to internal psychological practices intended to change the quality or state of consciousness of your mind, its efficacy comes exclusively from the meditation. Prayer, on the other hand, is effective insofar as there is a supernatural or non-ordinary order of Being or being who might respond to it."

There is a phrase in the East that talks about the "monkey mind". In meditation we are seeking to quieten this lively and sometimes obstreperous mind. It requires some patience and it's a bit like training a dog to a lead; we are trying to bring our thought process into line and focus. Meditation allows the outer "noise" of the world to subside, which enables contact with the inner or higher soul self. It also enables the person to be focused in the present in a state of mindfulness, which is the ability to

Meditation brought me more calming and powerful energies. My perspectives changed and my mental processes were different and my tiredness always disappeared afterwards and this lasted quite a few days. Afterwards, I was able to be aware that something was staying with me and working with me; I wasn't able to manifest it in a physical, practical sense to begin with. As time went on, I found I could even bring some meditation into every day even when I was going on the tube and bus.

observe one's own moment-to-moment changing experience. For the purpose of spiritual self-development, it has much value. It aligns us to the inner core spirit of self, which has the effect of allowing us to feel safe and letting us see ourselves as we truly are.

Meditation exercises

There are many meditation methods, including repeating a sound, word or mantra, which enables the mind to come into focus. Some meditation schools will give you your own special sound or word that can be utilized for this purpose. Equally, you can create your own. However, if you choose your own word take care that it expresses the energy you truly want.

When you start to meditate it might be quite difficult to just go into stillness, and some method or tool can assist you. It's a good idea not to make this too complicated. So, if you want an image to use as a focus, choose something that is close at hand such as a flower or a potent picture. A candle can be useful as it is a source of light and we are endeavouring to connect with the light part of ourselves.

One of the simplest tools is our own breathing. Breath, as discussed in Chapter 2, is a powerful tool and has been used for the purpose of meditation over millennia.

Transpersonal psychology sometimes uses altered states of consciousness as a tool in the psycho-spiritual development process. Meditation is a form of altered consciousness, and it has been found that bringing in these altered states may provide different or even more information for the individual's self-development. Because of the clarity that meditation often brings, it can be thought of as leading us into a higher or better state of awareness. In these higher forms of consciousness there can be a transformation where the usual sense of self is expanded. The sense of identity then encompasses more than that of a single

EXPERIENCE

"When we started doing meditation in the group it was immense. Suddenly it felt like electricity and it was such a strong feeling, I mean it didn't stay at that sort of illuminating state all the time, but when I was there in that meditative state it was fantastic. It felt really brilliant. To be part of a group where everyone was meditating and having a sort of energetic connection with each other. It was really a very strong feeling."

EXPERIENCE

"I had an experience within that focused breath which allowed me to relax from everything that was going on my head or around me. I find that even if I can just go and do it for five minutes a day I get a positive experience. It's a very good starting point."

Exercise: Connecting with the breath

Close your eyes and be willing to let go of the hustle, bustle and irritations of your everyday life. Do not give yourself unrealistic expectations at first, because it is not always the amount of time you spend meditating that matters but the quality of the meditation. Keep trying if you cannot achieve the meditative state at first. Like any skill, gradually over time you will find it becomes easier. To let go of the mundane world some imagery can be helpful so imagine a wonderful brilliant light coming down and massaging and relaxing your whole body. Alternatively, you could use the image of crystal clear water and imagine yourself having a shower, cleansing yourself of all disruptive energy.

Mentally scan the main areas of your body starting with your head and working downwards. See the light releasing and relaxing around your head; pay particular attention to areas that tend to hold tension like the jaw and mouth. Release the tongue from the top of your mouth; see the light moving through and around your neck. Release tension in your shoulders and upper arms down to your hands and fingers. Move the light through your torso down through your whole body into your upper legs, feet and toes.

Become fully aware of the natural rhythm of your breath – the relaxing rhythm of breathing in and breathing out.

Let your breath be natural – nothing forced or pushed, just the regular natural rhythm. Stay with this concentration for a few minutes and gently let that connectedness to your breath take you deeper into the part of you that is always still: the hub or core of your whole being. Keep the awareness of your breath and consciously breathe into that still place. Gradually, visualize gentle waves of light emanating from your core. Move this still energy outwards until it comes out of your body, creating a circle of stillness around you, with you and through you. You might like to visualize a golden band of light a few inches away from your body that will serve to hold this stillness. Stay with this as long as you feel comfortable and remind yourself that the stillness is there all the time, if you choose to acknowledge it.

isolated human being and with that expanded awareness the individual can connect and identify with universal and cosmic forces. Achieving altered states is thought to give students a different view of themselves and others, and meditation is often the first step. It can be seen as limbering up as you would before any form of exercise.

The goal of many meditation schools is ultimately enlightenment, a perfect wholeness in which we experience opening our hearts to all beings, allowing love and compassion to flow through our lives to everyone without judgment or limitation. To imagine this state is going to come immediately is unrealistic; however, if we achieve it for a few minutes at first, we can then learn to hold some of that energy throughout our day.

Exercise: Breathing into the heart

Go through the first stage of meditation as described on the previous page. Breathe into the area called the heart, which is placed in the middle of the body slightly above the region of the physical heart. Focus your breaths into this area expanding the heart energy, which is not emotional love but the energy of healing love beyond emotions. Expand the energy with each breath and feel the energy circling out and around you like invisible wings of love. If you wish, you can invite any energies that you feel are unconditional loving ones – an angel, Christ, Buddha or simply the energy of pure light. Hold yourself in this state for a few minutes. When you want to finish, try to bring that energy back into your waking state. Enjoy the healing note of love.

A variation on this is to choose what is called a "centre" word, which is used to impress a positive idea and a loving feeling, such as a flower, love, peace, light, tree, etc. Once you have taken care to choose the word, contemplate it and wait. Gradually some association will come to you. Reflect on whatever comes into your head for a few minutes. This may have some meaning for you, but whatever you feel, return to the centre word again and again. This has the effect of allowing you to train your mind to focus and also may bring some inspiration to allow you to see your life in a different way.

Visualizations

For the novice, deep meditation is not always easy to achieve, so having something to focus on is a helpful start and therefore some forms of visualization can assist you towards greater depth. Visualizations can aid the unfoldment and understanding of self, and can help us connect to aspects of self; the part of us that "knows" what we are not always able to see or face in waking consciousness. Forms of visualization are increasingly being used in psychotherapy to unlock and then speak to the areas of our unconscious. Here are two very simple visualizations to bring learning of self.

Exercise: The inner child

After taking yourself through the "connecting with the breath" meditation (see page 46) imagine yourself going into a safe and comfortable room. Into this room invite your inner child. Give attention to the way the child looks and acts and talk to him or her. Give yourself plenty of time and then ask the child what he or she needs and what will make him or her feel safe. When you have done this, embrace the child and feel it melt into your heart.

The child is a personification of that aspect of yourself that feels vulnerable and frightened, so give some thought to what occurred in your meditation and make use of it in your daily life. You can also bring a feeling into this meditation. For instance, if you feel hopeless, abandoned or fearful, you can ask for the hopeless, abandoned or fearful child to come in, take note of its appearance, and again talk to it and find out why it feels that way. At the end embrace it as above.

Exercise: Inner guide

Take yourself through the "connecting with the breath" meditation and when you feel completely relaxed, imagine you are walking out in the sunshine on a day that you have nothing else to do but enjoy yourself. As you walk on you come to a waterfall; you walk into it. Take some time to experience what that feels like and the sense of cleansing your whole self with crystal clear pure water. When you feel cleansed, see yourself come out into a pool of healing waters. Give yourself time to be aware of any images that come into your head, inviting the healing waters to help you work through whatever emerges for you. When you feel ready, imagine yourself sitting in the sunshine and invite a guide or friend to share your feelings and answer any questions that have emerged from your meditation. In this way, the guide or friend acts as a personification of your higher self and you are able to communicate with it, which will assist your learning of deeper aspects of self.

EXPERIENCE

"As a drama teacher I utilize both types of mediation for myself and my students. The visualization type can be used to set a meditation off and the purer form, which makes immediate contact with the inner stillness. Although the inner stillness was not there all the time when it happens I often see white and nothing else. I call this being in the whiteness. Nowadays I do not need to use visualization to get into this white open state. I now sit quietly for a few minutes each morning. Sometimes I ask for help if I am worried about anything and visualize light around it, I just send the thought out there, sometimes contacting angels or just allowing it to go into the ether and sometimes although I'm not quite sure what God is I send thoughts to God."

Subtle energies

It is understood that every living thing is energy and that everything vibrates or emanates an energy field out and around it. It is thought that this life force energy flows through and within every living thing. The idea of subtle energy is found in Eastern medicine, where it is thought that a balance of this life force in the energy field sustains health. While Westeners know it as subtle energy it is also known as:

Ankh: ancient Egypt
Gana: South America
Ki: Japan
Mana: Polynesia
Ntu: Bantu (S. Africa)
Pneuma: ancient Greece
Prana: India
Qi (chi): China
Ruach: ancient Hebrew.

The energy field is a vibrational energy that interacts with living matter through the chakra system. The seven centres of the chakras (see also next section) provide an emanation or flow of energy that penetrates through the body as though through layers or shells. This substance is called the aura or energy fields. By attuning to the aura, a sensitive person can sense the state of an individual's health, emotions, mind and spirit. Sensitives do this by perceiving the size, shape and quality of the aura, which alters with the physical, emotional and mental states of the person. Attunement to subtle energies also allows us to better understand our own state and what we are personally radiating out to the world.

The subtle body is the non-physical psychic (i.e. unseen) body that is energetically superimposed upon our physical bodies. It can be measured as

---

Exercise: Sensing energy

Although traditionally divining or dowsing rods were made from twigs, most commonly hazel or willow, you can turn an ordinary metal coat hanger into a set of rods. Using a pendulum can be just as effective and this is also easily accomplished by finding a strong chain and hanging on it a crystal of your choice. It is understood that thought is also an energy and that thought directs energy. So engage your thought and will to connect your energy to that of the rod and mentally ask for what you are seeking. In the case of sensing the strength of one's aura, use the rod or pendulum and work slowly towards each chakra area. You may fine that the pendulum or rod will react to each centre a bit differently and in this way you will be able to ascertain which centre is stronger or weaker than the others. Sensing other people's energies may also give you some idea of your own energy and how it is working for – or against – you.

electromagnetic force fields that are found within and around all living creatures (see also Chapter 2). These energy fields have been known throughout the centuries and there is a growing movement towards investigating how these ancient concepts might connect with modern ideas. Kirlian photography and dowsing are two methods being explored, which might enable us to experience and acknowledge subtle energies. Through these it is possible to see the aura and chakras and work with them to ascertain the health and well-being of any individual.

Kirlian photography was discovered in 1940 by Semion Kirlian, a Russian foreman who repaired medical equipment. It has been used to photograph the emanations of the subtle body in both plants and animals. Dowsing has been used for thousands of years as a way of finding water and more recently oil. With the use of dowsing rods or sticks you can tune in to the vibration of whatever you are seeking, and the rods will vibrate when it is found. The aura or energy fields around the body can be detected with dowsing also. Overleaf you will find some guidelines to interpret what you may receive. (See also pages 200–205 for more on auras.)

Exercise: Seeing the aura

You will need the assistance of another person. Put yourself in a relaxed meditative state in a slightly darkened room. Sitting 2 or 3 feet away from each other, look at the other person at a point slightly away from their physical presence. Allow yourself plenty of time for your vision to shift. After a time you may be able to see a slight hue around the body of your friend. This is their aura. You may find that either you physically see a colour or you may just "sense" a colour with them. Pay particular notice to not just the colour but the way the colour comes off the body.

Red Too much red in the aura might mean over exertion. If the red is being thrown off the body it might be indicative of anger. Crimson might mean a high sex drive and scarlet a strong ego.

Pink often shows unselfishness and sensitivity. If it surrounds the person it can mean that he or she is receiving spiritual healing or that he or she is a healer.

Orange denotes a person of great purpose and creativity. If you see dark or black bits, it could mean self indulgence and a person wrapped up in his or her own emotions. A reddish orange is indicative of someone who is devious. If the orange is being thrown off the body, it denotes sexual desire run riot and might even mean sexual disease or corruption.

Yellow is a sign of balanced emotion, clear thought and also compassion. Muddy or dark yellow shows a fearful person who might also be resentful and one that may be lazy and believe that the world owes him or her a living.

Gold indicates a person who is mystical and spiritually advanced. A highly developed intuition is also likely. It is interesting to note that gold is a colour employed by artists in depicting saintly or godly beings.

Green Grass green reveals equilibrium and healing qualities, someone who is selfless and adaptable. A soft pastel shade of green might indicate a healer who is connected to the earth. However, any darkness with green indicates selfishness and envy, particularly if it is being thrown off the body. Muddy olive green denotes greed and deceit and can also reveal a depressed person.

Blue This usually belongs to someone of an independent spirit who has discovered a way of communicating with divine energies. Often it denotes a devotional or religious nature. It is a healing colour. People with blue in the aura are incorruptible as they have a strength of character that is born out of their inner knowledge. Darkness with blue indicates dogmatism and stubborn qualities.

Indigo Colour of spiritual attainment. A seeker of divine truths. It is unusual to see this colour interspersed with darkness but if you do, it might mean that the person is overly concerned with his or her own perfection.

Purple/Violet High spiritual attainment.

Grey/Black Look at the part of the body where this appears. If it is over the head it could mean negative thoughts. If it is around the solar plexus or lower body, this is someone with negative emotions. If you see dark grey or black enfolding the body, it might mean that this is someone prepared to implement his or her dark ideas of revenge and deceit.

Brown is associated with a materially orientated person. Muddy brown might mean someone who is overly engrossed in material accumulation. He or she needs to get what he or she wants immediately.

Silver Erratic energy. This is someone with a lot of mental activity. If it covers the body, it might mean mental illness. It can also indicate someone who tends towards an illusionary state.

White This is rarely observed over the whole body; if it is, this would be a very enlightened being.

The chakras

Chakra is a Sanskrit word meaning "wheel" or "disc" and relates to seven vortices of energy, for the reception, assimilation and transmission of life energies. Chakras are a system of spiritual evolution, and their subtle makeup can be explored only through particular means, including meditation, yoga and self-development. In the Indian tradition, the centres are referred to as lotuses: like the flower, we are rooted in the mud and darkness of the depths but ultimately we blossom under the light of the sun. The lotuses are allocated a certain number of petals to each centre, which

THE CHAKRAS IN CONNECTION WITH SELF-DEVELOPMENT

Chakra	Key Aspects	Method	Statement of Intent
Base or *Muladhara* (red)	Survival, physical safety	How to survive in the physical world	I learn through what I have
Sacral or *Svadhisthanna* (orange)	Emotions, creativity	How one understands and uses feelings. Creative force and drive	I learn through what I want
Solar Plexus or *Manipura* (yellow)	Self worth. The lower mind. Sympathetic connection with others	How we measure ourselves within the community	I learn through what I can and can't do
Heart or *Anahata* (green)	Love without judgement. Balance	How to understand and forgive	I learn through love
Throat or *Visuddha* (blue)	Spiritual connection. Communication	How to communicate without fear	I learn through communication
Brow or *Ajna* (indigo)	Insight. The higher mind	How to perceive higher qualities and potentials	I learn through clear perception and intuition
Crown or *Sahasrara* (violet)	Higher consciousness. Depth. Inner knowledge	How to surrender	I learn through knowing

describes the increased rising of vibration or frequency as one progresses from the lowest to the highest chakra. They also correlate to seven colours that the chakras throw off depending on the speed of their revolution. Colour is light vibrating at different frequencies, and the analogous notion is that as the pure white light of spirit comes down into the physical world it splits like a prism reflecting the colours or energies through the human energy fields, breaking into the corresponding colours of the chakras. There are quite technical aspects to the flow of energy connected to the chakras which are not applicable to this work; however, it is worth noting that it is seen like a current of energy that flows and creates a pattern like the Caduceus or Staff of Hermes symbol of healing. This current of energy is called the *kundalini*. The kundalini concept of the unfolding serpent has long been associated with healing and its Caduceus logo is still used as the symbol for medicine.

Quoting from the yoga teachings, the concept is that we do indeed contain all the higher levels of consciousness as a true potential known in general terms as kundalini energy. This is said to lie dormant, asleep in the unconscious, initially in a state of slumber waiting to rise. Once this dormant kundalini energy is activated, it starts to unwind from the base chakra centre and gradually rises to the spiritual link of the crown centre. It is thought to travel in a figure-of-eight-like manner, rising through the pathways or meridians of energies to which the chakras are connected. This spiraling unfoldment process activates higher and higher areas of self and that movement is thought to change the energy of the individual.

The transformative process creates a series of shifts or initiations until the kundalini reaches the top centre, where connection is made to the highest spiritual energy bringing union to a source or god and a profound consciousness change leading to enlightenment. These qualities or centres connect to the physical by psychic subtle essences or energetic attraction, activated by the life force or "prana", "chi" or "subtle energy". The seven chakras, therefore, could be perceived as stepping stones towards higher consciousness and spiritual integration as the subtle force rises and heightens through each. They also should be regarded as learning tools, intended to enable insight and personal exploration as well as implementing health and healing. In this book I use them as an effective tool for spiritual self-exploration through which you can gradually build up strength and achieve transformation to higher states of awareness.

Over the years I have watched the different levels of intuition in operation and linked them to the chakra centres as below.

LEVELS OF INTUITIVE PERCEPTION

1	**Base**	Material	Instinctual
2	**Sacral**	Emotional	Tribal
3	**Solar Plexus**	Lower mind	Personal, auric
4	**Heart**	Love	Loving awareness/Balance
5	**Throat**	Communication	Inspirational/Channelling
6	**Brow**	Higher mind	Vision
7	**Crown**	Divinity	Alignment

1. Instinctual senses are those that put us on our guard from danger, most often equated with an animal sense of knowing.

2. Tribal senses connect with care for our group whether that is family, society or the environment. A sense of knowing what the tribe or family needs or fears.

3. Personal intuition alerts us to people's feelings, thoughts and what they are emitting, i.e. their emotions, thoughts. etc. A sense of sympathy towards others, but also an awareness of fear or threat. A sense of our own self worth.

4. Loving empathy assists any healing process whether in ourself or others. A sense of balance and being able to help or heal.

5. Inspirational links take us towards attunement to unseen forces, a sense of linking to some spiritual entity which is likely to be dictated by the beliefs of the individual, e.g. a Catholic might feel the presence of Mary or Jesus, a Muslim might feel the presence of Allah. These senses can also feel like an angelic presence and may be acknowledged as some form of information, advice or guidance beyond the mundane.

6. Vision gives us a sense of the greater picture beyond selfish personal concerns so that we "see situations beyond the clouds". Exemplars of these traits include the Dalai Lama and Mahatma Gandhi.

7. Alignment to the highest divinity is rare to see, but could be equated to the greatest and best, e.g. Jesus, Buddha, Allah, Yahweh.

Chakra exercises

On the right, you will find a useful exercise to awaken your chakras. And because the balance achieved by using the chakras can be so valuable to the unfoldment of self, on the following pages I provide some easy exercises to bring light into every area of life. Although these exercises are fairly simple, the results can be startling. Some latent or hidden issues may emerge; if they do and you find it difficult to manage, please find a competent group or therapist to assist you. Choose wisely as there are a lot of well-meaning people who know very little. It is sometimes the case that a group or person that has the most kudos or is deemed "special" turns out to be superficial and merely flim-flam. No matter how good a practitioner purports to be for some people, he or she may not be the right one for you. Use your intuition to guide you and don't be afraid of walking away if it feels wrong.

EXPERIENCE

"When we started working on the chakra system, it was incredibly powerful feeling the link with these separate centres. Funnily enough when I was meditating on my own, I instinctively went to the centres. I felt it was like an unfolding and what I was experiencing through these exercises was aiding me to unravel things in my life or they unravelled in conjunction with it. I went through immense changes and ups and downs, bringing up lots of negativity and all sorts of things happened to me but I was still going through this process safely, which was invaluable."

Exercise: Connecting to the chakras

Having gone through the "connecting with the breath" exercise (see page 46), direct your focus into each chakra one by one and simply breathe once, twice or three times into each centre point, starting with the base. While you are going through, pay attention to how each centre feels: ask yourself which centres are stronger or weaker than others. Breathe light into each one to expand. The Eastern approach is to see each chakra as a flower; the least petals are in the base, the most petals are in the crown. Visualize each chakra opening up like a blossom. Alternatively, you can use the image of pulling a curtain or opening a door. When you reach the top crown chakra, spend some time acknowledging yourself as a spiritual being.

Carrying on from this exercise, intuitively choose one of the centres. Whichever centre you choose, focus on that area and see yourself going into the "room" of that centre. Allow your mind to freely envisage the room or place in which you find yourself. Make note of the colours, furniture, pictures or scenery. At some point in the exercise, come into the centre of the room where there are two chairs. Sit down and invite some guide or teacher to speak with you. You can ask questions here. After a few minutes say goodbye to the person and walk out.

If you saw any colours, they may relate to the colours of the chakras and indicate something you have to take notice of about yourself. If there was a picture, what was it? The picture in this meditation is often an aspect of yourself. If there was any furniture, what was inside? Whatever you find there might relate to things you might want to let go of in your life. After each exercise, gently reverse the process and visualize closing the petals on your flower or shutting the curtain or door, with the exception of the crown and the base centre, as these are always kept open. Enjoy the sense of peace you will have obtained from this exercise.

EXPERIENCE

"The experiential work of the chakras really helped me, it was something I could hold on to and everything started falling into place. Breakthrough came by working with these week by week. I thought, I can see how this works and I can use this to stimulate my intuition so it was a link. I made a link through the imagery and suddenly in a meditation I have a sense of an altered state and I thought 'ah' I know what this is all about now.

Muladhara
The Root or Base centre

Colour
Red

Location
Base of spine

Area affected
The bones and lower back

Quality
Solidity. Satisfaction in one's
existing state and being
comfortable

Energy
Earth

The base chakra

The energy of the chakras often feels like a wonderful tree with deep roots into the earth and high branches that reach to the sun. The earth link is in the base centre and the spiritual contact is in the crown. Without the depth of the roots the tree cannot grow tall and so it is with our energies; our roots must be strong and deep. To obtain this depth is called "grounding".

The exercise that follows is very efficacious if you are feeling physically drained, particularly if you do it lying flat on the ground. Directing base energy is also effective for those recovering from operations or even a common cold.

Exercises

After putting yourself in a meditative state take some focused breaths into the base area. Visualize that energy connecting from the base of your spine through your legs and feet deep into the earth. Not just the surface level of the earth, but where the earth is a volcanic mass of liquid energy. The colour red is very appropriate here; visualize red energy being drawn up into your feet and base centre, which is around the bottom of your spine, just as though you were a tree sucking the energy up from deep within the earth. Allow your mind to focus on any earthy and natural thoughts. As you draw this energy upwards, embrace yourself as a living physical being at one with the earth and the universe.

Finish the exercise as usual, bringing back your experience into normal consciousness.

Another very simple way to connect with the base earth energy is by walking, which also can be a form of meditation. Choose somewhere pleasant and walk for at least 20 minutes, two or three times a week. Get into the rhythm of feeling each step connecting with the earth. If you can find

a tree and spend some time sitting with your back against it open to impressions and thoughts, this can open you up to inspirational messages.

Finally, an even quicker way to connect with base earth energy is to stamp your feet around the house and, as you are doing this, really mentally connect to the earth and consciously draw on it. The use of the base enables intuitive connection to our physical needs.

Svadhisthana
The Sacral centre

Colour
Orange

Location
Sacrum on the spine

Area affected
Fluid functions, i.e. urine
and semen

Quality
Creativity and drive

Energy
Taste

The sacral chakra

This centre is about creativity and movement and, if it is balanced, is a very powerful tool energetically. It is a bit like an engine or a rocket blast that gets things moving. Many people are frightened of movement and yet our planet is all about change. Indeed, as we speak, our Earth is hurtling across the universe at thousands of miles per hour.

Many cultures have an ethos of change and transformation and deities that personify this. In the Hindu faith, Shiva "the destroyer" breaks down the structure of form to bring change and that change brings transcendence. In Christianity, the crucifixion is about death and yet it encompasses the resurrection that gives us inspiration that life continues. And in all our lives we experience deaths of many kinds – not just physical death but death of childhood, relationships, jobs and situations. Indeed death and rebirth are constant in all areas of our lives. However, with any death comes space for the new.

It is not always easy to acknowledge, but it is often the situations in life that give us most pain and distress, those that make us feel pushed to the extremes, which are the ones that allow us, probably after some struggle, to reach inside ourselves and engage with a higher

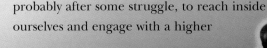

aspect of self. When this occurs we almost certainly emerge stronger and wiser and able to move on to greater things. Through the death of our "little self" we can obtain rebirth to higher levels of consciousness.

The expansion of sacral energy allows us to intuitively sense other people's emotions. It is a form of empathy. Unconsciously we are constantly picking up feelings from others; unfortunately, the noise and clutter of the outer world does not always allow us to acknowledge this. Using meditation helps us to become balanced and more aware of ourselves and our needs and the needs and feelings of others. With this information we are better able to understand one another and ourselves and respond with greater affection and truth. Because the sacral centre connects with the emotions it is important that we allow any emotions that surface to emerge and then allow them to pass away. Having a trustworthy person with you is advised.

Exercises

Having got yourself into a relaxed meditative state, breathe gently and purposefully into the sacral area, which is three to four vertebrae above the coccyx, using the colour orange to inspire strength and movement. Visualize yourself on a raft on a river. As the river moves, you acknowledge what you are doing when the water is both calm and rough. Go with the movement as the water carries you along. If you are troubled by the choppy waters ask yourself why – still waters are stagnant and stagnancy breeds disease. Without movement your life would be unhealthy. Consciousness thrives on change and through change we discover new things, our minds expand and we are therefore improved as we explore. It has been said that the greatest thing in man is his curiosity and his need for exploration. It is the food for transformation. Actively allow yourself to be at peace with both the rough waters and calm. Finish the exercise in the usual way.

Other methods of stimulating the sacral are dance, particularly those dances that activate the lower belly, such as belly dancing.

Manipura

The Solar Plexus centre

Colour

Yellow

Location

Just above the navel

Area affected

Digestive system

Quality

Expansiveness, warmth and joviality

Energy

Sight

The solar plexus chakra

The use of a connection to the solar plexus, like all the chakra energies, instigates change and transformation. In this case, change is connected to will and power. In order to progress spiritual self-development we need to re-define our notion of power to one that empowers and brings strength, as differentiated from the power that takes away another's will. In this work I am dealing with energies. Just as electrical energy requires a wire or channel to direct it, so your power needs direction and will. The transformation of the solar plexus centre emerges from the emotions of "poor little me" to consciously direct your power and energy to make things better.

To hold true power we need to embrace our responsibility and take action accordingly. If we let others have their will over us, that is equally our responsibility and choice, but if we submit to another without really wanting it, it is not a real energy and will create problems over time. If we live a lie, however lofty our intentions, that lie disturbs the atmosphere around us and this often has the effect of causing some form of communication breakdown, often with the people concerned not understanding the reason. This is why knowledge of your true feelings, thoughts and aspirations are vital to depth spiritual development.

An example of lack of will is the person who blames others – or even life – for all his or her woes. Power that is blocked often reveals itself as anger and, when it starts to spill over, it is destructive if it is thrown out on to others. Anger needs to be purged within ourselves and some form of emotional therapy here can be helpful. It is a strange truth, but we are often more frightened of our potential power than we are of our weakness. One possible reason for this is that to embrace true power of alignment to spirit means taking full responsibility for every aspect of our lives. There is an unconscious recognition that this means many changes, which we often resist. Inertia can also be our enemy but on an energetic level all movement is good, so the individual needs to engage his or her will and make a move.

Exercises

In a meditative state, visualize a situation from the past in which you felt out of control or helpless. In your mind, take yourself back to the situation and consciously change the scenario. Do this, not by the enforcement of anger over the other, but by quietly and lovingly stating your wants and needs to the other person or people involved. Observe how you feel and how the other person or people react. Then allow your mind to be unconditionally open to the changed outcomes from their changed attitudes. After finishing this exercise, surround the situation in a circle of light and visualize letting it go into light, asking that right be done in the future. Do this without any attachment to any possible outcome.

Laughter is often a good healing medicine for the solar plexus, so try to put yourself in environments where there is genuine laughter. Have a small group of people in a circle each laying his or her head on the stomach of another. One person has to say "ha" out loud several times. It won't be long before the whole group is laughing – enjoy the energy of group joy.

Anahata
The Heart centre

Colour
Green

Location
The level of the
upper breastbone

Area affected
Mobility and the heart region

Quality
Relationships or sympathy
with others and self

Energy
Touch

The heart chakra

As we come to the heart centre in our development we come to the pivotal point of energy, the bridge between the lower and the higher forces. In the energy of the heart we find the central concepts of most religions and faiths, many of which speak of the necessity to experience and move into the state of unconditional love for real depth transformation. This is present in Christianity as the "sacred heart", in Buddhism as the "middle way" and in the East the notion of "unconditional love". But what does unconditional really mean? Loving without judgment is something very hard for most people to comprehend as we love for all sorts of reasons, many of them to satisfy our own desires, including sexual ones. The love of the heart, however, is beyond personal emotions, wants and needs. It is an openness of love without aspirations for the future. This form of love is not common, as, even in the love of a mother for a child, there can be some personal aspiration and desire.

The unconditional form of selfless love requires some loss of ego and the ability to merge with somebody without any desire of what is required for self. Without really understanding our selves and those hidden repressed unconscious aspects, we can never really get to the point of departure from the mundane to the divine. As we move from the lower chakra energies we can break through to a glimpse of the infinite and a state of love that is removed from attachment. However, unconditional love is not just about loving others; the most important aspect is really loving ourselves, including our darker shadow aspect. It is profound love that enables us to accept things as they are; this is not a submission to, but rather an alignment of ourselves to the higher spiritual force of love beyond measure.

Exercises

Before starting a visualization and after taking yourself into the meditative state, spend some time really focusing on the rhythm of your breath. Breathe deeply a few times then regulate your breathing to be in tune with your heart. Focus your breathing into the heart centre and up to the throat, brow and crown on inhaling, then breathe downwards through the heart into the lower centres to the earth on the exhalation. Do this three times.

Another heart exercise is to visualize someone with whom you are having difficulty. Do this in a dispassionate way without emotions. Breathe into your heart, finding a balance of energy, and begin to breathe heart energy from you to that person. This might be difficult at first and if you find yourself feeling any kind of animosity stop the exercise and try again later. If you find you are getting emotional it can be helpful to see the other person as a photograph or two-dimensional image. With practice you will be able to allow an outpouring of heart energy to another without aspirations as to any possible outcomes. This point is very important as unconditional love means without judgment or attachment to outcome. Be honest with yourself. If you succeed, even if it is only for a few seconds, you have probably broken the negativity between you. It's easy to give love to someone we ourselves emotionally love, but the love of the heart has no separation and no boundaries.

Often, this exercise can really turn a situation or relationship around, but equally if it means that person has to leave our lives, accept this as part of the process of healing and transformation. Working with unconditional love means we can be in an unclouded space intuitively, which allows us to open up to others in a clear and receptive way.

Visuddha

The Throat centre

Colour

Blue

Location

Around the throat area

Area affected

The throat and ears

Quality

Communication

Energy

Space

The throat chakra

When we come to the fifth centre, we have crossed the bridge from the lower mundane into the higher realms. This centre opens us up to higher vibrational energy and allows a degree of sensitivity beyond normal everyday occurrences. Not surprisingly, the throat centre has a lot to do with communication and sound. Sound is a vibration and can affect us profoundly; it has been used in all cultures as a form of prayer, meditation and celebration of higher forces. Chanting is to be found around the globe and the rhythm of the chant has a peaceful and meditative effect on us. The Hindu term for the throat chakra, *visuddha,* means purification. It suggests that to fully obtain connection and openness, we need to have reached a certain level of purification.

The more subtle levels of the higher centres require greater sensitivity, which is fully in line with the idea that the higher the consciousness, the higher the vibrational note of the individual. Heightened consciousness requires a great deal of dedication and purpose. In reality, there are very few people who can take on this task as it requires scrupulous commitment to the real truth of who you are. Truth has its own clarity and vibrational energy so that when we hear someone speaking right from the heart and core of his or her being, even if we don't necessarily agree with him or her, we tend to listen and respect the individual.

Exercise

Having opened up in the usual way, pay particular attention to your breathing and try to get the rhythm of it in tune with your heart. The use of sound is extremely helpful here, so start by gentle humming. (When you use sound don't allow the sound to get stuck. Feel the vibration before you make a sound and then let it channel from your being.) There are various sounds

or mantras that can be effective; the traditional sound for the throat is "Ham". An English version of an appropriate mantra is "I am that I am". This mantra connects the individual with the universal energy. You can say or sing it. Other sounds that are helpful are the "Omm" sound, thought to be the original sound from which the universe was formed. The Hebrew mantra "Amen" is similar in sound to this.

Listen to the sound you make from within, and don't concern yourself with what it sounds like externally. Chant the sound as many times as you like. In your visualization for this centre, take yourself up into a spacious sky and feel as though you are flying like a bird, allowing your senses to be as graphic as they want to be. As you come back onto the ground, visualize a tree with a single bird on a branch and listen to his sound and try to absorb it into your being. Try to hum in tune with the sound you are hearing within, and let the sound float through your throat. When you have finished, visualize a golden cape around your whole body and be particularly aware of the feeling of the earth under your feet. Get up and gently walk around for a minute or two before you get on with you daily life, so you can be sure you are back in your body.

Ajna
The Brow centre

Colour
Indigo

Location
Slightly above and in-between the
eyebrows

Area affected
The eyes and ears

Quality
Perceptions beyond
the material

Energy
Vision/Time

The brow chakra

Opening the brow centre opens a window to what is described as the third eye. You have probably seen the ancient Egyptian motif of the third eye portraying the brow centre. It is synonymous with the true meaning of the word clairvoyant, or clear vision. This is the part of us that "sees" and has vision beyond the mundane. With this centre fully opened, one comes into a vision that has an overview. You see beyond and above what is going on. This view largely ignores detail but gives breadth of understanding that most people never see. The evolution of the individual at this level is someone who is beyond prejudice and sees things as they are and not coloured by what they want. It connects with light. Light is a very fast element and with it we step out of time and space. Light is produced by the excited energy of electrons; as they circle they jump to form a quantum leap. The raised energy from the brow takes us towards a leap of consciousness. This leap somewhat removes us from the material and our vision and view of life can radically alter. The view of a man at the top of the mountain is different to the view of the man at the bottom; they both have their reality and neither are wrong, but if they don't experience it for themselves they may not understand the other's view. Although the brow is a high vibration, many people find this centre opens automatically in times of great stress or danger when suddenly they "know" what to do.

A good exercise for this centre is to see a light streaming into your brow from the source of the greatest highest good. Mentally ask for light to penetrate through into your brain to stimulate the creaky doorways of your mind that are not used very much. You don't need to have any images at all, although they may spontaneously appear. Just enjoy the sense of connecting with a higher light vibration.

Exercising any muscle requires practice and work; so does exercising the use of the chakras. Don't be put off if you feel you are not succeeding. Although visualizations are a good tool there are some people who are not naturally visual, but will, however, have a "sense" of something, which is just as valuable.

Nonetheless, using visual images can help to train and focus energies so do keep trying.

Exercise

Having opened up in the usual way, focus your energy and attention into the brow just above and between your eyebrows. Focus on your mind as a clear, blank screen and onto that screen bring in an image of anything for which you need to have an answer. Maybe you wish to know something about the state of your health; if so, see your body as a silhouette and allow the images to form within it. You can also do this with an emotional or work situation; however, if you are emotionally attached to the problem. it is much harder to allow the clarity without your expectations and wishes getting in the way.

If you do this for someone else, it is important that he or she has asked you to do it. Making psychic connections with anyone who doesn't know is a bit like opening someone else's post. It is also energetically unsound and in some cases is a form of psychic attack. I will discuss this more later in the book.

Sahasrova

The Crown centre

Colour

Violet

Location

The crown of the head

Area affected

The head

Quality

The mystical marriage or union between the universe and self

Energy

The crown chakra

When the individual comes to the crown he or she is in a state of union or alignment to the spiritual essence of the universe. This is not something many people experience and it could be argued that it is not even conducive to everyday life. This is why people go to monasteries and ashrams to be away from the mundane world and concentrate on their spiritual energy. However, it is possible to manifest this higher consciousness in day-to-day living even if it may not constantly be present. In intuitive terms, the crown chakra is the "knowing" state. This is when one simply knows without the use of reason or rationale. You often hear people say "I knew I should have done this" or "I knew I shouldn't have done that". The task is to be open and free enough to have this knowing more of the time and the trust to act upon it.

Our brains hold billions of interconnected nerve cells and as a mechanism of the mind it is limitless. The stimulation of the crown takes us towards a sense of limitlessness and allows perception of a higher and deeper consciousness. As we move our energy up into each higher chakra we climb in consciousness and our reality shifts with every altered state. On a personal level the crown energy is beyond fear.

The major exercise for this chakra is meditation and subsequently bringing this state into our waking life. This is called "being present" or in a state of full awareness in any situation, place or with any person. Even though for most people this seems out of reach, it can be done in small ways every day. If you remind yourself of the feeling of centredness in the meditational state regularly throughout the day, it can become like an energetic tuning fork that brings your energy into in the present. Research on the effects of meditation (see also Chapter 2) show that brainwaves change into a state of deep relaxation, and oxygen intake and heart rate decrease and this has the effect of putting the body in a state of deep rest. From this state we move smoothly and we are better able to contact our in(ner) tuition or inner teacher – that part of us that "knows" what to do. All of the meditations in this book will assist the process but perhaps the best ones are those ones that simply connect ourselves with our breath.

Exercise

As the crown is connected with thought, having put yourself into a meditational state, mentally ask a question; wait and allow the mind to freely get some inspiration. Whatever images or thoughts you have, pick one and ask yourself where it came from. It might have come from the past, but keep following it back and further back to its origin. At some point you may find yourself connected to an infinite source which will give you a sense of blending with the universal energy. Being in this heightened consciousness does not mean, however, that you will not encounter all the myriad experiences and difficulties that life brings, but it does mean you will be able to come to terms with them with better understanding and hopefully see them all for the potential of growth.

Chapter 4

Stage two:
unfoldment of the spirit

Drawing on pyschotherapy, in addition to spiritual and

psychic techniques, this chapter offers further exercises

that provide the means to enhance intuitive abilities for

use in all aspects of life and living.

Looking at self

There are many traditions that hold that to be spiritual we just need to connect to God, whether that is through a religion or priest. Such spiritual connectedness undoubtedly has a profound effect and inspires, heals and can enlighten, but it also may disregard the personal aspect of self. Like many people before me, in my joy at finding my spiritual connections, I fell into the trap of ignoring unresolved personal issues. I felt so at peace with the timeless reality of my spiritual links that I believed this light would, in time, obliterate all the negative aspects of my being. But life has a way of not letting us forget we are in the material plane. When very difficult issues emerged in my personal life, they made me realize not just the benefit, but often the necessity, of using aspects of psychology to uncover past issues and pain, dissolve unwanted patterns and push through fears. The lower, and often the more noisy aspects of our psychological being, often obscure, veil or even obliterate genuine connection with the inner light. We see only through our eyes, and if those eyes are cloaked with old patterns, shadows and fears, we simply cannot obtain full spiritual integration. Therefore, we must consider the psychological aspects of self.

The four forces

Psychology has evolved greatly in the last 125 years, and today we recognize four major approaches – The Four Forces.

First Force What is now known as the "first force" began in the late 19th century with what is called "behaviourism". This attributes pain to the conditioning people receive, and it attempts to replace negative experiences with more positive ones, unlike spiritual systems, which encourage freedom from all conditioning. All types of psychology have their benefits and certain types of depression can benefit from first-force psychology. However, behaviourism is very limited in its view of the psyche because it concentrates on the outward and observable aspects of self and may not reach the underlying problems.

Second Force This is the psychology associated with Freud. It is concerned with a deeper understanding of the psyche. It acknowledges the unconscious part of our self and concentrates upon the emotional pain that occurred in childhood. Because the parents of wounded children are themselves often hurt, they cannot understand or even "see" their child's wounds, so over time the child consequently learns to repress his or her feelings and eventually loses awareness of them. On reaching adulthood, such children often continue to maintain these same defensive attitudes as a form of protection. The remedy is a process of remembering or re-experiencing old pains and working through them. The benefits of this form of therapy are obvious and clearly effective, but again it is not concerned with the deeper spiritual aspect of our being.

Third Force Starting around the 1930s, psychologists such as Maslow and Rogers, began to promote "third-force" or humanistic psychology. Maslow's well-known "hierarchy of needs" theory holds that when lower needs are met, space opens up for the individual to take account of his or her potential creativity and self expression. Once the basics are taken care of – we are fed and clothed, for example – higher needs emerge, such as altruism and a deeper understanding of self, and they lead us towards self actualization. Humanistic psychology contends that fear and lack of meaning in an individual's world make him or her avoid reality so that the person's life becomes a false or inauthentic one. People in a state of fear will gravitate to superficial things such as inappropriate relationships, drugs or non-stop entertainment, in fact, anything that prevents them confronting what is really present within.

Fourth Force In the 1960s, on the back of much of Maslow's work, "fourth-force" psychology emerged. This looks beyond the personal and thus is known as "transpersonal". The basic notion of transpersonal psychology is to integrate all the aspects of self with past traditions of spiritual wisdom. It takes into account the inner spiritual depth of the individual, and the process by which one connects to it is referred to as "unfoldment". It encapsulates the mystical idea that we are cloaked with veils of illusions – the outer persona – that mask our true inner being. When spiritual development takes place, there is a process of psychological unpeeling, layer by layer, until the deepest core of self is reached.

Our inner force

In chapter one, I talked about what Maslow described as our inner nature, the core and the real part of ourselves. It is a dynamic force that while apparently silent is all the time trying to drive us like an eternal engine. It is ever-present and although it can be inhibited, it won't go away.

One of the most common experiences I hear from students, especially when they first come into this work, is they feel they are "being pushed" and they do not know what or who is pushing. Often the person tries to ignore or fight it until finally he or she realizes there is something very important to acknowledge. This inner force is also a will-to-health on all levels. If it is frustrated, denied or suppressed, some form of dis-ease occurs. At our inner core is the quest for our true identity.

In transpersonal work, there is the means to uncover this core inner self and many of the exercises are very effective if the individual engages his or her will in the process. Together with this process of unfoldment, you can learn to listen to the inner voice; the in(ner) tuition or teacher. So alongside the transpersonal techniques, you can also employ intuition as a guide or voice, a light that illumines your path to your real self. Strictly speaking, this is a form of psychic energy as it is unseen, but it should not be confused with the psychism of the fortune teller or that which is associated with the "new age". Psychic development of a spiritual nature can be used very effectively to assist the process; unfortunately students, if not properly guided, may be side-tracked into the "wow" and glamour of psychic tricks. Deep intuition has no tricks; it is the most natural part of who we are; it is our inner true nature and to cloud it with trinkets that look like gold but are, in reality, nothing but flim flam at best and actually dangerous at worst, is a very real concern. This is where the student must examine very honestly his or her own integrity.

Questions to answer honestly

1 Do you want the truth even if it appears less appealing or even if it reveals things about yourself that are shadowy and dark?
2 Are you prepared to take this journey into the unknown whatever you may find?
3 Are you prepared for the possibility of all your constructs, models of life and beliefs changing?

If any of the answers to these are "no", in reality you are unlikely to find your true inner being, and you may not journey very far along the spiritual path. In many ways, no exercise however good can make up for the real determination to the will-to-good, the true, the real self.

Transpersonal methods

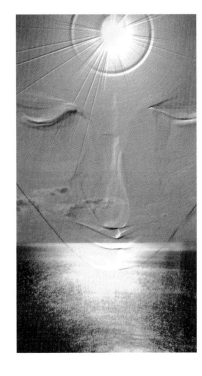

How do we approach the exposure of our deep core spirit in the process of unfoldment? What methods will assist our journey? Over the last 50 years, psychologists explored this matter and "transpersonal", "psycho-spiritual" or just "spiritual" psychology emerged. Much of what has been written is theory but an increasing number of practitioners are making use of methods that uncover a deeper layer of self. It is suggested that the psychological and the spiritual are interwoven and therefore can't be separated, and it seems that we need to address the whole person as a psycho-spiritual unit. Common methods employed use visualizations and dreams.

When the psycho-spiritual journey begins, it is not uncommon to experience more dreaming than usual. This is thought to be the unconscious mind trying to tell the conscious what it needs to know. Many people make the interpretation of their dreams more complicated than necessary. The unconscious is actually not trying to be mysterious or obscure – it wants you to know the truth. So it uses commonplace things to trigger the answers. Most often in dreams, every living thing, particularly a person, is an aspect of yourself. Even if you dream about someone with whom you went to school 20 years ago and have not thought about since, that person might be representative of a characteristic of yours, which is what the mind is trying to relay. If you have a dream about an aggressive or violent person, for example, he or she is a personification of the violent and aggressive part of yourself. Other aspects of the dream will tell you what is causing the dis-ease of self.

EXPERIENCE

"I dreamed I was in a small room like a cheap motel with a bed and I was talking to a man who means a great deal to me. Another woman entered the room and he lunged at her legs. I walked out in disgust and got in a brand new car. I could smell the newness of the interior. It was not a flashy car but obviously expensive. It was like a cabin with bold looking instruments. I felt safe. As I was setting off, in my rear view mirror I saw the man was running towards the car. I pressed the button for the electric window to close. He ran up to the window and tried to claw his way in. The dream ended with me having my foot on the accelerator wondering whether to let him in or drive off."

The dream described in the box on page 77, has many possibilities. It may be that the other woman and the man were personified aspects of the woman relating the dream. However, in real life, the woman was involved in a love triangle and decisions were being made, so it could be that the dreamer was playing out her real-life situation symbolically.

The most important part of this dream is the new car. A car or other vehicle indicates one's own mode of going through life. In this dream it was brand new, indicating that the woman is ready to embark on a new life. She felt safe in the dream so, whatever her choice, she has all she needs in her life to be safe.

If the people were aspects of her, then she sees herself as "the loose woman" and the male aspect of herself as weak. However, in both cases the car, her vehicle through life, is safe. It is a very reassuring dream.

Bias and prejudice

At any moment in time we are the sum total of all our experiences originating from our childhood, society, schooling and, if you believe in such things, your past lives. We all see a world coloured by these experiences; it is unavoidable. Some of these perceptions will be helpful to us as when, for instance, we have been brought up to believe that we must consider others and be kind to our neighbours. However, if we end up only doing things for others to the extent whereby we do not consider ourselves, it becomes counter productive to our spirit and our truth. Part of the unfoldment process, therefore, is to really look at our biases, prejudices and assumptions. This is not as easy as it sounds, as we all would probably like to think we don't have any. But we often inherit the fears of our parents. If they had a bad experience, say with someone from another country or culture, that prejudice may have been passed unconsciously on to us.

Biases, prejudices and assumptions will cloak our true self. It may not be possible to dissolve them completely but by being aware of them we can minimalize any potential problems in the future.

Bias Being in favour of one thing person or group in comparison with another. e.g. giving preference to or making allowances for a friend or a favourite.

Prejudice Preconceived opinion that is not based on reason or experience. Dislike, hostility or unjust behaviour formed on this basis; treatment of a person as inferior or nasty. Conditioning and programming by elders or other members of society against other sections, cultures or groups, e.g. racism.

Assumption Accepting something as true or certain with no proof, e.g. assuming a person who is immaculately dressed is happy and well or even that he or she is rich.

Exercise: Biases

List your biases, prejudices and assumptions. After you have thought about them take them into a meditation and ask for guidance. Ask whether they really assist you today.

EXPERIENCE

"I grew up in the 50s and 60s and there was lots of prejudice about people being black, gays, you name it and there was even prejudice about God. I felt all that was not right, I didn't want to listen to it because I thought differently. Consequently, as a child, I put a kind of umbrella around me thinking nothing is going to permeate through. But growing up in a family, going to school, going to work, a lot of prejudice seeped through to my skin and it was almost like trying to turn the Titanic at times. I worked in an area where there was a lot of prejudice and I began to feel inside of me there was something that didn't reconcile itself with the life that I was living. I remember thinking 'This isn't right, I don't know where I'm supposed to be and I don't feel right', but when the rest of the world is telling you 'Well this is the way it is' it was very hard. It took courage to try to change this, particularly in the very institutional organization I worked in; I tried to change it and I worked hard to keep my integrity but eventually I had to leave my career because it was destroying me. I had to get back to my soul and to get back in touch with my true self, into my authentic self, the part of me that has no prejudice. The spiritual work I did allowed me to alter these assumptions; it felt as though I was being reborn. It put me back on the path and it freed me from the negativity of separation between peoples, which in turn allowed me to understand myself."

Transference: the mirroring of self

The notion of "transference" was introduced by Freud after he noticed that his patients were transferring their own feelings onto him. This concept has now become well known in therapeutic situations. When transference occurs, people unconsciously transfer to the leader, therapist or healer the hurt child part of themselves, also their hidden and repressed feelings about a parent or some other

Exercise: Observing yourself

The art of observation of self is something that is always useful, as is the practice of detached loving observation of self. Pay particular attention to those people that frustrate and anger you. Are you reflecting your frustrations on them? When you feel antagonistic to someone ask the difficult questions, "What is the trigger for this? Could it be my own anger, frustration or any other emotion?" Be honest with yourself. You really can turn your life around and work to dissolve problems or actually use them to your benefit, if you know. Try not to be frightened by finding a darker side to yourself; see it as though it is just some unfortunate infection to be cleared. Remember, if infection is not dealt with, it can fester and causes dis-ease. Similarly, your unresolved issues can cause great disturbance to you. Better to have them revealed so that they can be worked through and healed.

important authority figure from the past. It's a bit like holding up a mirror and transposing the reflection of hidden aspects of self, either negative or positive, onto the other person. However, this doesn't just happen with authority figures; it can also occur all the time in everyday relationships. It is particularly prevalent when individuals project, often unconsciously, unresolved issues onto a "safe" person. Mothers, for instance, are often the targets of anger of their teenage children. Such anger is often a result of the adolescents' fears and uncertainties. It is not dissimilar to the idea of "dumping" stuff onto others.

Have you had a situation when someone accused you of something completely unknown to you? This could well be transference. It can also arise when individuals fear a sudden and/or unexpected situation in their lives; it arises when there is a change from feeling in control of things to losing control of them. The fear, when not identified, is projected onto others. It may have little or nothing to do with the person to whom it is directed. Observing this is not always palatable but can bring about awareness of one's own difficulties. For the purpose of looking at self, the knowledge of this concept is useful to understand what really might be occurring. Transference, therefore, can be put to work and used to motivate learning more about oneself.

AUTHOR'S EXPERIENCE

"While running a psychic development group many years ago on the first evening of the term as the class came to an end one of the participants got up, briskly pulled her jacket down and addressed the group. 'I cannot possible stay in this group; you remind me too much of my mother!' At which point she abruptly turned and walked out the door never to be seen again. I have no idea what her mother was like, but have observed many times since that, as a woman leading a group where sensitive energies emerge, students have often projected an image of a mother figure onto me. In this instance obviously this student's mother was not deemed safe so she could not stay. At the time I had no notion of transference but this particular student alerted me to the notion of what I called mirroring (transference) and I now use it in a pro-active way to help students understand themselves."

Cutting the ties

At some time or other we all find ourselves in a situation with people who are very difficult. This might occur in your work environment, when you feel you are beating your head against a brick wall and are just not being heard. It might happen in a relationship when you find it very difficult to be yourself without pressure from another. This often happens between parents and children, when the children sense that the parents do not understand or want them to do something that, if the children are honest with themselves, they don't want to do. It also happens in a relationship that is not working out the way you want and this is particularly painful for you to accept or come to terms with. You may feel helpless, unable to move within the situation or with the person concerned. Such situations have the effect of making us feel tied and trapped. We may feel there is simply nothing we can do. It is certainly true you are unable to make another believe or see things your way and, on a spiritual level, you do not really have the right to try: free will is sacrosanct in spiritual law. If you try to alter the will, persuade or cajole another against his or her will, no good can ever come of it and usually what occurs is that the other person just builds up resentment, which at some later time will result in separation and much regret. However, it is not true you can't do anything about it. Energetically you can change the vibration and bring some healthy space between the will of yourself and others. The second quote on page 84 is from a student who found it difficult to be himself.

If you are really going to do this exercise on an unconditional level you must be very firm and resolute with the way in which you implement it. It is important to let go of your own personal will in the process and one of the ways to do this is to intentionally, and with focus, make your energetic links only through the higher consciousness both of yourself and the person or situation you wish to clear. This point is vital and without it nothing will really change.

Although strictly speaking you do not have to be in meditation, it is likely to assist the process.

Exercise: Cutting the ties

Consciously, with clear intent, invoke the highest greatest good and take your own energy up to your higher self. It will help if you can visualize your energy a few inches over the top of your head; this has the effect of removing the personal wish or desire. Visualize the person with whom you are having difficulty. Direct your energy and thoughts to his or her higher self. Again, you might find it helpful to direct your focus to an energy above the person's head. Mentally ask the person's higher self to give you permission to connect with him or her and allow healing to occur. Then look at the image of the other person and feel where it is linked to you; you might see some tie, chain or other material join between you. Take particular note to which part of the body it is connected. Imagine a tool that could cut away this tie. For example, if you see string, a pair of scissors would be able to cut it. You can be as inventive as you wish – use fire, water, an axe, etc. Again, make sure you are working with your higher self and then visualize dissolving, cutting or whatever it takes to remove your tie to the other person. When you are sure this has been implemented, go back to that part of yourself previously joined and flood it with light. If it was a chakra point, fill that centre with its natural colour. For instance, if it was the solar plexus (and in this exercise it often is), flood your solar plexus with yellow sunlight energy and then seal it up. If it was the sacral, use the colour orange and the image of pure flames. When you have completed this healing, take your energy into your own heart centre. Breathe healing light out and around you, feeling the energy as though it were the wings of a healing angel wrapping around you. If necessary, keep reinforcing the clearance of the centre and drawing your energy into your heart. This exercise should have the effect of letting you feel more of the real person that you truly are.

> "I was 43 and my mother was phoning me every day telling me what to do. It was really aggravating me. Day by day I just felt increasingly angry. When you suggested using the 'cutting the ties' exercise I didn't want to because I love my mother even though she drives me mad, but something had to change. After I did the exercise, she did not stop phoning me but what happened was I found I simply was no longer affected by her calling. In fact, our relationship has altered and there is more acceptance and we have become more like good friends. I really appreciate that."

> "I've been using the 'cutting the ties' exercise on a day-to-day basis as I find I absorb or connect with other people's energies rather easily and find it helpful to quietly just take a step to one side and break down energy connections. I use it as I go through the day if I feel I've meshed too much with somebody else's energy. I have got caught in other people's emotional issues or fear states and I feel like I touch those and feel them resonating within me. I feel that I'm kind of running along in somebody else's tracks rather than my own.
>
> I used to feel that somebody else's thought patterns or emotional patterns had triggered my thought patterns or emotional patterns and I found it troublesome. Now I can simply will myself back, will myself clear again or will my own energy. At work if I'm working with somebody who has a different systems of thought, or emotional belief that is very different from my own I find that there is a gradual erosion of my clarity and I realized that I needed a little quiet time to separate this. Cutting the ties felt like letting daylight in somewhere that had been needing it for a while.
>
> It gave a level of a sense of reconnection. Sense of something that was familiar that had been clouded or closed. I could connect more to the source, to my own place of information and inspiration. I've been somebody who analyzed. I would say too much, now I try not to, I can just say what feels right and my ability to stay in my own energy space increased."

My next-door neighbours were driving me mad. They were a couple who were both musicians. She practiced her piano every day and I could hear it in every room of my house. I love my home but I felt as though I was in prison. I had asked her not to practise and got really angry. She is a concert pianist and she said she had to work. I got very anxious, couldn't concentrate; I didn't want to move but it became intolerable. When I heard about the 'cutting the ties' exercise I felt I would not be able to do it because I was just so angry. I couldn't put it up to a higher source. I didn't feel I could let go of my hostility enough to implement it properly. I thought I might make it worse, but as time went on I just knew I had to do something. I did the exercise although I couldn't hold it for very long. At first nothing happened, she went on playing although I did manage to feel a little bit more relaxed. Then all of a sudden it stopped. I don't know what happened — she was still living there but she did not play anymore. Three months later they moved and I have my own space again. It was miraculous!

I have had real problems with two old girlfriends that previously had been very close. It started when my son got really ill and I guess at some point I felt 'needy' towards them and had expectations of these relationships. The pressure was on and it reached a point when it just blew. My poor husband bore the brunt of it. One girlfriend lives in Scotland: I had to wait until last week to see her; it had been over two years. I was really nervous about it and thought I'm OK but I was actually very angry and instead of blowing the anger out on them, which was one way of what I wanted to do, I knew I had to transform that pain into light to let it go and all weekend that's what I have been working with. I could feel the pain, I knew it was stuff that had to be dealt with.

I actually felt that I did transform it last night with the help of my daughter. When I told her 'my solar plexus feels like I've got to work in there'. she said, 'Oh mummy what do we do with the stones that we can't lift'? She was just joking and I said 'I don't know', and she said 'We smash them up into little pieces' As she said this I knew she was right and I visualized it; the anger as stones being broken up, and it just went, it just went 'ting' and cleared.

We had a lovely laugh about it and it brought a lot of joy and I felt it. I've been doing 'cutting the ties' exercises; my intent was to clear it and heal it for myself. I also called on angels before I cut the ties and when I saw my friends we all went out for a meal and the kids were there and it was OK, it was fine and I'm sure that what ever will heal.

The main thing I guess that has come out of this, was when I separated from these two girlfriends, I felt that I maintained, created, accepted, opened up to a relationship with a deep spiritual energy and now this is where I take my energies to find inner peace. It was a very traumatic time for me but what occurred was the creation of a profound connection through letting go of my fear.

Transforming conflict

As I have described earlier, it is possible to transform and change positively your energies and the way you relate to your world. Not everyone is good at visualizing but everyone has some form of imagination that can be put to good use. Energy follows thought; how you think about yourself and the situations you find yourself in really can make a difference. We all sometimes react to a situation in a way that, upon reflection, is unproductive or even destructive. With practice you can, in a state of awareness, be present in the moment to learn how to respond constructively and not react defensively. "Being present" in the moment comes from meditation and a form of concentration that can be achieved in activities where you have to be totally focused in the now. A tightrope walker, a footballer or a ballet dancer cannot afford to lose concentration for a second. This state is not dissimilar to a form of conscious meditation.

The next exercise can clear and heal a situation after it has happened. As with all the exercises it is important to go into it with a clear and open heart and mind: without that no real healing occurs.

EXPERIENCE

"I walked into the restaurant where I was going to be having dinner with a few friends. When I arrived there was a person I was not expecting and did not know very well. At the time I was a smoker and asked the waiter if it was OK to smoke. He said not at that table but he could move us to a smoking part of the restaurant, I thanked him and asked the group if they minded. The woman who I was not expecting and was not very well known to me was the only one that emphatically said she could not move and was rather dogmatic and stubborn about it. Something about her lack of flexibility just brought anger up in me. What transpired was neither of us would budge and it ended up with me in floods of tears and having dinner at the other end of the restaurant. I realized that it was much less to do with smoking and more to do with my extreme stress at the time and I felt bad about disturbing the evening. Two days later I was able to throw light on the evening and found my friends were able to understand each other better and no hard feeling has been left."

Exercise: Transform conflict

Often in the heat of the moment our good
sense and awareness of self is forgotten. If
there has been a situation where you might
have felt uncomfortable or irritated and that
brought out anger or resentment, and you
allowed them to be vented on another person,
you can look at how this occurs and move the
energy to a different, more productive place. In your
mind, go through a situation that was uncomfortable for
you. Really be in touch with the feelings you had at the time and
recall how you felt and what you said. Remember in some detail what
occurred. Try to identify the presence of the person, looking in detail at how he or she was
dressed and what he or she looked like. Be in some kind of empathy with how that person was
at the time and try to understand why that person reacted in the way he or she did. Keep
reviewing the incident imagining being the other person; begin to recreate the situation from
his or her perspective. Hold that situation in light. Breathe very purposely into your heart.
Then imagine that you were back on that day at the start of the problem and as it unfolds in
your mind, consciously change your feeling and reaction to it. Because you "know" a little
bit more about the way the other person feels, watch what happens. Change the way you
respond. Keep going with unconditional feelings towards the person. When you have
brought the situation to a conclusion surround the situation with light. Of course, you cannot
literally change what has gone before, but what can occur is that the person with whom
you had previously fought may well soften his or her feelings towards you and you are
likely to soften your feelings towards the person. If nothing else, you will be more cautious
in the future about how you respond in a similar situation.

Good use of energies

Much of our time, thoughts and energy are spent on issues from the past and anxieties for the future. Consequently we may find that we are wasting energy in areas which we may be unable to change. Although it may not be possible all the time, we can with practice train ourselves to hold our consciousness. This allows us to focus in the moment which is not only energetically sound but also gives us a clearer awareness of our true needs. Being present in awareness then gives us the option to alter anything we wish. Of course it is possible that we may not need or want to change anything but if we keep looking it will reveal what we might best be able to do in order to transform any situation.

EXPERIENCE

"I realized I was spending most of my days with the pain of a bereavement from a boyfriend leaving me. I really really loved him and thought we were going to be together for the rest of our lives. I spent all my days going over and over in my mind what had occurred. I couldn't understand why this had happened. I was obsessed with it. I then realized I was living with that pain for over 90 per cent of my day. This made me distracted, I was not working properly, my friendships were put under strain and I was tired the whole time. I also realized that all my thoughts would not bring him home. It was hard but gradually every time I thought about it I just sent it into light. Gradually I was able to be in touch with my power and strength came back into my life."

Exercise: Understanding your energy use

After putting yourself in a comfortable space choose any day from the last week. Use your intuition to choose. In your mind, take yourself back to the start of that day. What did you feel when you awoke on that morning? Then take yourself right through the morning of that day. What did you do? What did you think? Where was your energy? Next take yourself back to the afternoon of the same day; go through the same procedure. What were you doing? What were you thinking? Where was your energy? Finally, recall the last part of the day up until the time you went to sleep. What were you doing? What were you thinking? Was that a good use of your time and energy? Now ask yourself what thing or thought took up most of the day and what percentage of time you spent on it. Was it 20 per cent of the day, 80 per cent, or another figure? Breathe into your heart and ask yourself if that was a good use of your energy. If you find that most time was spent on thoughts from the past or with some painful experience, really be very honest and ask if that was productive for you. It might be that it was productive, in which case surround the day in light and breathe back into your heart. However, if you think it was not a good use of your energy, imagine that whatever it was is somehow tied to a part of your body as a wire is linked into the exchange of energy (as connecting plugs were used in old-fashioned telephone exchanges). Ask yourself if you want the drainage of energy to continue. If you know you don't, visualize unplugging from the mains and holding for a moment the plug in your hands. Ask, "What have I learnt from this?" When you feel satisfied with the answer, let the plug dissolve from the part of your body to which it is tied and breathe into your heart centre where it will melt away in light.

Self identification

Roberto Assagioli saw the higher self as the transpersonal or spiritual self, the "essential beingness". It is not identified with the roles we have in life and is not affected by the conscious experience. The higher self is not the experience but the part of us, the "One" who we are, and, as such, the conscious self is seen to be merely a reflection of the higher self. It is this point that can synthesize the whole being and allow a more essential beingness of human existence. The following exercise originated from Assagioli as a way to be more connected to a real and true inner being.

Exercise: Acknowledge who you are

Put yourself into a relaxed state. Close your eyes and breathe into your heart. Become aware of your body and how it feels. Pay attention to your bodily sensations. Acknowledge that you have a body and that it serves you every day of your life. It allows you wonderful experiences and you therefore value it. It is a gift. Examine how your body was different when you were a child, the different size and shape it was. Acknowledge it had different sensations when you were younger and also realize it will change as you grow older. It is necessary in the material world to have a vehicle in which to live. That vehicle is your body. Ask yourself "Who is aware? Who has the feelings?" Acknowledge that your health may change. You may be sick or tired but that you, the real you, is not your body.

Next, acknowledge your emotions. Become aware of what you are feeling right now. Watch them for a while; acknowledge that they change. Sometimes you feel happy, sometimes you feel angry, the feelings change and they move from joy to sorrow. At times very strong emotions may seem overpowering but acknowledge that even those change in time. Remember, if you can, your emotions as a child. Be aware of how they might have changed. Go deeper within and see that although your emotions may swing from one feeling to another, something within yourself remains the same.

Next, look to your mind. Again in an impartial way watch your thoughts. What are you thinking now? Give yourself some time and watch your thoughts move and change. Think about your thoughts as a child. Are they the same as they are now? Acknowledge that you have a mind and that it is a very valuable tool for expression and for learning. Acknowledge that the contents of it are constantly changing – new ideas, new information. Sometimes your mind is clear; sometimes it is confused. As you observe this, make sure you also observe that your thoughts are not you.

In the light of your questions ask again, "Who is aware? Who has feelings? Who has thoughts?" Try to experience yourself beyond the mind, emotion and body

at a point of awareness within. Think about the being that is the real part of you that does not change. If you dis-identify from your body, your mind and feelings, you are left with the essence, the spirit of yourself. State out loud, "I am a centre of being and will, and I am able to do all these things. I am a luminous being, an awareness encased in flesh. I am a being of light; I am a centre of pure consciousness, love and will."

Round table visualization

There are many ways to access aspects of yourself in order to create a more healthy life. Using an active imagination in the process helps. This section ends with an inventive exercise, which can excite the imagination using the concept of King Arthur's round table. The image of the table is one of safety and can be very productive in finding out more about yourself. Like all these exercises, this one requires you to be honest with yourself. This exercise can be done on your own and is also very effective if you implement it with the help of someone who has some notion of psychology.

Exercise: Sit at King Arthur's table

Take yourself into a comfortable place and make yourself as relaxed as you can. It will help if you implement the "connecting with the breath" exercise first (see page 46). Close your eyes. Imagine King Arthur's round table. The centre is gold, which represents the heart. Around the table are seated King Arthur and Queen Guinevere and other knights and/or people. King Arthur represents your male side and Queen Guinevere your female, and the others represent additional aspects of yourself. Pay attention to how you feel about these people.

What do the table and its location appear like? If the table is located in an unpleasant place, change it to a more favourable one.

Invite part of yourself to a place where the table is present. The self you invite could be any part of you that you have given up; it could be, for instance, your younger self, playful self, or naughty or creative self. Be as inventive as you wish. The idea at this stage is not for that part of you to come up to the table, it is more just to meet with it, and find out what it wants from you. If you have any concerns about the self with whom you are going to work, bring in some help in the form of a friend, a positive person you respect, or a spiritual leader or guide.

As the part of you comes to the place where the table is, take account of how you perceive that part of yourself. Use all your senses – sight, sound, smell, taste, movement and emotion. Thank that part of yourself for coming and ask it, "What do you want?"

If you have chosen an aspect of yourself that feels neglected, it might be angry. It may appear shocked or surprised. Bear in mind that it cannot do anything bad to you because in doing that it would be destroying itself. Sometimes it may appear masked in a nice image, which, when removed, can reveal a very different face. Take account of what is wanted; acknowledge and respond to the need. It may need space, attention or love.

Now request that part of yourself to come to the table and join the rest. If it does not want to come, accept this and remember you can invite it another time. If it does come, watch where it goes. If it leaves, imagine it back. The other self will present you with a gift. Acknowledge the gift and thank your other self. Ask it what the gift means.

Notice if the table or its location has changed. You can continue the exercise, inviting other parts of yourself if you wish. When you have finished, breathe the image of the other self into your own heart and breathe the whole image of the people around the table into the golden centre of the table. Dissolve any image and breathe firmly back into your own heart centre.

King Arthur experiences

The round table exercise can be very powerful and useful. It embraces ideas from psychology and human experience. It is somewhat similar to Gestalt psychology, which concerns itself with the integration of self, seeing the whole being greater than its parts and completing the circle. The idea of parts of yourself being separate is based on people's life experience and Jungian psychology. Jung describes the way we choose to recognize certain core qualities and push the opposites into what is described as the "shadow" or the "dark" side. Unless we are some kind of saint or highly evolved being, all of us will have, to a lesser or greater extent, some darker aspects of self. Nobody really wants to see these and yet do we really want some dark shadow lurking unconsciously sabotaging us or creating difficulties for us? Like a cancer going unnoticed, isn't it better to see it for what it is and therefore be able to cut it out?

Hiding these darker aspects may or may not be intentional; for example, if I want to be recognized for my kindness or courtesy, I may hide my unkindness or discourteous thoughts, feelings or actions. Jung considered the process of what he called mature individuation as accepting the parts of ourselves that assist the transcendence of the ego.

The concept of King Arthur's round table originates in Celtic legend, and therefore is likely to be based on Celtic religious and spiritual tradition. In more recent history, the round table has come to represent democratic leadership as it allows an equal voice. Using this metaphor for integration suggests a holistic process in which all aspects have a part to play. Many people have done this exercise; here are just two people's experiences.

I called for any destructive part of myself to appear and two youths came and said they were "infanticide" and "patricide". This seemed rather extreme and I questioned it. They certainly did not look like anything that would be so sinister; actually they looked very handsome and appeared really sweet. But then they removed what appeared to be masks, which just peeled off their faces and what was there underneath was horrible and shocking — they looked like demons. One immediately grew and grew, he got really big and overshadowed the whole table. They ran riot, they tried to break up the table and were unruly, aggressive and violent. I was quite scared. I asked them to return to the table; thankfully they did and the golden centre absorbed them. I was quite shaken by the whole experience but actually what I found was that the fear of negative aspects of myself diminished and there was some feeling that whatever dark bits of myself may be lurking I could melt them away and they could never destroy me. The extraordinary thing was the gift they brought was life. So for me there was something about the shadow side being destructive of life itself: like a boil or wound it must be dealt with so it can be healed.

Ages ago when I did the King Arthur exercise I invited my little hurt bits to the table. Immediately there were hundreds or even thousands of lemmings hurtling onto the table. I did not know what to do so I imagined a hole in the table and invited them to go through it. They disappeared. The gift they gave me was joy. I think this related to my reaction when I feel hurt. 'Cos I do kind of rush at things. I don't mean violently, but I don't take time to really understand and see where I am going. This exercise made me see how destructive that aspect of myself could be.

Chapter 5

Stage three: psychic sensitivity

Once the more basic exercises are mastered, more

advanced techniques are offered that enable you to

progress to learning how to connect and attune with the

aura and astral – inspirational and channelling

energies that provide a deeper revelation of self.

> *Many years ago I had a student who went to a tarot reader because at the time she was experiencing great difficulty in her marriage. She thought to herself, that if only she knew whether her marriage would work or not she could cope. The tarot reader correctly picked up from her that there were marriage difficulties, however she then went on to say 'you might as well pack your bags now the marriage is over'. My student said she walked out the door knowing one thing and that was she did not want her marriage to end. From that moment she did all she could to turn the marriage around and 20 years on she is still happily married. What many untrained psychics do is to read off the aura, the energy the person is emitting and read it back to them as fact. In this case the tarot reader was likely to be picking up her fear.*

Intuition

For the purpose of spiritual self-development we are looking to use a deeper form of intuition to act as a guide, an inner teacher, a directive tool to lead us closer on our pathway to the core, the truth or who we are. Intuition by its nature is a psychic experience. There are different levels of psychic perception and the student needs to distinguish between these to be able to discern the real from the superficial or false. This is a very important factor in understanding what is real. There are many different forms and reasons behind psychic experiences. For instance, a common experience is when we walk into a house or building and feel there is something good or bad. This could be for a number of reasons; it could just be that we are picking up some kind of very different feeling we have never experienced before and this makes us feel on guard or wary, when there may be nothing negative present, or it could be a connection to a discarnate spirit. It could even be a type of psychic memory imprinted in the building. Whatever it is, it is a very different sense to that of a deep inner knowing.

Learning psychic perception is a bit like learning an instrument. It takes time to attune to the very many different energies, to trust your feelings. It requires constant practice and attunement because although people have some psychic faculties naturally, an untrained psychic often does not realize the difference in the levels. This can be misleading at best and dangerous at worst. Most books you read on psychic development only cover the first three levels. These are commonly called the auric levels; the physical, emotional and lower mental (thought) level. This means that the untrained psychic usually connects to the lower areas. This can be very helpful, particularly for those people who do not realize what energy, thoughts and emotions they are emanating out to the world. However, the problem with this for an untrained psychic is often the hopes and fears of the person are seen as actuality. For instance, if someone has just gone for a job interview and they believed it to have gone very well the psychic will pick this up and might say they have got the job. If someone expects a lost love to return the psychic may say your boyfriend is coming back. In either example this might not actually be the case but only the hope of the sitter. The nuances of energy are not easy to decipher and, just like learning any instrument, it is only by constant practice and attunement that the psychic can become competent. Also as we have seen in earlier chapters there is the problem of the psychic's own bias and assumptions, not to mention transference, getting in the way. If the psychic has not gone through their own self-awareness process they will be unlikely to be conscious of these things affecting the reading. The psychic reading then becomes very unreliable.

The aura

The lower level The lower auric levels help us in daily life. On the base instinctive level we may pick up danger, putting us on guard and enabling us to literally get out of the way of harm. Animals in the wild use this level all the time, and it can be just as useful to us. If we meet someone we may pick up they are not to be trusted; alternatively we may psychically pick up that they are going to be someone to whom we can go to in times of need.

The second level is a psychic awareness of what our tribe or families need. Again this is present in the wild with herding animals. This can be very useful in a work environment when we have to work as a team. On this level we can also pick up emotional energies. We must sense, for instance, when someone is frightened or fearful, we may sense if they are unhappy or if they are fulfilled. This allows us to be good friends with those around us. It gives us the ability to be sensitive and empathetic. This sense is very useful in therapeutic and healing situations; however, although it is good to have a feeling about someone, it is not good to hold on to that feeling. If someone is crying you do little good by crying with them. Many untrained psychics pick up energies from others and find they can get drained. Talking to a friend in trouble on the telephone can also do this, so by the time the

Many years ago I gave a sitting to a lady who was greatly distressed; she had been to a psychic who had told her that both her daughters would die. Apart from the ethical consideration of such a dreadful thing to say, it was incorrect. This woman's greatest fear was the loss of her daughters; the psychic had picked this up and read it back as an actuality. To someone of a nervous disposition this could cause a great deal of stress.

phone call is ended your friend may be feeling much better but you are worn out! Learning to be centred and focused in one's own energy is not just good practice as a psychic but also is profoundly useful to us all in day-to-day living.

The third level is where most psychics get their information. Psychic connection on this level alerts the psychic to the person's thoughts and feelings, their sense of worth and where they are directing their energy. It often comes with images of what is occurring within the life of that individual and it can be amazingly accurate. How that psychic advises on that subject, however, is fraught with difficulties. If the psychic is not confident and balanced in their energy they may well project their own fears onto the sitter. When I train a student in psychic development I always try to advise the student to say exactly what they receive. If this is an image they must describe the image without putting any interpretation upon it. When this is implemented properly it is not only much more accurate, but it can also cut out the psychic's bias and prejudice of their own feeling around the image.

Individual will can also be a problem in the third level. We all know the feeling of being with someone who is very wilful. Sometimes it can make us feel physically uncomfortable and when it does it is usually felt in the solar plexus area. Energetically the person is draining our energy; however this is rarely anything they are consciously aware of. All the person would know is that he/she feels more empowered, whereas the person from whom they are taking the energy feels uncomfortable and sometimes depleted. Linking with this area a psychic can find out what the person fears and hopes but there is a down side of an untrained psychic working on this level. The human emotions are very powerful and this might lead an inexperienced psychic to feel these as predictions. This may not only be incorrect but could be disempowering by allowing the person to think they are absolute. Emotions and thoughts can easily be put across as faits accomplis, not just possibilities.

Auric exercises

There is no real alternative for learning psychic development other than in a good group. The group dynamics and the evidence and attunement one can receive week after week is irreplaceable. The problem with finding a good teacher is that there are many people with integrity and talent, but unless they have gone through their own unfoldment process they may be incompetent to really understand what is going on with the student. Depth psychic work is not just about evidence, it is about how it is relayed, what quality of energy comes through with it and, most important of all, how much clarity is in the transmission of the psychic. What has all this got to do with spirituality? The beneficial aspect of sitting in a psychic development group is in understanding another person's feelings, and being empathetic and sensitive to others. This serves as a reflection of oneself and most importantly you are likely to receive inspiration for and by yourself, which is something that anyone can and does

SIMPLE GUIDELINES FOR WORKING IN A GROUP

1 Use simple uncomplicated meditation exercises like "connecting with the breath" on page 46.
2 Remember it's all right to get things wrong; we all do and only a fool thinks they are right all the time.
3 Learn to listen to members of the group; they all have something to teach you and the one that aggravates you most is the one that you will learn most from.
4 Be humble but don't just be nice for the sake of it: speak your mind with kindness.
5 We are all good souls. People are difficult usually because they are feeling at odds with themselves. People behaving badly are usually ones that have had bad things done to them.
6 Be true to yourself, but don't be afraid to look at the shadow side. Like any infection or cancer it's best to know about it so it can be healed.
7 Trust your own feelings. Be discerning. Usually the most elaborate-sounding evidence or guide is the one most likely to be false. True guidance comes gently with love not glamour.
8 Never be afraid to say NO.
9 Exercises can only work if the person is really engaged into the process.
10 When in doubt, go back to the heart. Work with unconditional love.

benefit from. Of all the psychic development groups I have led over 25 years probably only 1–2 per cent of participants are working psychics. However, the benefit that it has given them in any walk of life is immeasurable. Knowing oneself will lead to being a better person and the process of unmasking oneself takes one deeper and deeper into one's core self towards spiritual attunement.

Unfortunately, often in psychic development groups pettiness and political aspects can creep in. We are all equal in the eyes of God. However, there can be a sense that people in the development groups are vying for being the most enlightened. Who or what can possibly evaluate spirituality? What method would one employ? Good deeds, in themselves, may not necessarily be coming from the heart and if one does something merely to earn "brownie points" the energy is defective and probably no good will come of it. If you are connected to a group where there is backbiting and nastiness I would strongly suggest you vote with your feet and leave. If you really can't find a good group, gather about six people together and meet regularly. If there is no one of experience to lead it, run it as a democratic concern. This is a lot harder than it sounds as the simple truth is everyone likes to think he or she knows best.

Psychic training

When we start working with psychic and intuitive energies, it can be quite a turbulent time for students.

I had only vague feelings to begin with, which I now can identify as intuition. This was verified by doing simple psychic attunement exercises and allowed me to trust my intuition more and realize I did not necessarily always have to have some rational or logical explanation for things. Sceptics might argue that these experiences might be explained by all manner of things, even eating the right food!

In other words this student is saying that people might dismiss intuition for a number of seemingly more rational explanations; however, this was "not her explanation".

Exercise: Simple psychic sensing

Together with a couple of friends, after doing the "connecting with the breath" exercise, put some objects on a tray. Make sure the objects are not antique but have only been owned by one person. Choose an object and engage the will in attuning, linking and "making friends" with the object. This is like an energetic arrow of communication; like dialling a number towards the object, if you like. Then wait and be open to any impressions you might receive. Do not discount anything. Whatever you feel, see in your mind, hear in words or whatever, relay exactly as you receive it. Check with the person if the information is accurate. This exercise is used very often in psychic development groups. It is not of a particularly high level but it does allow students to verify that they can gain psychic information. Often even students who have never done it before receive really good evidential information. They then begin to know that something is going on and something is working.

During this period of development there can be a kind of inner tug of war happening. In this particular student's case, it was a fight between her logic and rational thinking and her inner feelings, of which to the latter she "still has allegiance". The rational mind told her not to continue, but was counterbalanced by her own inner feelings that drew her back week after week. For many weeks she thrashed about with these contra feelings, often requiring discussions after class. Her protestations were listened to and although she was given reassurance that she was all right, the decision to stay or leave was very much put back into her own hands. She describes one of the first exercises she tried:

I thought this isn't going to work. This is fairground stuff, I thought, this is mumbo jumbo magic and very silly. But I thought well I'm here and I'll have a go and I was scared because... I'm going to fail and I'm not going to be able to do this ... I picked up somebody's ring and had all these images and so obviously I was linking to something and thought, oh that's a bit strange, I can do this...this taught me to trust more, go with the flow, not immediately to have a rational explanation, a logical explanation.

She was initially not sure of anything and she found it all "very difficult" but the fact that she received positive confirmation of her own intuition through the exercises was the major factor to her continuing the development programme and she relays that "deep down I knew there was something in it". At the beginning, she realized that she was "only skimming the surface", "there is obviously a lot more there".

On page 103 you'll find an exercise that is used very often in psychic development groups. It is not of a particularly high level but it does allow students to verify that they can gain psychic information. Often even students who have never done it before receive really good evidential information. They then begin to know that something is going on and something is working.

Psychic energy

As we saw in Chapter 2 there are some scientific explanations of how a psychic picks up energy. One student who is a scientist explains:

I now understand human beings are energetic creatures in the sense of having electro-magnetic variation waves around and I believe that all thoughts and emotions are stored in their energetic body. I'm not sure whether the use of the word energy is quite correct; it is a misnomer as this may mean something different to physicists. However, we are spiritually energetic and the term is accepted in spiritual and psychic studies so I cannot think of a better one. I now find myself slipping between the accepted rational and energetic approaches quite easily as I feel different senses are used for different tasks.

There is also a very powerful self-awareness aspect to psychic training and one that is not always comfortable. To do these exercises you are put on the spot. You could try and bluff it, but that would not work permanently. The psychic has to be in a silent still space, an open channel to be able to respond to the energies and be an open receiver of information.

I often felt exposed doing the psychic exercises, which was quite hard; I felt vulnerable and they were sometimes frightening. I started feeling people's energies more and feeling people's emotions and feelings and I didn't like it. That was sometimes a bit uncomfortable, I mean it was incredibly useful and I think it's something that I have always been able to do but it was highlighted and I didn't like feeling what people were feeling because it wasn't me . . . I was vulnerable, that's what it felt like, being made to feel vulnerable.

When asked what, if any, value there was in this, she said:

It gave me another awareness of myself, so in that way it was helpful. I didn't want to be defeated by it . . . It was definitely a big challenge to be able to do it.

She also said that the psychic exercises made her less judgmental.

Because when we linked with people and said things we must never try and impose things. Whatever you came up with was theirs not yours, so you weren't there to judge and you were never there to say you "should" do. That was a very difficult lesson for me. I am in a position every day of my life to tell people what to do, not just in terms of the work but in terms of their lives; they bring the most ridiculous things to me and expect me to solve them and just through doing this and also through the discussions I hope I've learnt to do it less, to be able to say this is your journey, even if not in those words. And it was through linking with people and realizing you're linking with something completely different. I got crazy images at first because that's how I worked and the teacher would say "what do you see?" so I think it taught me a lot.

Here, the student is describing the unpicking of psychic information whereby the student has to say "exactly what impressions they see without interpreting or judging them". Students are encouraged to be very succinct, clear and precise. She said she felt this process allowed her to become very much less judgmental in her day-to-day life. She also learned to use her "intuition differently". It taught her to listen to others, particularly in her work as a teacher. She said "you have to listen" and "you have to ask questions, to get them to think for themselves by asking intuitive questions, getting them to use their intuition". She enjoyed the group as she found herself "being good friends with people I would never normally meet" and with whom she would normally have had nothing in common.

Auras

Every living thing has a field of energy around it called aura. How can we use this to assist our own awareness and possibly help others? You might see healers waving their hands around and wonder what they are doing. They are directing and balancing energy within the aura of the patient, which is thought to have a profound effect on the health of the individual. The aura is not a static energy field, it vibrates and fluctuates as the person's consciousness changes. It can also change more permanently through personal and spiritual growth.

Exercise: Visualizing the aura

Auras can be photographed as described earlier with Kirlian photography but they can also be drawn. Get a large sheet of paper, preferably cream, and some paint, markers or coloured pencils. Have a subject who will allow you to do this. Try to put yourself in a relaxed or meditative state. Attune your thoughts and energy towards your subject. Draw a rough outline of the body (it doesn't matter if you are not particularly artistic). Around the outline draw three circles, then colour them in any colour that you feel intuitive to use. The inner patch is the physical aspect of the person, next is the emotional and the third is the mental or thought aspects of the self. If you find yourself using different colours in each circle that's fine. Very often we expel a number of different energies at the same time. Look back to Chapter 3 for interpretations of the colours in the auras.

You can also boost or even change your energy, by visualizing light into the area that you feel is unbalanced. Make sure this light energy is not coming from you personally but is coming from a higher spiritual source. Also, make sure you are drawing this light in a loving and unconditional manner.

Exercise: Sending arrows of communication

This exercise will give evidence that you can fine tune your psychic talents. Again this is best done in a group; however you can ask a few people to volunteer. It's better if you do not know too much about them and their lives. After relaxing and putting yourself in a clear space by the opening meditation: send out an arrow-like energy of communication to the aura of a person in the room. In your mind, ask for some information on a physical level only. Relay this back to the person. Do this again, asking for information on an emotional level. Relay the outcome to the person. Finally, attune and ask for information for the person on a mental level. Again, relay this back. You will find you get different pieces of information. Often with auric attunement you sense this as a feeling, you might, for instance, feel some discomfort in your body when you are linking with the physical and you could feel sad or happy whilst linking on the emotional. Please make sure at the end of this type of exercise that you very firmly bring your energy back to yourself. Breathe into the heart centre and feel your energy ground under your feet, like a tap root of a tree. This is called grounding your energy.

You can also do a scan on your own energies; a simple way to do this is to lie on the floor and breathe into each chakra. Feel and sense what chakra point is not flowing and breathe light into it. This is particularly good if you are physically under par. You might also take note of any inspiration you may receive during this exercise as it is likely to help your body recover.

The tarot

The 22 major arcana, or trumps of the Tarot are not just a fortune-telling device but a powerful description of spiritual transformation, which can help us understand deeper aspects of our lives and can go some way to enlightening our path. We all encounter many trials and tribulations but every situation can, if properly understood, be turned to our advantage. It is often the very things in life that push our buttons and that we find most hard that are the ones that build up spiritual muscle and in-depth learning.

The whole of Chapter 7 (page 138) is given over to a journey of self, which is described with relevance to the symbolism of the Tarot's major arcana. Though the story is fiction, the characters' experiences are drawn from my many years of listening to thousands of spiritual encounters.

HERMIT

There are times in our lives when we have to "go it alone", and yet the card illustrates that we all have an inner light and guide within us. All spiritual aspirants go through some stage of isolation, but this can push us to find some inner quality, some deeper meaning and purpose in life. When this has transpired, great awareness and empowerment occur and we discover a permanent feeling of safety that creates a sense of invincibility, which means we will never feel alone again.

I had lived all my life on the surface and I came to a point where everything conspired or pushed or I pushed myself to go inward. Something was missing and I realized that actually the inside of myself was extremely important and full of depth and this realization brought tremendous change and personal growth

MAGICIAN

This card talks to us about the power of thought and asks us to look at how and what we think. Muddled thinking creates a muddled life. Focused thought allows us to put out into the atmosphere more positive energy that creates its own magic. Beliefs are not fixed; what we believed as a child changes as we grow and, as we grow spiritually, our beliefs often alter to reveal a different picture. We shape our world through our own notions and beliefs but we can choose to believe whatever we want.

Intuition cuts through the imagination and it can occur when a person reaches rock bottom and there is an awful turmoil but in that moment there is an awareness and realization occurs. I believe that anything that makes you think beyond where your mindset is stuck assists you because it broadens the way you look at things. So, making me reassess things has actually made me reassess everything — the whole nature of belief if you like.

DEATH

This card is often used in films to predict physical death but its true meaning is about death of some aspect of ourselves. Life is full of ebbs and flows and we all experience some form of change or death of situations that perhaps no longer serve us. There is little certainty in life and, as with the seasons, things come and go. Just as spring follows winter the initial menacing idea of death opens us up for new things, new beginnings and better times.

My world seemed hopeless; I had come to the end of a major chapter in my life. Yet even at that time, I was aware of new growth and movement in the shoots of spring and there was the potential for something more real and important to emerge.

Experiences of psychic development

Developing the intuition and psychic faculties as part of a spiritual self-development can be problematic. It is important that the student sees this stage as only part of the journey, not an end in itself. Some students feel it is unnecessary to do psychic exercises, but if they can engage in them they all feel the benefit. Below are some experiences from psychic development students:

EXPERIENCES

"I felt extremely put on the spot and had to deliver so to speak with the psychic exercises and that was really hard and every week we used to talk about it outside the class and think, well it wasn't as bad as we thought this week. I actually felt determined to do it, I really wanted to do it, I knew I could do it. Sometimes I used to think by myself the more fearful it is the better, so I knew that if I pushed through enough fear then it would be really helpful. It seemed to me that I was slowly working through the worst fears in my life. Every fear that I ever had started to come up over a period of years, it was so horrible but actually facing them wasn't as bad as I thought in the end. I felt I needed to pursue things as they came up and I couldn't ignore them, it was so horrible and I wanted to run away, yes I gritted my teeth. But what I gained from it was tremendous."

"We were learning to open the heart, which was quite new. It always felt fantastic to me to actually focus on that part of my being, to be honest and it really had, over a period of time, quite a profound effect on me, you know focusing on your heart and understanding that things worked though the expansion of consciousness though your heart and that was an ongoing process. I understood it mentally, but it took a while for it to actually physically manifest itself; I felt it and it was definitely quite a strong feeling."

When I started the classes it was really a very difficult time. I split up from my relationship and I was going through tremendous turmoil and at times felt incredibly depressed and felt really you know on the edge of things, so I think it was a real focus point coming to the class. It enabled me to practice at home. I used to sit down and have time to myself and try to centre myself and that helped me to go through the things I was going through at the time. I used to really like listening to the people I have to say because everyone else's experiences were so interesting and so different and also it was nice to be able in a way to compare yourself with other people because if you knew somebody else was feeling similar sort of things then you felt on the right track as well, in a way I needed the sort of reassurance of the group.

I started to become aware of people having energy and also that I had energy which I didn't really realize before and then I begun to realize what they were then doing with their energy. It made me feel a bit more withdrawn, because I initially felt very exposed. It made me feel sometimes quite uncomfortable with some kind of new knowledge if you like and I remember I did go through a phase of being quite anti-social, I didn't want to be around lots of people that were you know sort of zapping my energy and I felt quite energetically manipulated because I then started to realize how people were able to drain me if I let them.

Mediumship and the astral

In the fourth level of psychic attunement we come to mediumship. The word has come to mean different things, but basically it is when a psychic is a medium or channel between the material world and the world of spirit. The psychic is able through this link to communicate with discarnate spirits, guides and teachers. The astral plain is a difficult subject and one on which we cannot delve much here and one might ask why should it even be included in a book about spiritual self development. We do this for a couple of reasons. One is that when students of spiritual development are opening to spiritual truths there is often a period when they are unable to contact their own wisdom direct. When the consciousness of the individual is rising they automatically emanate a call for further knowledge and wisdom.

In the early days it is not always easy to receive spiritual truths clearly. As we saw earlier, often in the beginning of development, the students have more dreams and some of these are not just of the psychological type and there is often a sense that some piece of spiritual knowledge has been received in their sleep, although they may not always be able to relay these in words. In sleep we go into the astral plains and when the students are open to receive, this can act as an open frequency to spiritual inspiration and knowledge.

It is possible to connect with guides through the astral, but whereas this can be inspiring and helpful, one must be very careful because it is very easy to contact a lesser astral energy. On the lower levels of the astral there are many energies that are very good at masquerading as benign beings. Two good ways of identifying these are that they will either give inflated names, such as some known identity: an enlightened being needs no names. Also they will give messages that either inflate the ego or bring fear. For instance they may tell you that you are "special" and have been chosen, or they may say if you don't do a certain thing something awful will happen. Good common sense must be used; remember, no divine being will ever tell you what to do. They may advise, guide and heal but they will never abuse the sacrosanct law of free will. That said, a good link to a guiding teacher energy is of extreme value for the student at this stage of development.

Just as there are levels of the chakras there are levels on the astral as well. The lower levels are to be distrusted and ignored. The place that most mediums link to the departed is often referred to as "summerland". This is where you will find a loved one doing the things they most enjoyed in life. For instance if you connect with a relative that loved his garden, the medium will often tell you he or she sees that person in a beautiful garden. If the relative was particularly musical she may have found a place where inspirational music is made. Many creative people feel a connection with this. Composers have been heard to say that they awoke in the morning with a piece of music composed for them in their sleep. Writers talk about muses and inspiration; sometimes they say they feel something else has written it for them. This is a form of channelling and most probably from the astral layers. It's a bit like having access to all radio frequencies and being able to tune into whatever is appropriate. So for spiritual growth it has something to offer us. Be careful though, as it is only one stage of the spiritual journey, a means to an end and not the end in itself.

Astral attunement for healing

Another good reason for including some astral work in an intuitive spiritual development programme is that it is very hard to get a fix on the energies there. It attunes the psychic sensitivity in a way that no other exercise does. To begin with it can feel very nebulous but as the student progresses they fine tune their connection, and they become discerning and much benefit is to be gained.

When working on the astral level students often have difficulties:

On this level I never felt strong, it was like something smoky that might be there and might not and I'd try and have a go and it never worked. I accept there are angels and people in spirit but I was not so sure about talking to dead people. The concept was problematic because I was brought up to believe that such practices were wicked and we just weren't meant to do it. I consequently did not fully engage in these exercises and although I felt the presence of my dead father, I would never say I clearly spoke to dead people. Nonetheless, as the classes progressed I lost much of my fear and would be intrigued with what other people said.

When asked if these concepts had a purpose or if they assisted her at all she said:

I think anything that makes you think beyond where your mindset is stuck at the moment assists you because it broadens the way you look at things, even if it's only to look at it and then say no. That has to be preferable to not looking at all. So I feel that the whole thing, by confronting me with things and making me reassess things has actually made me reassess other things as well, the whole nature of belief if you like.

There is another reason for linking to those in spirit that is little used but has some similarity to transpersonal psychology. I have found that putting someone in touch with a relative or friend that they had great difficulties with can bring enormous clearing and healing. The experience below illustrates this.

EXPERIENCE

One day when I was with my mother when I felt the need to contact my father in spirit. Suddenly he was there and it was so profound. He actually sort of gave me the feeling of so many things that I never experienced with him while he was alive and it was almost as if the whole thing had gone round full circle and he was able to open his heart to me completely, which was absolutely fantastic and I never in a million years would have anticipated that would have happened and so on a spiritual level, it was absolutely amazing. Then what happened was my relationships, especially with men, completely changed. I'm now with somebody who is so different from anybody else I've been with before and I felt the whole thing had completely healed and it was an immense realization that actually you can heal very difficult things in your life and they do come right.

This connection to spirit had a positive therapeutic element as I was able to be present with the energy and watch it transform. After this experience I felt more open, more loving than I had ever felt before to people and circumstances. It was also an incredible healing for my mother, because my father was saying things to her also, which she accepted.

Channelling in the astral

Channelled material is now accessible in many publications. Astral channelling can be classified usually by the name of the link. Such names as "Seth", "Emmanuel", "White Eagle" etc., are classified as astral as these are entities that come through via a medium. They usually have distinctive names and personalities. Often the information in these kinds of material is loving and inspirational and sometimes thought provoking. The best of these are very good and do the job that they have intended, to inspire, heal and help, and these types are a good introduction to further spiritual knowledge, as described earlier. Sometimes the medium is in some kind of trance. However, trance is very demanding on the medium and it is not absolutely necessary. If the psychic or medium works at progressing their level of consciousness they can obtain just as good material, or even better, than through trance. Trance means that the entity completely takes over. This can drain the physical energy of the medium and it takes years to completely amalgamate the energy between the medium and the entity. There are various levels of inspiration but everyone can link into some form of inspirational information.

EXPERIENCE

"I was visiting my mother and our conversation shifted to my father's sister, my aunt who lived about 80 miles away. We very rarely discussed her and the conversation got quite intensely detailed about this lady ... at one point I stopped and I was aware of my aunt momentarily, I could see her and there was a feeling like a rush of wind around my shoulders, I could feel her, sense her, for about 30 seconds, a very very strong feeling and I was completely unaware of what was going on in the surroundings ... the following day I got a telephone call to say my aunt had died unexpectedly at that exact time.

This was beyond coincidence as I was not particularly close to this aunt. I believe I had contact with her spirit and this incident encouraged me to investigate and develop my intuitive side and become a competent practitioner as a sensitive healer and medium."

Psychic protection

There are now many books on the market that refer to psychic protection. Some give elaborate exercises to help build up an energetic layer of protection. Below I will give a few simple examples that are very effective, however please remember nothing can be more effective than you holding a good true open loving heart. This does not mean just being nice to people. Being nice does not always mean you are being honest and there is no spirituality in falseness. In short it simply won't be effective long term. In the next chapter we look at the importance of practicing unconditional love and in terms of protection there is nothing better.

The media and films love to present the horrors of psychic attacks. These things are grossly exaggerated and mostly never occur. Most people

Exercise: Linking to a higher consciousness

Take some time to go through the "connecting with the breath exercise" and any further meditation that puts you in a higher state. Of particular value when working with the heart is unconditional loving energy. Firmly engage your will and send it to the very highest level. Intention is all. Make sure your intention is real. Ask for the highest greatest good, and then go even higher and even higher still, remember there are no limits other than those you put upon yourself. Having sent the arrow message to higher consciousness, be open to any information that pops into your head. Speak it out loud. You might wish to use a tape recorder to help because if you are properly linked you are unlikely to remember the words you have spoken. When you have finished, make sure you bring your energy firmly back into your own body. Breathe firmly into your heart and send that energy down below your feet. Then breathe at least three times into the heart again and focus on the room. Some hot drink and/or food will help to ground you. (Apologies to vegetarians but meat is the fastest way to ground energy.) Listen to the tape and transcribe. Be discerning; just because you receive information in this rather unusual way does not necessarily mean it is any better than other methods. Take the inspiration that you can and meditate and work with it.

The use of an astral link, if it is done with care, is valuable. Refer to the experience of a maths professor on page 115 that led him to develop his intuition.

who think they may be possessed are most likely to be possessed by their own fears. Thought forms can be extremely powerful and if someone is constantly giving energy to some fear or obsession they will over time build up an energy in their aura. This is often seen as some personification: a bad spirit, an unpleasant creature. Nobody needs to have this kind of experience. Bad energy feeds on fear, so working to release fear is the most important part of clearing any disturbance.

A good healer can be very efficient in helping in such cases but even the best healer will be unable to completely clear a negative energy if the person is perpetuating it with their own fear. Exercises, such as those in Chapter 3 and the two below, will help considerably.

Exercise: Encase yourself in a protective circle

Life presents us with all sorts of challenges and sometimes our emotions are our worst enemies. In the work environment, for instance, often a petty quarrel or a feeling of being unappreciated makes life very hard and can build up resentment that is often projected towards one person. In this case do one of the "cutting the ties" exercises. The simplest way to do this is to be in a good space through meditation, see the person concerned and circle them with light. Do this without any preconceived ideas but ask that healing come and watch the person in their circle drift out of view into light.

In a personal relationship you may be feeling very drained, usually this is because there is some emotional connection. It doesn't matter if the person concerned is miles away or even if they are dead. After putting yourself in a good space through meditation, really call up to the highest spiritual light and see that light coming down and around you as a shaft or funnel of light. Fill your whole being with this light and then visualize a brilliant steel tube encircling your aura. Make sure in your visualization that there are no holes in it and it is completely sealed. If in doubt, visualize a lock or bolts that keep it fastened. The top is open, giving you access to spiritual light, but nothing else can get through. Keep reinforcing this image for at least 5–6 days. You should begin to feel your own strength and energy coming back. If necessary after this time do the visualization again several times.

When there is animosity or even love that is unrequited, there can be a lot of drainage of energy. Although it sounds wonderful to say you have your heart open, when the emotions are involved it is very difficult indeed to reach unconditional love so the steel exercise is a very good one to get you back into your personal energy.

Chapter 6

Stage four: integration of self

This chapter contains exercises for transformative experiences that lead to spiritual self-development and explains how this form of self-development can be merged into the reality of everyday life.

Opening your heart

Integral to most faiths and cultures is the notion of arriving at spiritual truths by connection with the heart. Christians talk about the "sacred heart", Buddhists speak of the "middle way" and other Eastern religions refer to "unconditional love". It might seem, therefore, that a similar philosophy runs through all cultures, one balanced through love. If we regard the chakras as a model, we see that the heart centre energy is the bridge to higher consciousness. Connection on this level can energetically release us from the lower levels that restrict our growth. This concept is central to forgiveness.

Many faiths speak of the necessity to let go, and as the prayer says, "forgive those who have trespassed against us". In many cases, this is not an easy thing to achieve. We are all fuelled by righteous anger at miscarriages of justice that affect us personally. You could argue this is perfectly acceptable, and it is certainly true that for evil to spread often it just needs good men to do nothing. But hanging on to resentment, regrets and anger mostly hurts the person who feels them. It is vital that the individual lets go of lower, unproductive energies. When this happens, I have observed an enormous shift that frees that individual from his or her pain and restriction.

To gain some kind of unconditional acceptance of others requires that you learn to love yourself. This is not the love of ego, or being satisfied with your role in life, job, house or status, but a love that comes from really knowing who you are. Many transpersonal exercises, like the cutting the ties exercises in Chapter 4, can be enormously helpful in this process, but nothing can work if the will and intention to look within are not present. Really engage your will in your meditations and contemplations and be connected to wanting the truth whatever that might be. It is like looking in Pandora's box, but I have found that most people, when they do, find that they are not so bad, and any shadow aspects of self can be cleansed and healed if the will is there to do it.

Exercise: Asking for revelations

Be relaxed, and carry out the "connecting with the breath" meditation on page 46. Breathe 1–3 times into each chakra centre, spending some time making sure there is positive balanced energy in all areas. Try, if you can, to consciously align your breath to the breath of the cosmos. Go back to breathing into the heart centre and with each breath imagine healing, loving energy flow out and around your body so you feel perfectly safe. Send a powerful energetic call to the highest greatest good and ask that what needs to be revealed to you will be. Hold the meditation for at least 10 minutes. You may not receive any information at the time of the meditation but you will be opening a doorway to greater knowledge and further possibilities. You are likely to get some insight within a couple of days or when you least expect it. It often comes when you are busy with something mundane, like cleaning a floor, driving a car, etc. The mind in that state is often freed and opened to insights.

There is a saying, be careful what you ask for, and it is very true in any energetic work. Here, we are asking for revelation about ourselves. This almost certainly won't be what you might think. It will manifest itself in your life and can sometimes come with disruption. However, disruption is part of the clearing process and, in the end, can only be to your good. If your intention is true, you will want to know where there are difficulties whatever they are.

Mysticism

Contemporary spirituality has concepts in common with mysticism, as do all cultures and religions down the ages. However, like spirituality, the meaning of mysticism often appears confusing. Indeed, the word mystic has, in some circles, come to stand for something nebulous, and is little understood. However, it is generally thought to mean a belief in a personal "union", or "marriage" with a higher source and "being mystical" refers to a transcendence of human understanding. It is thought to be a sense of "connectedness" or "oneness" with a universal force, the living world, God, or "all that is". Mystical experience comes in different types.

Nature Mysticism: This refers to a sense of oneness with nature and the living world. It is a sense of immanence – operating and experiencing the wonder of the communication and connectedness within the self.

122

EXPERIENCE

"When I was in Australia I visited Ayers Rock. I made the most amazing connection not just with the land itself, although that was breathtaking enough, but I also made a link with the history of the rock, the aborigines and their culture. I felt their feelings — it was completely overwhelming. It took me to another place altogether — it was healing and expansive and the connectedness I felt I will never forget. It still inspires me whenever I think about it."

Soul Mysticism: This is the notion that the soul can be put into a state of complete isolation from everything other than itself. It is the quest for right knowledge of oneself.

God Mysticism: This is when the inner core self is thought to be assimilated or totally attuned to the essence of the divine so that the individual personality and the world are felt to be dissolved. The soul or spirit is deified without losing its identity by a process that eventually brings transformation of the lower self by the highest self. This process is your own spiritual journey.

Exercise: Connecting with nature

Gather some objects of nature around you – leaves, stones, fruit, crystals, cones or anything else from the living world. Spread them out in a comfortable place and put yourself in a relaxed or meditative state by simply connecting with your breath. Breathe into your heart chakra and move the loving energy outwards and around you, so you feel protected and loved. Take your time doing this. Next, choose one of the objects of nature, pick it up and "make friends with it" that is, make an energetic union with it. Surround and attune with it through the loving energy you have built up. It's important you do not project your own feelings on it, just be open to what the object has to say to you. When you have finished, consciously dissolve the link between you and the object. Once you truly connect with any living thing the connection will always be with you, and you may find you want to keep this object and connect

The mystical journey

An age-old phenomenon, the journey of a mystic is present in the Jewish Kabbalah, Sufism, Buddhism and other Eastern religions, and Christianity. It is often referred to as an inner personal journey during which the individual develops and grows by passing through different stages. The story of spiritual development is that of a loving, strong inner spirit, which although affected by fear, pain and longing, is never overpowered by these feelings. Its challenge is one of re-vision of life and living. Its process is analogous to that of the matrushka Russian doll – each time you open one there's another inside; all represent the person at different stages.

Models of this journey include that present in the chakra system discussed earlier. The 16th-century nun, Teresa of Avila, spoke of the seven "mansions". The contemporary writer, psychologist and philosophical thinker, Ken Wilber, also gives us a number of models. He sees self travelling as a journey that is taken step by step through the layers as a ladder of self growth. He describes the stages as the "archaeology of spirit" – the more superficial layers of self are peeled off to expose deeper and more profound waves of consciousness. This concept is present in the unfoldment process of spiritual development.

with the healing of it at another time. This exercise can give you very different perceptions of energy of the living world and can be done in your own home but even better if you can communicate and attune to any part of nature when you are actually outside. If you attempt this, remember to approach the tree, rock or whatever you link to slowly and gently. It has a very subtle and different energy to the ones you are used to, so take your time. Stand away from it and connect before you move towards it, find a place to sit and embrace and merge with the energy. The communication with all aspects of nature can give you healing and a chance to experience different senses.

"In the course of my teaching, particularly in London where students come from multi-cultural backgrounds, the experience of the connectedness is extremely similar. It is a sense of divine unity, whereby any separateness of self melts away into a feeling of transcendence and unity. It does not seem to make any difference whether the person believes strongly in their own faith or has no faith at all. Science tells us we are all made of the same stuff. Is there some core part of ourselves that knows this and longs for this marriage or union with the ultimate source of life? When it occurs it seems to bring a profound sense of oneness with everything, and promotes healing and strength. There is even a sense that whatever occurs in the life of an individual it is always safe as life is eternal and indestructible."

Although the spiritual mystical journey is not always chronological, descriptions of it seem to imply there is some intentionality of self from the individual in the process. St. Teresa suggests that "It is absurd to think that we can enter heaven without first entering our own souls, and without getting to know ourselves and reflecting upon our nature". She, together with mystics down the ages, acknowledged that the individual takes an active part and not a submissive role in the process. For St. Teresa and many others, the soul is, in effect, acting as a magnetic force throughout, drawing the individual towards the divine union.

In a recent research study, as I delved deeper into the meaning of these three spiritual models, I was struck by their similarity – particularly between the seven mansions and the seven chakras – even though they are centuries apart. Did St. Teresa have access to knowledge from the East or could these similarities give weight to the notion that there is some immortal universal collective consciousness or a "perennial philosophy" – knowledge across faiths and cultures, and evidence of a possible transcendent unity of religions? Maybe the concept of unconditional love suggests that it is not so much a perennial philosophy but a perennial self that exists within us all.

Visions and synchronicity

Having obtained some link with the unconditional heart energy brings the student into a very different world and all kinds of possibilities can emerge. However, connecting with the heart rarely comes overnight and even when it comes, is unlikely at first to be constant. The student still needs to be vigilant so that imagination and possibilities do not lead him or her down blind alleys. If, as science tells us, we are all connected with the whole universe, it seems possible to be able to communicate with any aspect of the cosmos. Whereas theoretically this may be true, it can lead the student into cosmic fantasies. The questions that need constantly to be asked are, "Is what I am doing making me a better person now? Is whatever information that is coming to me helping my journey now?" Just as you can attune to auric, astral and higher conscious energies, so, too, can you link to cosmic ones. Whatever the channel or link and however good the medium is, be discerning. It is my experience that spiritual energies encourage, inspire and heal; they do not express anything that creates fear.

In previous books, I have already written (see box) about the inner connection of strength to a spiritual source, which can help you transcend, learn and grow for and by yourself. Depth spiritual knowledge comes in the form of a knowing what to do, what is right and who you are. When you are in a good clear energetic space – being in the zone as it were – and vibrating in a positive sense, often wonderful synchronicities happen. These can feel like a kind of magic. If you think about this energetically, it is because there is a clear flow, an openness to receive. This has the effect of a positive magnetic attraction, drawing you towards what you have projected. In this open state, jobs, good situations and helpful people seem to be drawn towards you.

For most people, synchronicities won't occur all the time. It is our fears, prejudices, lower wants and desires that get in the way. Sometimes, however, having what seems like a restriction in one's life is also right. So, if things are not flowing, have a look; maybe the block is allowing something else to occur that would not otherwise do so. It might, for instance, be keeping us away from something of which we should not be part. Look deep inside yourself honestly; you will know whether it's better to persist or let go. If you take the analogy of life being like a river and you are in a boat, sometimes the water is gentle and you can lift your oars out and go with the flow, sometimes it is turbulent and you need to row like mad. Knowing when to move and when not to and what to say is always a challenge. Do you want to pretend all is well when it's not? Do you want to live a lie? Somewhere deep inside us, we really know the answers.

AUTHOR'S EXPERIENCE

Not long after the publication of my second channelled book I led a workshop in London. There were 29 participants, 23 of them had read my book and misinterpreted it. They had somehow interpreted the words to mean that there was a spaceship coming and thought I could inform them when and where the pick up was! I was horrified. Certainly my books were about change, but change of consciousness and certainly not the death of our planet — and no spacecraft was ever mentioned. I had to gently relay the real meaning of the book and tell them that although I would personally love to have a trip in a spaceship I had no knowledge of one coming. There were 23 very disappointed people!

Dealing with pain

Spiritual development is full of change, deaths and rebirths. We all, from time to time, particularly through turbulence, experience pain from disappointments, grief, separation, or when our expectations have not been met. When we have physical pain it is usually because something in our physical bodies is out of balance; something is wrong and our pain alerts us to this. Emotional pain is just the same; it alerts us to something being off balance, something that needs to be addressed and, as such, it is not our enemy but the kind of good friend that will tell you the truth. So one effective approach is to make friends with pain, and change your mindset to understand that it is trying to help, not hinder you. Obviously, this is not easy. It might feel that you are making friends with your enemy but often in psycho-spiritual terms, it is your enemy that will teach you more than any other person. To be able to genuinely make friends with pain is to be in an advanced state; most of us would try to push away, ignore or deny such difficult emotions, but denial will ultimately not work as they are likely to reappear over and over until you do something about them. Pain is not something most people can just confront, but any psycho-spiritual work, particularly if it is enforced with unconditional energy, is likely to help.

EXPERIENCE

‘Come out’ said Lucifer, taunting me. ‘Are you afraid of me?’ I said nothing but sprang onto him and hit him. He returned my blows a thousand times and lashed out and scorched and slew me which felt like hands of flame. My body just lay there still. But then I sprang upon him again with another body and with another and another. And the bodies which I took on yielded before him and I flung them aside, and the pains which I endured in one body were the powers which I wielded in the next. I grew in strength till at last I stood before him complete, with a body like his own and equal in might, exultant in pride and joy. Only then did he cease and said ‘I love you.’ And with these words his form changed and he leaned back and drew me up into the air and floated me over the topmost trees and ocean and around the curve of the earth under the moon till we stood again in paradise.

Exercise: Passing through your pain

Imagine your pain, fear or anger or any other negative emotion as a person. What would he or she look like? Be very graphic in your descriptions. Give the pain a name or, if you like, simply call it "pain". Draw a picture and write a list of the qualities you perceive the pain to have. Communicate with pain; keep asking why it does the things it does. If, when you do this, you find it hard at first, leave it for a while and come back to it later. Keep a note of it all. If you persevere, gradually pain will explain its purpose and you will embrace it as your friend. When this has occurred, visualize pain dissolving and integrating into yourself.

An analogy from Edward Carpenter, a 19th-century mystic, describing the angel Lucifer is very similar to the process of the transformation of pain. His notion is that Lucifer is actually the angel of light and illumination in disguise, and can assist us if we allow him. In this experience, Lucifer is transformed from being something we fear to something of real value; he becomes a teacher and friend.

Experiences with higher consciousness

Emotions are often signposts for many aspects that affect our lives; positive emotions aid us in allowing us to feel good about ourselves and enjoy life and living. Negative emotions restrict us; nothing is quite so debilitating as emotions that spill over and cloud our true vision. Learning to deal with them is part of the spiritual self-development process.

It was an incredible lesson to me that being too emotionally involved with people does not work, even with my daughter. It was incredibly difficult to realize that at the time and you had to let go and then it brought up the questions of what am I doing? And who am I doing it for? I thought that if you have healing or psychic ability or skill then surely you must be able to use it for people that you love the most? Now I realize you have to do it with complete and utter detachment and you can't always do it for the people that are close to you. That realization was hard, I wasn't aware of my own limitation and that's something I'm probably still learning.

Another profound lesson that needs to be addressed is forgiveness. Many faiths and religions talk about the need to do this. We may think we have forgiven someone but it's not until a situation or circumstance arises that puts it to the test that we really know. Below, a spiritual facilitator describes a student's reactions in class.

There was a woman who felt that she had done a lot of work on herself and was vaguely insulted by the idea of looking at herself, but there were so many suppressed feelings and emotions. I think she was challenged by it and was most resistant to going into things like forgiveness and letting go and how that corresponds to an energetic processing. A lot came out. When she eventually started talking about her abuse as a child she said I forgive him but I don't think I want to speak about him or see him again. We were doing something like group healing and she was in tears the whole time and she told the group the whole of this, but she kept saying I forgive him but I don't think I want to speak about him or see him again. So we opened a discussion on what forgiveness really meant and within the process of an hour and a half she went from a point where she said oh you know I've dealt with all of these things to coming to a point at the end where she was basically saying I haven't. So I think it was a very powerful thing and with the help of the group she came to her own conclusion about it because she couldn't hide the fact that it was still so painful. Gradually through the classes she opened up, and was able to let go. She had a serious skin complaint all her life and it all but disappeared and now her whole energy has changed, she even looks different she is very much more free.

This episode was beneficial for all the group because it gave a first hand opportunity to look at forgiveness in our life, to question whether we really know what forgiveness is. Listening to others talk and hearing their experiences is a very powerful tool that gives you the permission to look at yourself. People often tell you they know a lot and tell you that they don't need any of this stuff and then learn the hard way that they are not exactly where they think they are. Letting go of pain releases energy and makes profound beneficial changes in one's life.

Dark night of the soul 1

If you are still reading this book you must realize by now that spiritual development may sound pretty and blissful but it is actually quite hard work. The process of unfoldment of self allows all sorts of patterns, hurts and pains to emerge so they can be healed:

Things come up, and looking at oneself so honestly can hurt, but I found once I worked through the hurt bit by bit and again looked at myself unconditionally it worked. I said, "OK, fine that's in the past and next time let's do it differently." Now I have the tools to see things differently and to react differently.

Because the journey of self is one that has to be experienced in the real world, it is a process that plays itself out over time. Bit by bit, stage by stage, individuals get closer to their cores, real beings and strengths. It would be foolish to suggest this can be done without any disruption and, as one gets deeper, there is often a stage when the journey is very hard indeed. This has been described as "the dark night of the soul". It is often relayed as a form of deep spiritual transformation, which may come with trauma, sacrifice and even martyrdom. When it occurs it could be defined as a profound sense of loss of self; one's ideas, notions and beliefs are shattered. However, it also can mark the beginning of a new life. Old systems and constructs of behaviour break down and you are forced to ask the ultimate questions: "Who am I? Why am I here? Where am I going? And how ought I to live?" This might have the effect of making you feel naked, unprotected by the roles and masks of the outer world, and all that seemingly protected you in the past.

This age-old question of "Who am I?" is often asked when people are on the verge of investigating their spirituality. One of my students, who had been an enthusiastic student and had progressed well in intuitive development, around the second year began to attend class much less often and when he did come to class, he seemed agitated and angry. Below, he writes of his great difficulty with this process as he, too, had started asking similar questions to those above, about all areas of his life.

I was asking "What was the point of me coming to the groups? What was the point of me doing the job I was doing?" And I also started to wonder, "What was the point of the life I was living?" And I realized these questions led directly to my unease. I couldn't concentrate. I felt like I was drifting and falling asleep and I think now when I look back it was part of the process ... meditation was difficult for me, if you weren't quite focused in intent and there was something about your own energy, it didn't work. It was something like a process going on in my own energy ... I wasn't happy about this and I seemed to be seeing things in terms of getting it right or wrong.

Around this time it began to dawn on me that I was actually uncovering myself. My dilemmas lasted, a long time and I was becoming increasingly uncomfortable with myself. It wasn't very pleasant because it was all about me, wasn't it? I did every possible thing I could to mask it, avoid it whatever, but I now recognize it as a valuable part of my personal process. I learnt it the hard way. I also noticed a lot of changes going on with me physically ... it was a stage that I was unprepared for ... Physically, my body started to come out in different kinds of rashes and things. I became really angry, very irritable and emotionally slapped a lot of people around at the time and I kept blocking it and I realized that something strange was happening. It all built up and finally culminated on a particular day when everything in my life turned upside down in one morning. It was a catalyst point when everything that had built up just came out ... There wasn't any more blocking off to do. I was not in control. I had an inability to hold on to money, which was my biggest problem and it had come to the point of no return on the same day. Also, the relationship just collapsed overnight which was probably the right thing to happen but that wasn't the way I saw it at the time and I realized the reason I was holding on to the relationship was the wrong reason. My world fell apart mentally because that was where I was holding most of these things and things could not have got any lower. All the constructs around me were just wiped. I couldn't physically or mentally cope with that moment so I just had to surrender to it.

"Masking" and avoiding it, and then finally reaching a break-down point when his world fell apart, is a graphic description suggesting some form of death of self. The student continues:

Finally, I just sat down and thought I'll ask for some help. I felt that the only way to understand it was to let go. And when I did I had this overwhelming experience of peace and by the evening I felt so balanced and so peaceful. When you let go, all fear evaporates. I just had to surrender to it and when I did that I had this overwhelming experience of peace . . . and that for me was quite a turning point . . . the most difficult bit was learning to be more of who I am and actually taking away all of those things that I thought were right and weren't. This was a crisis point in my mind, in my fears and they evaporated almost as fast, but at the same time it didn't mean that some of the situations disappeared. And I think that's quite important because many people come looking for solutions to things but the solutions aren't necessarily the way they expect them to be and it doesn't mean that you look at the world really differently but it is different if you feel different or see it differently but actually the same things are happening. It affected me to the very core, but I had a sense that I would have to go through it.

"All the constructs around me were just wiped," and "it affected me to the very core" are very pertinent descriptions of a dark night of the soul experience, when one's structures of living disappear and there is nothing to hold onto. Finally, as this student experiences, "surrender" to a higher power comes. This form of experience could be seen as a form of death, the death of the past and the self that belonged to it, with no turning back. This death of self process has some correlation to the known phases of bereavement: denial, anger, bargaining, depression, acceptance. His experiences finally led to surrender, which is thought to be necessary for healing to take place.

Dark night of the soul 2

Of all the quotes and descriptions I have read on the experience of the dark night, one stands out in its heart-felt potency. A psychologist and writer said that:

After his "dark night" experience he became: a more sensitive person, a more effective pastor, a more sympathetic counsellor, but he would give it all up in a second and if he had a choice he would forego all the spiritual growth and depth which has come my way because of our experience. This is how it is with dark nights of the soul. Our souls grow strong and we develop an authentic capacity to console others but we cannot celebrate this growth like an egoistic victory because the price we paid was far too high (Elkins).

Losing everything that makes sense of your world is very hard and consequently can induce spiritual transformation, but change and death is part of the human condition and to believe otherwise is folly. We so desperately want everything to continue as it is that we have to believe that things will always stay the same. This process has been described as "dying to the self" but it is not really about dying. It is about letting go of all that has held you back. This might mean the actual construction of how you believe life exists. Belief is not set in stone. As children we believe all sorts of things that turn out to be incorrect and as we grow spiritually, our beliefs change, too. But letting go needs to come alongside some connection with a spiritual force, whatever name you choose to call it. If there is a connection to spirit, whether within self or beyond, it can assist you over the bridge towards self-awareness. But letting go of any aspect of self is not an easy process. Another student explains:

I think the depth of knowledge gets deeper with the process, almost like an onion, where you keep taking the layers off, and as another layer comes off it's a thicker layer, that's how it feels and so therefore in a way sometimes you think, well hold on a minute, what is it giving to me in my life? I'm not going to know the answer maybe never but invariably the answer as to why I had that lesson will be revealed in my experience. It has been revealed a few times however one is impatient in it, I have been in there in that pain. I do not know the answer as to why I had that lesson but it will be revealed and it is coming much quicker, the answers.

As described here the peeling of the onion of the outer layers or lower aspect of self can be a painful process and requires confrontation of difficult personal issues.

I do remember feeling a tremendous amount of fear. I felt I had to confront things and this felt right ... I hadn't felt such depth before. Opening the heart felt fantastic to actually focus on that part of my being to be honest and it really had quite a profound effect on me.

Transformation 1

Confronting yourself is often seen as part of the self-awareness process and "opening the heart" is an expression that means finding the heart, the core or spirit, the soul of who you are, in order to communicate with the authentic self; that part of you that is real, genuine, or pure. To reach the heart level it is thought to be important to be able to transcend at least some fears. The heart level is seen to be the link between the physical and the spiritual worlds and many faiths hold that you cannot journey up to the higher, more spiritual energies without experiencing this heart energy – love beyond judgement and conditions. But it is thought that to arrive at this, one often has to examine oneself, and, as the data and the literature confirm, the release of unproductive fears and negativities through this process can be disconcerting. A student relates that in the early part of her development, she was "worried":

In the beginning, when I didn't have anyone to turn to with the first exercises, when I didn't know what was going on, I didn't feel I could talk to anyone, yes that was a worrying time and I thought, in fact I wrote it down; "I think I am going mad," but I was too busy to go mad. It also had another effect when I went through a terrible patch with my husband on the marital side because even that needed looking at but I feel we have come out so much better.

When constructs change you can feel you are going mad, and, in some cases, change could bring chaos to your personal life. Having a good mentor at this stage is advisable. When asked what made her continue with her development she said:

I think once I'm in I might as well go through it, that's my attitude, why not look at everything and sort out all the cupboards and see what's there?

"Sorting out all the cupboards" suggests looking at various aspects of self and once again the need to implement an act of will in the process. To a lesser or greater degree, students passing through depth transformation undergo a similar process:

It was definitely like an unfolding, so what I was experiencing was then aiding me to unravel things in my life or they unravelled in conjunction with it and that's what I felt. I went though immense changes and ups and downs and bringing up of lots of negativity and all sorts of things happened to me but it was allowing things to process, that's how I felt it.

Observing negativities and what is described as the shadow side of self is rarely an easy process and takes courage and determination:

I have to say that the whole thing to me has been an integration so I can't really separate what has happened to me in a way because it just feels that it has all worked in conjunction with everything else. And it didn't always feel like that realistically it's only since I started on this path that everything changed, you know, my path of life, my intentions have changed. They have definitely changed for the better in so many ways.

Transformation 2

The extreme aspects of spiritual transformation as in the "dark night of the soul" may be transformative but they can be terrible to live through. Even if it was possible for any practice or teacher to instigate transformation, which is debatable, you would have to question the rationale and explore the minefield of ethical consideration of sending someone down the road of the "dark night" which, historically, has taken mystics close to the edge of sanity. Nonetheless, research suggests that no authentic depth spiritual transformation occurs without change and some dying of self:

Facing my fears wasn't as bad as I thought in the end and after I got over them I realized it wasn't as though I was being rewarded but what I gained from it was wonderful. And after every set of circumstances something wonderful happened even in my own transformation or events or you know something great happened and I felt like, for me anyway, I needed to pursue things as they came up and I couldn't not look at them. So when it was a horrible fear, although it was so horrible and I wanted to run away, yes I gritted my teeth.

Reading this account, it sounds like spiritual development is putting students through a form of torture, but spiritual and mystical literature also imply that any depth spiritual process may necessitate a clearing out that can at times be disorientating. Change is rarely comfortable and can induce anxiety and fear. So the question that emerges is, "Is it possible to minimize this or is it essential to development?"

The effects that spiritual development make in the lived world of each student varies from the heavy "dark night" scenario to the person being able to have a greater sense of self worth. Research reveals that crisis can lead to greater transformation. As one student related earlier, the external aspects of his life did not change, but the response to them did. Nonetheless, the data generally reveals that changing perspectives can upset life considerably and can upset a student's equilibrium. Spiritual self-development seeks to help the individual obtain a better life, mind, body and spirit, but change often comes at a personal price that for some is just too high to pay.

Spiritual emancipation is something each individual has to see in his or her own way. Each person is different; each has a world made up by different experiences and coloured by many personal elements, such as family influences and genetic inheritances. This means every individual will have unique components to look at within his or her life, with different things to transform. Transformation can be achieved only by the individual sensing and feeling his or her way through the

process. Intention, engagement, purpose and will are essential; this is not a passive development and it takes time. Some are impatient:

Well I suppose that's what I've been trying to do but it, took me years and years and years just to get to ... Just to sometimes make a phone call takes me years literally. With a fear of something, it's difficult to let go of traumas because when fear is linked with a trauma it's just very hard.

Transformation 3

All the elements seem daunting, so the question arises, "What could counteract these difficulties?" It has been suggested that a real sense of connectedness between the self and a higher force is necessary to be able to come through this process. This connection sometimes comes in the form of awe. Awe is the opposite of fear because in fear we desert ourselves. Awe enables us to transcend ourselves through what is known in mystical terms as "surrender" or letting go. When this occurs, fear cannot touch you. In that sense of wonder, you may be able to set aside your need for certainty. At some stage of your journey you need to feel safe without certain knowledge and to feel safe with whatever happens, wherever you go or with whomever you may be.

If you consider awe to be reverential wonder and profound respect, an inspirational experience usually related to some religious or spiritual experience, it could be said that the opening to a higher power could lead one to surrender to higher forces which, in turn, might to some extent, at least, transform the life of the individual. There are many descriptions of awe leading to transformation of self in varying degrees. However, no programme is likely to be able to contrive the experience of awe in an actual lived experience. Nonetheless, it may be able to facilitate the opening up of the individual for this experience to occur, and some of the comments concerning meditative exercises seem to show this is true.

As a facilitator of spiritual groups I know only too well how easy it is to get a group of people into a state of bliss, however this is usually of an astral type. A large group of people together often indulge in a mass reaction. Something takes over. We can see this in football crowds and concert audiences, and the reaction can be pleasant or sometimes it can turn to violence.

A powerful orator can instigate bliss quite easily. But the trouble with this form of bliss is that it will not last and the student needs to return again and again to receive a "top up". True bliss is very personal; it is not incited by a charismatic preacher or leader but from a deep meaningful connection between the self and spirit. So any experiential group leader must be mindful of this. The leader must realize that he or she cannot facilitate a personal connection for others. A leader can prepare the ground for the seeds of spiritual alignment but it can only be the individual who does it for him- or herself.

Many exercises will assist the process but an exercise in itself is not the answer. It is how it is implemented and what energy is used. There is no more powerful energy than the energy of intent to good, intent to truth, intent to what is really right. This is how it is with depth spiritual connection. There can be no conditions, no judgement of others and of self. This is not an easy place to be. Very often you might think you are there but only experiences as they unfold will really let you know whether this is the truth. Through depth intuition you can know what to do, what is right, and then you must accept what occurs and work with it. All paths lead home eventually and through your own unique experiences you come to realization and ultimately enlightenment.

Chapter 7

The self and tarot revealed

In this chapter I use archetypes to bring alive a story of development. The story is fiction; however, the characters' experiences are ones that I have encountered in my work time and time again. I hope you find it readable and it helps you understand that your spiritual processes are unique to you and yet you are not alone on your journey.

THE FOOL

Life is said to be a journey of self discovery. I was young and the world was all there ahead of me. I felt enthusiastic and had no fear of what might occur. I had energy and youth. I did not even take the time to think about my actions or even know I should. I wanted adventure, I wanted to explore, I climbed high mountains dived in the sea and did many reckless things. I had many girlfriends; some I loved with a small l. I wanted variety; I wanted change and adventure. Nothing seemed barred from me.

My name is Chris and I believed I was the nicest person I had met, but then I was young. I had little experience of life. As a child I had a sense of presence; something with me, I couldn't say what it was. I felt I was not alone and that there was some power beyond myself. God was on my side but I did not think too much about God in those days. Sometimes I would pontificate to friends about religions and the violence that they have caused around the world. Sometimes we would talk about different beliefs and that some people needed theirs and it was right to accept different faiths. At that stage I did not believe much at all, although when I was a boy, I sang in the choir and went to church. The only time I attend church now is for weddings and funerals. I liked the singing, but the priests seemed somehow removed from the world and seemed to have nothing much to do with the life I was living. In fact, I suspected they would have been horrified if they knew what I got up to. Like most boys of my time I dabbled in drugs, drank too much, sometimes got into a few scraps, but I always thought I would be OK. Death and

A fool doth think he is wise but the wise man knows himself to be a fool

Shakespeare, *As You Like It*

tragedy had not hit me then. I took risks with most things, even my own life at times. I had fun but strangely everything I did quickly became tedious. I was acting the fool and there was not much evidence of wisdom. In this stage of the spiritual journey, one is barely conscious, a spiritual baby where every new thing is amazing. We dive into life without a care. No deeper meanings clutter our world. We have no boundaries; we just live.

I drove too fast and I crashed my car a couple of times but that did not seem to stop me.

On one occasion I went sky diving and jumped over the cliffs. I hadn't really had enough training and the equipment was faulty. I must have had a very busy guardian angle on that day because somehow I landed, albeit with a bump. I was bruised and had broken a leg, which meant I had to be confined. I made the best of it. It was at this time an aunt who was staying with us left a book. In boredom one day I picked it up. I read it, unprepared for the contents. It was a metaphysical theosophical book about an initiate, a wise teacher who lived in the world affecting everyone's life just by being there. It touched on philosophies I had never known although, as I read about them, they seemed strangely familiar. I suppose you could say it changed my life. My leg healed and life went on but my life was never really quite the same again.

THE MAGICIAN

I was bright at school; I did only the work I really had to and somehow managed to get through college. I was an entrepreneurial type, excited by the kill of getting new business. I made money but spent it. Never saved but always seemed to just have enough for what I wanted. Around my early 20s I craved something big. I needed a challenge. It was the 80s with the money-making culture in full swing, and there was a feeling you could obtain anything you wanted. I set up my own business and worked hard and long. It paid off in material terms and I hardly had time to spend the money that accrued in the bank. On the occasions I went out I drank far too much and there was always another pretty girl that took my fancy. Mostly the girls were one-night stands.

When to the sessions of sweet silent thought I summon up remembrance of things past, I sigh the lack of many a thing I sought, with old woes new wail my dear time's waste

Shakespeare, Sonnet 30

At this stage of the journey we are excited by the mind; thoughts and ideas abound. We think we can make magic but the magic we make may turn out to be an illusion if we haven't discovered the true magic of life, the spirit, the core, the truth. I was full of tricks in the disguise of negotiation. I noticed my intuition was extremely good in business and I was able to make instinctive decisions that always seemed somehow to pay off. I never doubted these and looking back I was incredibly arrogant; it never occurred to me I would not get what I wanted as mostly I did.

In many ways I was more alive than I would ever be. I felt in control of my destiny but could not have told you what that was. Many times all sorts of wonderful synchronicities happened; it almost seemed that all I had to do was think of something, make a phone call, and it started to manifest.

Useful people seemed to come my way in the strangest of situations; in fact, everything seemed to fall into place so much I began to feel invincible. In a very short space of time I made a million. I had a fast car, I bought fashionable property in London, and when I had the time, I went to high-class clubs.

There was nothing to indicate that anything in my life was wrong, but one day, sitting and thinking about my life, I had the overwhelming feeling I was lost. I analyzed this. I had many possessions. I was certainly successful in a material sense and yet there was an emptiness that once identified simply would not leave. I did not realize it at the time but I was in some kind of spiritual void. It wasn't that I was lonely but I felt very alone. There was a hole inside me that I felt unable to fill. Something was missing. The ability to obtain what I thought I wanted was losing its appeal. The thrill of the kill was subsiding.

It was at this time that I began to investigate a deeper meaning to life. I looked at some of the many workshops flooding the scene. I found a group of people that seemed sincere; they needed someone with financial acumen so I offered my services and started involving myself in the promotion of a spiritual way of life, doing good by making money for spirit, but I knew deep down there was still something missing.

THE EMPRESS

I watched her out of my window; I saw her get out of her car and go into a neighbour's house. There was something about her, the way she moved. I wondered whom she was visiting. Lucky guy I thought with a girlfriend like that. I saw her a few times and then on one occasion I was getting out of my car as she walked up the road. I smiled, it was a sunny day. "Lovely day" I said. I stopped to talk to her but she was in a rush, she seemed sad. "My father is very ill; I visit him a lot these days." "I know, I have watched you", I replied. She looked surprised. "Oh good", I thought, "she is not visiting a boyfriend." "Would you like a drink some time?" My whole life depended on the answer and some deep intuition in me knew it. "That would be lovely". Before the week was over I was completely in love with Jane. We were close friends from the start and I loved to watch her face as it moved in such expressive ways. It felt safe, wonderfully right and I knew I had met the woman who I wanted to be my wife and who I would love for all my life. I believed I had at last found what would fill the emptiness in me.

Less than 18 months later we were married. I spent my days doing anything and everything to please her. Her face would light up; it made me feel alive, it gave me a special kind of purpose that I had never felt. The day our first child was born was amazing. I looked at Jane in the hospital bed holding our child and I could not express my feelings towards her. She was a great mother right from the start and those days of our children's childhood were so comfortable. We would go on all the outings, take them to shows, make them laugh. What is ever better than a child's laugh – so spontaneous, so natural, so real. Jane was feisty and could just make things happen, we both could. The spiritual group grew and became well known. Jane was intuitive and had caring, healing gifts. When the kids permitted it we went to meditation meetings together. On occasions when she was practising healing, I felt such profound love coming from her energy. My God I loved that woman.

A child of our grandmother Eve,
a female, or for thy more sweet
understanding a woman

Shakespeare, *Loves Labours Lost*

Jane was hugely protective about our two children; she always put them first and she never let any ideals get in the way of the practical reality. When I looked around at the misery of the world I could barely believe my luck; I must have done something very good to have this in my life. Our children became the centre of her world and in human terms that is how it should be. Mother love has an unselfish quality rarely seen outside that relationship. It touches and inspires us and in seeing this we get a glimpse of the possibility of unconditional love. Jane was the archetypal mother and I thought of her as the best wife ever. The whole of our children's childhood years were the most special of my life. We were meant to be together and nothing and no one would ever part us – at least that's what I truly believed at the time. We were the perfect couple; people would comment how much they could feel our love. I would never have envisaged that it would be me to break us up.

THE EMPEROR

I continued to make a good living with the business and increasingly put energy into the spiritual group. There was a feeling of a mission about it; at times I felt it was the most important thing I could do – after all, what could be better than promoting a spiritual way of life? I came across many cranks and many blind alleys. God there are some flakes in the world! I researched other forms of spiritual models, took various courses, spoke to endless people and worked really hard. Fortunately, Jane was sympathetic to my stance, and I had the strength and love of my family.

Exploring the entire subject brought to bear my whole feelings of spirituality on a personal level. So many people with different ideas. Some believed we were star children and were waiting to come home; some took a psychological approach and believed that spirituality was merely part of our nature, some were fundamentalist and adhered to a particular model of belief that probably had not changed for hundreds and thousands of years. And then there were the "new agers", who did not seem to mind what they did or whom they followed, but seemed less good at taking responsibility for their own growth. Mystics down the ages tell us that the truth is within, that we are connected to God, we just have to listen. I tried to listen and sometimes the messages came so clear I could do little else but to follow them. Sometimes I was less sure.

Jane and the family allowed me to feel the Emperor – empowered, the father, the male, the action force and drive that is evident at this stage of growth. At this time, I was able to provide material comfort for the family and establish a good structure for us to live. And in the echo of that kind of determination, I could catch sight of a greater determination to rise beyond the physical world to do something more altruistic. But the real inner strength I needed was not yet in place.

I dreamt my lady came and found me dead, strange dream that gives a dead man leave to think. And breathed such life with kisses in my lips that I revived and was an Emperor

Shakespeare, *Romeo and Juliet*

I used my business acumen to make money for the group and that was not always as easy as it sounded. It's one thing to make money in a normal business but in an area that is not supposed to think about money, it was hard. However, money came in for the group and I took very little out of it, barely expenses most years. I spent very much more time on this than my other business, but I believed it to be sound. I had good people working on it and it seemed to be ticking along nicely. I should have realized that if you take your eye off the ball it bounces away.

I explored and researched teachers and gurus, many of whom I discovered were not what they seemed such as those who would stand up and speak pretty words on a platform then get off and be abusive to their colleagues. If spirituality is to work, surely it must work all the time. You can't just be holy on a Sunday and think it's right to get away with bad behaviour every other day in your home with your family and friends. I felt very strongly about this and was so very grateful for the loving wonderful family I had. I would never do something like that I thought.

THE LOVERS

The years went on, the children grew. I was so proud of them even through their teenage angst. Life was ticking away, I felt I was happy, which makes what occurred even more puzzling.

I was at a conference, one of many I had attended over the years. Adele came in late, but we got talking in the break. She had a remarkably similar view on life to me; she liked the same things and thought the same way. She was married and so was I and at first there did not seem to be any harm in exchanging contact addresses, after all we were in the same field. We e-mailed each other about various aspects of the work. I really enjoyed our exchanges and thoughts, and then she phoned, she was in my area, could we meet up. Again at this stage it all seemed so innocent. We had a drink, talked about the work, and then got on to subjects more personal. She was bored, unhappy with her life, her husband was a workaholic, and she was lonely. This brought out the protective element in me. I felt she was far too beautiful to be treated in such a way. Something about the way the light caught her that evening made my stomach jump; I watched her face, her smile, I enjoyed her intelligence and then suddenly to my horror I realized I was very attracted to her physically. We parted saying we would meet again; I went home thinking that I must stop this now and I had every intention of doing so. I threw my arms around my wife and thanked her for her love; she seemed surprised at my burst of affection. How could I even be thinking about another woman? But the trap was set and I was hooked.

I could not stop thinking about Adele and I did not put a stop to it. She was younger than my wife. I was at that certain mid-life age and Adele so excited me I could hardly work or think. Maybe it will blow away I thought naively; I let it progress. Months went by; my wife knew something was wrong but I just put it down to pressure of work. I would sneak off to meet Adele whenever I could, usually once or twice a week. We wanted to be together; I could not stand being apart. This made me make comparisons with Jane and for the first time in 20 years I would find fault, pick fights. I did anything that justified me wanting to be with Adele. My marriage had always been so good. Why was this happening? I even persuaded myself it was karma that Adele and I were destined to be together; why else would it happen?

Excuses abounded and Adele wanted me to leave my wife and be with her. What to do? I was in torment; agonizing days, weeks and months went by. I could not connect with spirit; I could not even meditate; I was angry with God. What is the purpose, why is this happening? What could I do? How do you choose between two women you love? The passion was overwhelming. In heightened emotions one day I blurted it out to Jane. She was very quiet, no recriminations just an awful look that said "Why?" The day I left home it felt like my soul was ripped apart but Adele was there waiting – a new life, a good life, a better life.

But love is blind, and lovers cannot see the pretty follies that themselves commit

Shakespeare, *The Merchant of Venice*

THE DEVIL

The children took it badly; my son would not speak to me, my daughter came to visit and pleaded with me to return. "Dad, why are you doing this? You and Mum had something wonderful; everyone said so." I looked at my lovely daughter; I remembered the day she was born. I loved her so much. All I could find to say was "I had to go."

The first few weeks and months with Adele were intense, wonderful. We could not take our hands off each other. We had a constant wonderful sensuous passion. I took time off work and dropped the spiritual group. My thoughts and mind were dissipated; I could not concentrate. It's difficult to describe my feelings. At the time I would have told you I was blissfully happy; when I look back, I realize I was in a kind of madness that I had little power to resist.

We made love endlessly, getting more and more experimental – animal, lusty sex. My God, it took me over; I was obsessed. Nothing else seemed to matter. I lost contact with my friends and had minimal contact with my children. I barely did any work. I was caught in the chains of passion. As the months went on we started to argue. I can't say why. Our fights were just as passionate as our sex and we would throw plates, scream and shout, but it always ended in us having sex so it made it seem all right. Days would go by and we would fight again. At first it never occurred to me that there was anything wrong in the relationship. After all, the passion was still there; we wanted to be together. If I was honest with myself, I would have known how miserable I became. I begun to feel disempowered in everything except lovemaking. All the things that I thought we shared became inconsequential, but I still wanted her. Months went

by, I became a shadow of myself, nothing seemed to flow. I could not be bothered with the business and was often abusive on the phone with colleagues. I got more and more depressed, I did not want to talk to anyone, I was sliding into an abyss and getting deeper.

Tell the truth and shame the devil

Shakespeare, *Henry V Part I*

Our fears, our lust and greed overpower us when experiencing this stage. The feelings are so strong it is a rare man that has the necessary power to resist. We think we have something great, we call it love but it is merely a shadow of the real thing. It deceives, grieves and overwhelms us and somewhere deep inside we know it is not right, but we dare not admit it. We make excuses, lie, to others and ourselves. It is fear, which must at some time be faced. It must be driven to the light so it may dissolve and we can finally see the falseness of the devil's promise. How can it be done?

When Adele and I rowed I once caught my reflection in the mirror; it was like looking at someone else, someone dark. Was this really what I had become? I did not dare think too much of the spirituality. The fights got worse and one day she stormed off saying she needed a break. I pleaded with her to return; it would get better I implored, I could not live without her. God I was pathetic, I would have done anything; she had me in her power but I did not care.

THE HANGED MAN

She got an apartment nearby but we continued our relationship; neither one of us had power to resist but she began to tell me she was more busy and couldn't see me very much. I would wait, like a dog on his mistress's lead. When we were together is was a bit easier; we argued less, but then we spent most of the time making love, which was still wonderfully intoxicating. Because I spent more time alone, I started grieving for my life, my children, my home. I had heard from the children that Jane had started an M.A. and was ploughing her energy into her studies. Sometimes I felt guilty but it was too painful to think about what I had done. Adele waved the carrot of us being together for always; inside both of us probably knew this would just never happen. It was much much later that I was finally able to admit that the love Adele and I had was not a soul connection but just another fatal attraction.

Having delegated much of my business to others, I was having minimal contact with work, but being so much on my own, my mind wanted stimulus. I started reading up on different cultural beliefs, I made notes which turned into pages that I knew could be a book. There seemed to me some link between the faiths, something that was mystically present in all of them. I studied many religious documents, found interesting articles that touched on similarities. Perennial philosophy is fairly well documented but many religious texts had been distorted over the years and the dogma of the beliefs were obscured making any direct comparison almost impossible to authenticate. However, when I looked into the experience of spirituality, I begun to see some patterns emerging. Models of the spiritual

The ancient saying is no heresy; hanging and wiving goes by destiny

Shakespeare, *The Merchant of Venice*

pathway had similar processes. What I did not appreciate at the time was that I was searching, searching not just for some academic proof of God within everything, but some proof that God was in me. But at this time Adele would always come first. I would drop everything as soon as she rang and when we arranged to meet I would be on tenterhooks all day with expectation. Then no work was done. Sometimes I tried to talk to Adele about my research but she seemed only to pay lip service to my thoughts. To Adele the deeper things meant doing good when she could. There is nothing wrong with that but I had noticed she only did these things when it suited her. Maybe that's unfair but it's how it seemed; in fact she only did anything when it suited her – even making love to me.

There are times in our lives when decisions have to be made, it is hard to let go of anything whether it is an intellectual idea, fantasy, love or some precious attitude on life. If we do not we are doomed to a life of being blown hither and thither by the dictates of the wind. Somewhere inside us all is knowledge of what is really right for us. Somewhere we know what our soul really needs and it is often not what we desire or would wish. We may curse God or the universe; but there's no point – ultimately sooner or later we have to take responsibility for what we know to be true. The distress this may cause can create a darkness that could swallow us up, but the human spirit calls softly at first, it gets louder and gradually, finally, it draws us home.

146

THE MOON

How many nights I just sat and watched the moon. I got to know every movement of the stars. Sometimes it gave me great comfort to know that the circle of the stars would revolve and be there. Sometimes I would just curse and think we all were like hamsters trapped on a wheel. What was the meaning of life?

The mysterious depths of our unconscious come to entice us to give a glimmer of a meaning and then it's gone. My thoughts were often chaotic; sometimes I thought they were genius, sometimes I thought I was in madness. I was awash with emotions in a sea of consciousness that I just did not seem to be able to grasp. It felt like I was swimming in an ocean that had no shores, no boundaries. I was powerless to do anything but wait. Sometimes the torment of this was so great I wanted to drown in these waters. Shifting moods and confusion, I could not quite grasp what it was I was supposed to be thinking, feeling or doing. I was in a wasteland of uncertainty, a place I had never experienced. Sometimes a thought would come into my head that seemed plausible – some dim awareness – and then it would dissipate, dissolve into the waters of illusion.

O swear not by the moon,
th'inconstant moon that
monthly changes in her
circled orb, Lest that thy love
prove likewise variable

Shakespeare, *Romeo and Juliet*

THE HIGH PRIESTESS

Through the murky waters of emotion she would come, the priestess, the energy of the unconscious and I caught a glimpse of daylight. The things that we believe are reality are shown in bold awareness of what they truly are. Our intuition slowly grows. The unconscious holds the secrets of ourselves. The priestess within us knows; she is that part of us that knows the secrets of our inner world. She sometimes comes by night in the form of dreams so that we catch some reality and she comes to us by strange happenings that have profound meanings. Like the moon of emotions we cannot immediately grasp it, but unlike the moon it is not the nebulous energy of dissipated emotions it is a sense of knowing, a conscious realisation of what we have to do. It is a call to truth, which sets off an opening to a more healthy path. Gradually our dreams take shape, our sense of something more than the obvious remains. She is persistent that priestess part of ourselves, she will never give up or leave us, she is constant. We begin to listen, we finally begin to hear. But it comes with confusion out of the murky waters of emotion but with the alarming reality of the truth that we have been unable to face. At this stage there is very little evidence of action in our lives. From the outside it might seem we are doing nothing and in earthly terms this may be true. But what is going on below the surface is more profound that any action or movement we do in the physical world. How we think and know ourselves will change our lives for ever. A small shift in perception will have the effect of altering the whole trajectory of our lives. My perceptions of me were altered 360°. I would never be the same. Somehow I just had to trust my newly born intuition and that it would lift me from the ashes to fly once more.

No automatic system can be intelligently run by automatons - or by people who dare not assert human intuition, human autonomy, human purpose

Lewis Mumford

STRENGTH

I started to get really angry at everything and everybody. There was a rage burning up inside me; even with everyday phone calls I noticed my tolerance level was low. I dare not take it out on Adele – I wanted to keep her too much – so sometimes I would just take off, drive off in the middle of the night. I wanted to hit out, hurt anything. There was a beast within me which I could barely handle and sometimes did not handle at all. My body came out in rashes. I refused to see a doctor, I guess I feared he might suspect my rage and put me away. Nothing seemed rational and although I continued my research, I often ended up tearing up the paper I had written on. This could not go on; sometimes I felt I would explode with the pressure. Like Forrest Gump I took some therapy in walking and walking and walking. Hours of it. I can't even say where I went. I deliberately exhausted myself so when I got home I just collapsed into bed to find some comfort in sleep. This did not always work, my sleep patterns altered and my dreams were nightmare monsters. One dream I had a lot was of huge beasts that would try to devour me. I had read a bit about dreams; I knew that anything in a dream could be an aspect of yourself. If the beasts I dreamed of were an aspect of me I was in big trouble!

I was like a child demanding that the world revolved around me. Patience was nil. Even standing at a check-out queue made me angry. I was aware that in energy terms my beast was incredibly strong and it occurred to me that if that energy could somehow be managed and used productively it could really do great things. How I could do it in this state was another matter. I was pushing Adele to do things she

As thy days, so shall thy strength be

Deuteronomy 33:25

did not want. I wanted her to go away with me for several months. She told me she could not leave her job. I was sure if she wanted to she could.

The key to transformation is that individuals own their lives and what they do and that they look, really look at reality, whatever that might produce. As the months went on I felt more and more like the sacrificial lamb. I began slowly but surely to realize that the relationship with Adele was not going to work. I tried to fool myself for a while but once awareness comes it does not leave. Somehow I must find the strength to sacrifice my passion for a better life. To seek a better truth. Making the decision was very hard. Unlike the direct action man of the past I felt emaciated, inadequate. I had left my wife and my friends; I had abandoned my work and my spiritual contacts. I had torn many lives apart for what? Just to say it did not work. When people say let go of your ego they have no idea what they are asking; letting go of your ego and pride feels as though your whole self is being seared with flames. I had always thought I'd win. I never thought I would lose. I always thought I was right. At last with all the courage I could find I did what I should have done before: I told Adele it was over and in doing so I walked away from the dream of a life with a perfect woman. Perfection, like fantasy, does not exist.

THE TOWER

I realized I wanted to go home, home to Jane. I had increasingly been going over the past. When we were together it was the happiest time of my life. I remembered her love, her compassion, the wife, the mother, the friend. I knew that love was real. I'd made a mistake but our love would survive. I tried to phone Jane over several days but I just got her answer machine. I phoned our daughter. "Mum's away; she's gone to America for six months to work and she's found a man. It's great to see her happy again," she said. As I put the phone down the awful realization that I had lost the best person in my life seeped into my consciousness. I was still in shock when, minutes later, the phone rang again and I automatically pressed the button. It was my business manager. "Where the hell have you been?" he said. "I have been trying to reach you for days. This is serious, we need to talk." I told him I was going away. "I don't think you will when I tell you what has happened."

I met him an hour later; he had a determined and pale face. I knew immediately it was bad. He explained that in delegating, my business had been destroyed. I laughed. "Its worth millions," I said. "It was," came the reply. Some kind of embezzlement had occurred. "What's the damage?" I asked. "I'm afraid I have to tell you you have lost everything." At first the words did not sink in. "Come on, there must be something left," I said in desperation. "No, nothing; in fact, it's so serious we could be personally liable. All your accounts are under investigation." "Why? How?" I said. "I'm sorry to say this to a man when he's down, but if you had spent more time looking after the business rather

Nor stony tower, nor walls of beaten brass, nor airless dungeon, nor strong links of iron can be retentive to the strength of spirit

Shakespeare, *Julius Caesar*

than chasing rainbows this would not have happened. You used to be so on the ball, Chris, where did it go?"

Hindsight is a wonderful thing; looking back on how it occurred it would be obvious to a simpleton that disaster would be likely to strike. I used to be good at business, so much the man of action; where was that person now? And more importantly what the hell was I going to do?

On that day my whole life collapsed. I had nothing – no job, no home, no love. My world collapsed utterly. I walked for a while then I sat down on a grass verge with my head in my hands; I watched the sun set and that evening, exhausted, alone and afraid, as though some invisible lightening flash had struck me, I was laid bare. Suddenly I saw myself, really saw myself for the very first time. This brilliant piercing light filled my whole being. It was like a huge electric shock. The light was too bright; I had nowhere to hide, I had to see myself. I was shaken to the core. No peripheral masks, denials, or prevarication would come to my aid. All the constructs of my life were shattered. All previous ideals, impressions of what I wanted to be and not what I really was were dissolved. They say one can get instant realization; what they don't say is what leads up to that point. At that moment I surrendered, finally surrendered to life. A light filled me, it surrounded me and in my vulnerability I finally found peace.

HIEROPHANT: HIGH PRIEST

I did not want to deceive myself about anything again. I was scrupulous about it; I even underwent psychotherapy to see if there was anything I had missed. The therapist and I spent time talking about the family, patterns of behaviour that started as a child. We talked about conflict and how I dealt with it. I acknowledged the male quirk that only wants to please women. Have you any idea how this one trait in a man disables him? I learned about men, I learned about women. I learned about relationships and I learned about me. I learned that the things I did to bring success were compensation for lack of attention as a child. I needed to be loved – don't we all?

I did not want to leave any stone unturned. I gained enormous self discipline and began to take mastery of my desires. There is a deep part of ourselves that is our own teacher, our own guru, but how many of us really listen to the inner part of ourselves that really has the truth? Yet it is there all the time in the background. We know, we really do know, so why don't we listen? Are we really so afraid of the truth? This might mean changing your way of life but isn't it better to live with truth and not lies? Maybe we do not have the strength to administer what we know to be right. My invocation was "Divine light of consciousness, open me up to greater possibilities, to greater truths, and give me the wisdom to deal with it."

Wisdom is the principal thing,
therefore get wisdom

Proverbs 4:7

THE HERMIT

The lawyers were dealing with the business; it was not going to be quick. I had no bank account, but I did have a very expensive car. I drove to the sales room and sold it for cash. I went to the airport and bought a ticket to Spain. There was a place in the mountains I'd always loved; it was as good a place as any to be. I rented a small villa that looked over a valley with no other houses in sight. I looked out and saw the beauty of the landscape. I was still bereaved and in shock. My days were spent doing simple things – shopping, cooking, walking, a bit of gardening and hours of just sitting. Even in my angst I was able to realize it is still a beautiful world.

I felt like a hermit in his cave. Quiet contemplation. I felt strangely at peace. I had connected with what could only be called some force or deep energy source that was not outside myself but was within. I realized that in some shape or form I had felt this all my life. But why did I not really listen to it before? It hummed inside me like an ever- present engine. Was it my soul? Bit by bit I felt myself align and attune to it. When it really was active I felt invincible, unafraid of anything that life might bring. It would sometimes slip but knowing where to find it, gradually it became easier and easier to connect with it again. It was comfortable, safe, safer than anything on an external level. I had a metaphorical lantern to guide me but the light was not external to myself, it was within. It had always been

there but like most people I sometimes had not known, sometimes I ignored it but mostly I let the noise of a busy world distract me from it. Contact with this deep inner being made me aware that on a soul level I, the real I, could never be destroyed and I knew therefore I was indestructible.

The mind can weave itself warmly into the cocoon of its own thoughts and dwell a hermit anywhere

James Russell Lowell

DEATH

In those months away in Spain it was like being a different person. I had always been very active, always looking for the next deal, but the time spent with Adele, and my state of mind at that time, dissolved the man I was – or at least that's how it felt. When our life is destroyed what do we do? Some people would try to pick up the pieces and try again. Deep inside me I knew I could never live the same life. My priorities had changed. I had no desire to make money for the sake of it. I'd had the life style that money brings and it held no attraction for me. I was empty. I lived the life of a monk: walking in the hills, speaking to few people. Frequently I sat in a kind of meditation; I was aware that some invisible process was occurring but I did not know what it was or what it would bring. What I did know was that nothing, absolutely nothing would ever be the same again.

> *Of all the wonders that I yet have heard, it seems to me most strange that men should fear, seeing that death a necessary end will come when it will come*
>
> Shakespeare, *Julius Caesar*

With the wonders of technology I was able to trawl the internet and started researching for the book I was continuing to write. Sometimes I was excited by a particular finding or thought. Sometimes I thought I was on to something really important, other times I just thought it was mediocre at best. I was in mourning. Not just bereavement of relationships and my business but bereavement of a part of my self that was gone for ever. The child part, the bit that wants its own way. The bit that is "I must have, it's mine". I felt naked, deprived of the mere falsehood of my previous existence. The masks I had worn were torn away. The persona I had previously used was gone. I had no coat of protection; I stood bare. In those months I thought a lot about my actions, thoughts and feelings. When we look, really look at ourselves without the pretence of having to think we are right or we are Mister Nice Guy, all sorts of things emerge from the depths. I could see how selfish I had been in my life. The person that was supposed to do all the right things for people was really only doing it so I felt good about me. The egoist sense that I was something special or different from the rest was an illusion. I examined my motives. When illusion and delusions are shattered and we see things for the first time and realize our motives were not as we thought, it is devastating and I could easily have plunged into self indulgence of what an awful person I must be, but we can only work from what we know and I had not known. I berated myself a great deal. What a bastard I was to my family, my wife, my friends; but as time wore on I realized the person I had hurt most was me. I could not drown myself in regrets, what I could do was make it better. In death there is birth and renewal and in any birth or beginning there is death of something else. Some rite of passage was occurring, I wasn't sure what, but out of the depths of despair a tiny glimmer of hope survived.

THE WHEEL

And so the ever turning of the wheel of life moves on and on. I felt a bit like you feel when you leave home for the first time. The loss of a home and all that it means; the loss of a woman in my life felt like losing one's mother, but I'm no psychologist. I was like a newborn baby and was aware that only through time could I begin to form my feelings, my true feelings. When I looked backwards I did not like myself; I did not much like many of the things I had done in my life. I berated the fact that I had been so unaware. But that was the old me; I had to somehow put that behind me, forgive the past, forgive myself, let go and walk on. I felt empty and yet there was this inner light, revealing to me that my life was a blank page and on it I could write whatever I wanted.

It was a full year before I came back to England. The dealings on the business were still being sorted out. It seemed there was at least something to salvage, albeit very little. The problem for me was I had no desire to start another business. The whiz kid was gone. I had no stomach for the driving force needed to push that kind of animal forward. What would I do with my life? I had to work: what could I do, what did I want to do? The new me was still forming and I did not know what that would manifest in the material world. I would have to trust in the process. I had to be OK about not knowing, not always trying to solve things, just be.

It was good to see my children again. They seemed to have their lives together much more than me, so something productive had come from my existence on this earth. A

Let us sit and mock the good housewife fortune from her wheel, that her gifts may henceforth be bestowed equally

Shakespeare, *As You Like It*

friend let me stay in his flat and I finished the book. A good thing about being a successful businessman was that I had many contacts in all sorts of areas. I knew a publishing firm and I presented my work. I wasn't happy but the despair was finally subsiding. Most of all I felt that whatever happened to me it really did not matter. Everything we experience happens for us to learn. Everything we do teaches us something.

I was trundling on when I received a call from the publisher. "There's a lot of work and some rewrites to do with this but I think its worth a shot," he said. I was amazed. It had been written for my own discovery to find out more about what really is behind the spiritual concepts old and new. The book came out in the autumn and sales were good. My publisher called. He wanted a chat. He'd had a call from a TV station; they thought the book was well researched and wanted to run a short series. Apparently the publisher had told them of my abilities and they wanted me to be involved.

Life has many twists and turns. Opportunities come and it's up to us to grasp them. I had nothing to lose and although these were very new waters for me, I was willing to give it a try.

JUSTICE

I had discovered myself; now I was being asked to create an image for publicity. I could not pretend; if they did not like me as I was I really could not do it. I had in the last few months found an inner peace that I had never felt before. I did not want to lose it for flimflam. But we are in a material world; I had to do some work and I believed in the book I had written. Life, it seemed, was presenting me with an opportunity to express my thoughts to a wider audience, and on one level it seemed too good to be true. Life is ironic; if this had been ten years ago or even five, I would have been jumping for joy. Now I just felt wary of all the limelight. There were promotions, interviews all over the place; it seemed I had struck a chord and the subject of contemporary spirituality was unfolding with interest coming from many diverse areas ranging from the new age to academia. Of course, not surprisingly, I trod on some people's toes. I got lots of good letters but some that said how dare you suggest you can be spiritual if you don't believe in our deity. I personally had no belief and basically took the stance that anyone's cultural background was probably the best method towards his or her spiritual roots. But it's only half the picture. The real essence is manifested within the experience of the individual. This does not sit too well with set dogmas that upon investigation often come more from the people subsequent to the original roots of the religion.

How to keep balance in my own feelings as I was getting more and more attention and admiration? I was told I was a natural behind the camera. Initially I took it all with

It is enthroned in the hearts of kings, it is an attribute to God himself, And earthly power doth then show likest God's when mercy seasons justice

Shakespeare, *The Merchant of Venice*

a pinch of salt; I thought they were just flattering me. But as more and more people said the same thing, I started believing my own press. Men and women of standing told me they thought this was a really important work. It's easy to be at one with yourself if you are on your own; with all the excitement of the success it was more difficult. However, intelligent understanding of what was occurring just about kept my feet on the ground; we all have to learn to think clearly and to cultivate and maintain a balanced mind. We have to learn to cope with whatever life throws at us. We have to keep a sense of self that is the core truth in amongst the hustle of the world that can cloak our true being. In many ways it's like being a tightrope walker. We cannot afford to loose concentration on the moment in which we exist, or we may find living in the present enables us to be aware and in balance it enables us to walk on.

In amongst all this I was also dealing with court proceedings from my old business. The culprits were finally coming to trial. I did not feel angry towards them; in many ways I now believed they did me a favour. If I still had the business I would be stuck in a world in which I no longer belonged. As I walked finally from the court seeing the motif of Athena's scales, it felt as though life was telling me the most important thing is a balanced mind, heart and body.

TEMPERANCE

Time is the great healer they say and I had found some kind of peace, but my emotions were still frayed. I actually started to believe I would never have another relationship. How could I take the risk? Without the burden of the emotions I felt safe, free. All those feeling getting in the way of life. I really did not think I could go through it all again. Life however allows us to forget the feeling of the pain even if it does not allow us to forget we have had it. We can remember it happened, how and when, but the feeling does not stay with us. It's probably similar to how a woman can experience the pain of childbirth, and forget it enough to do it again.

Time hath, my lord a wallet at his back wherein he puts alms for oblivion

Shakespeare, *Troilus and Cressida*

Gradually as time wore on the pain subsided. I was comfortable in my life. I had a good relationship with my children, the work from the book had all kinds of spinoffs that enabled me to travel all over the world. I was comfortable in my own skin, happy to give advice when asked but equally happy to stay quiet. I felt the need to have quiet times often. I would either take myself off to some remote area or sometimes I would go on retreat to various monasteries or places of rest. I gave myself quality time. I learned not to drink too much; I ate well with food that suited me. I exercised and swam a lot. My life was balanced and yet, in retrospect, only because I did not have the encumbrance of an emotional life. I was into my middle age and time seems different when you are older; you start thinking about old age and death. Time becomes more precious; you think how to fill the last part of your life.

My daughter announced she was to be married. I liked the guy; he was sound, easy to talk to, if a little naive, but who isn't at that age? He made her happy: that was the main thing. The wedding was on a bright summer's day. As I led my daughter up the aisle I caught sight of a woman in Madonna blue; something about her movement attracted me; she turned – it was Jane. I had, of course, spoken with Jane about the arrangements, but I hadn't seen her for a couple of years. The years had treated her well; she looked bright, empowered. I remembered why I had been attracted to her and my heart missed a beat. At the reception we talked. She was doing well, her life had taken different turns. She had a job that gave her satisfaction. It did not quite seem the appropriate time to ask but I found myself asking if she was happy in her personal life. There is no one special she said. "But I thought you had a man in your life?" I said. "I did, but it didn't last; he was a good man but ..." she paused, "You are a hard act to follow." "I'm not the same man as I was; things and people change," I said. "But the essence stays the same," she said, and drifted away to talk to relatives.

It was a happy day, filled with laughter and good food. I had forgotten the wonderful feeling of being with the family, that comfort, warmth and friendship. I did not want it to go away. After the bride and groom had gone I sought Jane out. "Would you consider having lunch with me tomorrow?" Her head turned to one side and she smiled. "OK."

THE CHARIOT

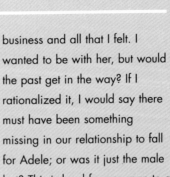

We found a good country pub and sat in the sunshine. We chatted about the kids, what they were doing and how they had grown up intelligent and healthy. I looked at her and said "I still love you, you know." "Why did you leave then?" she said. "Oh, Jane, how can I answer that? I just had to. It's been hard, you know." "Why?" she said. "Because it didn't work with you and Adele?" There was a trace of bitterness in her voice which I ignored. "Partly," I replied, "But it's difficult to talk about; I've been through some kind of transformation." "Yes," she said. "I see the grey hairs on your head!" We laughed. "No, I've achieved some profound awareness that means I will never be the same again." I opened up; I had forgotten how easy it was to talk to her. "I'm not the same either, Chris," she said. "Being on my own taught me many things about myself, it made me examine life, too".

Men and women are so different; how do we ever get together? The action of the man, the receptivity of a woman. The emotional needs of a woman and the emotional needs of a man are different. A man needs to have a sense of worth, a standing. A woman needs to know she is loved. But somehow at this time of my life I began to see the feminine side of myself. I had abandoned the warrior male for something more spiritual. Ironically, Jane seemed to have done the reverse, she seemed powerful and direct and she had drive and determination of which I had previously been unaware. I only knew I wanted to be with her.

We met again and surprisingly our friendship picked up as though it had never left. She let me talk about the spiritual shifts, the torment of the relationship with Adele, the

But at my back I always hear time's winged chariot hurrying near. And yonder all before us lie deserts of vast eternity

Andrew Marvell

business and all that I felt. I wanted to be with her, but would the past get in the way? If I rationalized it, I would say there must have been something missing in our relationship to fall for Adele; or was it just the male lust? This is hard for any man to acknowledge and very few do. Did I really go off with Adele just for passion? It's a question I felt uneasy about confronting; I daren't look. The only answer I could come up with was I don't know. There had been no real crisis in my relationship with Jane and yet I had been bored, restless. Could it have been that life presented me with the situation that enabled me, albeit with some pain, to bring about the changes of consciousness. Can life be so cruel? And yet do any of us really put ourselves deliberately through such turmoil unless we are pushed? I doubt it. We want things the same, familiar, but change is part of life, change is necessary, change instigates movement and life is movement. Had I invoked the emotional conflict myself? Had some deeper part of me known I needed change? But out from it all I had fought a battle both in the inner and outer worlds and come to some equilibrium. Could I dare to put myself in such a space again? And then there were the human considerations; what if it didn't work with Jane, that is supposing she wanted me back? Could we both go through the terrors of another break up? My feeling persisted, I wanted to be with her.

THE STAR

Jane seemed so independent these days; she had really got her life together. She was away for several weeks on a working trip. What if she found someone else? What if she just wanted us to be good friends? I rationalized what was the worst thing that could happen? She could say no. Would that really be so bad, I asked myself. After all, we both had separate lives, we both had gone through a massive amount of self discovery over the last few years. She had told me that after I left she went through a dark period that made her realize she needed to examine her life and herself also. She had reassessed her whole life and she had realized that she had never really looked at herself outside her role as daughter, wife and mother. This process brought confusion and she simply did not know what she wanted from life because she did not know who she was. I understood this feeling well. It seems that most people are constantly playing a role, that may or may not have anything to do with who they really are. They are born in a certain family, in a certain environment where people have certain norms of behaviour. We all automatically take on these norms just as if it is right. Most people never even consider the possibility that there may be something else. And when that hammer hits home that all is not what it seems, it is extremely uncomfortable. Most people are too frightened to look. Too much embedded in the status quo. They do not want to change, they do not want their models of life to be disturbed, and who can blame them? But it means they are forever moving through time living a construct that they have never questioned. It may or may not be a good construct but it certainly isn't one that they have

When the sun shall lose its light, when the stars shall fall down from the firmament, when the mountains shall remove from their places ... then shall a soul comprehend what it has shaped

The Koran

thought out or created themselves. To be self determining we need to look within and be brave enough to open Pandora's box. We may find things inside we do not like and have to adjust accordingly. However, alongside the darker aspects of self, hope is also present in Pandora's box and hope is a quality within us that despite disease, imprisonment or terrible disappointments allows us to carry this spark of light that intuitively tells us that eventually we will be OK. Yes, it's scary to look inside ourselves without a clue as to what is inside, but what is more scary is that people are walking around playing roles they did not create and even worse do not realize they are doing it.

I had hope but hope is fragile, with all the possibilities of fear and disasters. But to have no hope is to live with gloom, to allow ourselves the self indulgence of feeling sorry for ourselves and feel that nothing will or could work. Is hope connected to our soul I wondered, and what of those awful stories of people whose child goes missing and they wait and wait, sometimes for years only to be told their child is dead? I put that thought aside as I endeavoured to keep my eyes fixed on the vague, irrational and inexplicable sense that soon there would be a dawning of a new and wonderful time. In my heart I now knew that Jane and I were partners – for better, for worse. I only hoped she knew that as well.

THE SUN

I had been commissioned to write another book and I was also being asked to appear on TV as an expert in the field. Success was good, but I had known the other side, and consequently knew that both success and failure are impostors; they mean nothing. Everything is transient, everything changes, particularly in our fast-moving celebrity culture where if we have some fame it is merely a speck of dust in the clutter we call life. We might think we can change the world and we can, each and everyone of us. But we change our world by the energy we give out each day and good energy can be emitted just as easily in the supermarket, and in any day-to-day activity. The world is changed not so much by luminaries who win prizes or look good, but by all those good things that are done each day, by all of us. What is success? Maybe true success is really love, not the love of desire but that of unconditionality. At its best it seems to release a clasp that allows us to be free; it dispels the dark. Something in the human psyche pushes out from the weeds a tiny blossom that emerges into light. It might remain unnoticed or little understood but it has driven humanity through the millennia. It is the indomitable spirit of the human soul, which we can never analyze or know, but love is the closest we get; perhaps that is why all cultures speak of it. The human heart, the sacred heart releases us from bondage and allows us to journey home.

Jane was due back from the States on the Friday. Apart from a couple of e-mails we had not had any contact for several weeks. I phoned her on the Saturday; she seemed surprised to hear my voice. We talked about her trip and the success of my ventures. "Can we have dinner?" I said. There was a pause. "OK." Love, they say, is not everything, and in a material world that is quite possibly true, but without love there is very little meaning, very little purpose and little joy. Love has many meanings; we can love our pets, our favourite TV programme, we can love our friends, our lovers; but depth love is not so common and it fills our whole being with light. Not the light of passion or emotional support, not the highs and the lows but the constant eternal flame that is ever alive. Dear God, I was so thankful that my love was still alive, even with the possibility that I would be rejected. Was it St. Augustine that said, "There is a place in people's hearts that does not exist into which pain enters so that it might exist."? The pain of love can be torment, but somehow as it subsides it allows more knowledge, more strength and eventually more love. I knew I would love, really love, Jane all my life and somewhere within all my doubts I knew she would always love me too.

It was autumn; the colours were particularly beautiful as I drove with her to a country restaurant. It was tasteful; good food and quiet tables. I didn't know how to start the conversation. "I love you, Jane; I think I have always loved you even through the last few years." She started to speak but I said, "I want to be with you the rest of our lives. Can you forgive the past and be my wife?"

> *We make guilty of our disasters, the sun, the moon and stars, as if we were villains on necessity, fools by heavenly compulsion*
>
> Shakespeare, *King Lear*

JUDGEMENT

She looked shocked. She did not speak. At last she held my hand. "I love you too but you must give me time to digest this. I'm sorry I can't say anything at the moment; let's just enjoy the meal." I have no idea what food I ate that night or how I got home; the rest of the evening was a blur. When I dropped her off she said she would be in contact.

During those next few days I examined the past we had shared; I examined my motives once again. I had now done extensive therapy on myself, but each step of the way creates a different view. If we change, even slightly, our whole perception is altered, and consequently the trajectory of our lives alters also. Was it madness to try to get back with Jane? We had in the last few years done our own thing. We had both changed. Maybe we had changed too much for it to work. Could the very real love we once had and still had, be the lighthouse that would help us through the next stage?

Jane phoned three days later. "We need to talk," she said. We met at her place and she started to tell me about all her feelings when I left. She had never really talked about this before. She told me of her resentment, her grief, her feeling that somehow she must have been at fault. For months she spiralled downward finding it extremely difficult to be positive. It was at that point she had taken herself off for counselling. She talked and talked about her feelings and how gradually she came through knowing she was not to blame, and knowing she had a kind of strength that would allow her to move through the torment. She had cut the ties to me she thought permanently. She smiled and said,

Great men are not always wise neither do the aged understand judgement

Job 32:9

"Now I know what it must feel like for those women who believe their soldier husbands are dead and they arrive at the door. Sometimes they have remarried or are living a life that they do not want to give up." "Is that what it is like for you, Jane? Do you have a life that you don't want to give up? You know I would put no restrictions on your life." She replied, "Just you being there would alter what I did. I never stopped loving you, but the pain of the separation made me shut the door." My heart stopped when she said this; I was waiting for her to say "No" to my proposal, steeling myself for the worst.

"I never really shut you out completely; I think that is why I couldn't be with another man. But have we learned?" she said. "Have we really learned enough to make this work? Would you go off again?" "Oh Jane," I said. "I would be lying if I gave you definite answers to these questions; the affair with Adele completely took me by surprise. I did not plan or want it. All I can say is that I am older, hopefully wiser, and I will do anything I can to make this work. I love you beyond measure." "Yes," said Jane, "but I couldn't bear it if it happened again." "I know there are no guarantees in life but we can minimize any potential difficulties. We can work together, step by step. We will be honest with each other, we can have a good life." She said nothing for a while, she looked me straight in the eye. "I'm up for an adventure."

THE WORLD

In fairy stories it is always "happily ever after"; would that real life was so certain and always provided us with the perfect future. It was wonderful to explore each other in our new skins; we fitted back into place like a lost jigsaw piece, and we were comfortable together. The children were on their feet and we now had a blank page ahead of us. We could do anything, be anywhere. We had always promised ourselves to travel to places far from tourists, and over several months our plans took shape. Jane took a sabbatical and we began to tour.

We started in Canada, then through the States, and down into Mexico and Peru, Colombia and Chile. From there we went to Antarctica where the surreal views of the ice were sublime. We crossed into Africa, and it was while in some fairly treacherous terrain that Jane started feeling unwell. At first we thought it was the effort of all the travel, but she did not improve. I looked at her one day and something told me I had to get her home. We got on the next available flight. Jane was insistent that after some care and a bit of rest she would be back; unfortunately this was not the case. The hospital immediately admitted her; she was seriously ill. I nursed her through her treatment, but to no avail. The end was quick and she died in peace in my arms.

How can a human being dig deep within to rise when beaten down again and again? I could have gone into deep depression, berating the fact that I had lost her, taking on guilt for the pain I had caused; but those absent years allowed us both to grow and we were at peace with ourselves. The individual's challenge is to know and be able to act upon spiritual authenticity. The development of the

All the world's a stage, and all the men and women merely players

Shakespeare, *As You Like It*

spiritual self brings a form of unconditionality not just present when we love another human being and he or she loves us, not just when things go well, but also present when tragedy strikes, when our love is unrequited and even with death. This is the alchemy of the human spirit. Somehow, some deep strength emerged and finally gave me acceptance of all life's conditions. I missed her dreadfully and was only grateful that we at least had many months of fun and adventure and we had been so in love.

After the funeral I decided to continue the trip alone; I knew that was what she wanted. I knew I would see her face in every place I went, and in every step I took, and in my heart I would share with her what I found. Through Jane I had learned the real meaning of love. For love to be real it has to survive the hurdles and hardships, it has to forgive, understand and be grateful even when the person is no longer with you. Like an eternal flame, it cannot be destroyed.

We never really know what experiences are there for us to learn and grow. Life is an adventure and adventures have their joys and traumas. And so on a crisp early spring morning when I set out again, I had love in my heart and hope, not knowing what the future would hold, but knowing that whatever happened, with the connectedness of a firm inner strength, I would be able to encounter whatever life would throw at me.

Psychic powers revealed

Introduction

People often refer to "gut feelings, or instincts". This is a sense of knowing what cannot easily be rationally expressed or intellectually confirmed. People are often heard to say things like, "I knew I should have done that" and there is usually an overriding feeling of something being either right or wrong, without having a specific reason for it. Where does this feeling come from? Is there an innate psychic or intuitive faculty from which we could all benefit? How do we access it? And if we do so, why won't we trust this extra sense that is often referred to as the sixth sense?

Throughout this part we will investigate how much you use your psychic senses and how you might further train any psychic potentials. Taking the mystical view that we all possess divinity within, is it possible for us all to tap into higher awareness, to tune into information beyond normal means?

Many people regard the very notion of being psychic as something that belongs at a fairground. But most people, at some time in their lives, have consulted their horoscopes in the papers, or read some of the increasing number of articles or books on affiliated subjects, or even have been to some form of psychic or medium. Over the last 20 years, there has been massive interest in psychic and spiritual topics, so much so that psychism has emerged from the secular into the mainstream. Why then is there so much interest in this age-old subject?

To access psychic information, the seeker needs to be a clear instrument, which often necessitates some kind of self-development or transformative process. Psychic refers to an unseen force; it derives from the word psyche, which means of, or pertaining to, the soul, mind or spirit. In the allegorical Greek story of the mortal princess, Psyche, she had to endure many tests and trials to prove herself worthy of being the companion of the god of love, Eros. When at last she is given the cup of immortality, she sprouts butterfly wings, which are ancient symbols of the soul. This story suggests that in seeking unconditional love, we, too, might be transformed.

Perhaps one of our greatest attributes is our curiosity, our desire to learn, to make our existence a life-long learning venture. In this part we will explore some interesting questions about who we are and whether we are psychic and, if so, how we can enlarge and possibly use any psychic talents we may possess.

We will explore avenues of sensitivity, to help you assess how much you can rely on your inner knowing, to aid you in your own voyage of discovery. What you ultimately do about your gifts only you can decide. Anyone with 10 fingers on his or her hands, with enough dedication and perseverance could learn how to play a tune on the piano. Few, however, will become concert pianists. Psychic abilities could be seen in the same way; anyone with a strong desire to use these attributes will be able to access his or her intuition, very few are able, or indeed would want, to work as a professional in the field.

The following pages are laid out for interactive exchange. They contain simple questionnaires and exercises that will immediately give you some feedback about your approach to and potential success in the various areas of psychism. Often, there are suggestions about strengthening your "gifts" using the various exercises and practices given. If the process of discovery is successful, you should be able to use your intuition in beneficial ways in your day-to-day life. You will be able to see for yourself how a new perspective can aid you in not only being conscious of what's around you now, but also help you take charge of your own destiny.

The first chapter of helps you discover any latent psychic talents. How intuitive are you? Are your senses sufficiently awakened? Do you understand your will and use positive thought? Can you exert mind over matter? The chapter also provides you with insight into how meditation, sharpening your psychic vision, and comprehending the chakras and auras can lead to profound discoveries.

The next chapter tackles Extra-Sensory Perceptions. Is it possible to read minds? Travel to places without leaving your armchair? Look into the future? Or decipher dreams that inform you of your needs?

Chapter 3 considers the psychic aids at your disposal. Astrology, the I Ching, Tarot, Scrying, Palm Reading and Divining – all can provide insights that no other form of communication can.

Chapter 4 is concerned with spiritual healing and with simple approaches to balancing energies for health and well-being. Does the body speak to us through illness and if so can we do something to heal ourselves? Can you sufficiently develop your innate powers so that you can heal not only yourself but others? Readers will be advised on using particular "tools" such as crystals, music and colour. This section ends with glorious colour pages, which not only inform, but can be used for meditation and healing purposes.

Chapter 5 looks at communication with non-physical beings. Have you ever encountered a ghost? Are there such things as poltergeists? And do angels really help us throughout our lives? Could you be a shaman, someone who allows spirits of nature to talk through you, or become closer to a spirit guide?

The penultimate section covers psychic protection. If you are looking at developing your intuitive powers, you need to be discerning and protected. Some psychic self defence is used to aid you through your progress. Finally, in the last chapter, I discuss the implications of beginning to see the world through higher levels of consciousness. How can you best channel these energies and does karma really work within our lives? What is the transpersonal self and can it assist the function of our intuition effectively?

In entering the psychic world, people often lose sight of the joy of living and the fun of the adventure. In these pages, I hope to inject some enjoyment into the crucial subject of how we manage psychic forces in our lives, and what we therefore may achieve.

Keeping a psychic journal

One of the best the ways to develop your psychic skills is to record your insights, ideas, dreams and observations in a special notebook. This can help train you to be increasingly self-aware and will provide you with a reference base to help you to keep track of your progress and problems. You might like to start by asking yourself the questions set out on page 169 in order to direct your psychic growth. There could be things on the list that you are trying to overcome, achieve, or improve. Keep the notebook by your bedside; this way you can record whatever dreams you have (see page 224) as well as your day-time thoughts. Before going to sleep each night, review the day's events, recalling not just your own

feelings and experiences, but the reactions of others. Avoid getting caught up in the emotions of any situation—stay objective. Keep asking yourself questions. How do people respond to you and what energy from you attracts that response? Be honest in your assessment – that way you'll achieve the necessary overview for success in psychic work.

The golden rules

Write the following guidelines in your journal as a constant reminder to use your psychic abilities ethically and responsibly:

Never offer psychic insights unless asked for them.

Don't exaggerate your psychic capabilities.

Under no circumstances manipulate or control others.

Never tell someone when or how you think he or she will die.

Avoid judging or condemning someone else's behaviour.

Journal notes: Food for thought

One very good reason to develop your psychic abilities is because they may be able to change your life for the better. Therefore, you should give some thought as to what needs changing. The questions below are really prompts to start you thinking about your ultimate goal(s).

- What have you always wanted?

- What gives or will give you the most pleasure?

- What do you spend your time thinking/wishing about most?

- What behaviour in others do you most admire but feel is lacking in yourself?

- Is there anything that you were deprived of as a child that you still yearn for?

- Is there a difference between the things/people you value and the things you think most about – and how do you go about changing this?

- What are your priorities? What are you doing about them?

- What beliefs would help you to experience more fun, trust and joy? And help you deal with anger, fear and grief?

- What is preventing you from making the necessary changes to become the person you really want to be?

Discover your psychic potential

1

How intuitive are you?

Intuitive intelligence is a valuable tool for living. Your "sixth sense" gives you access to information that seems to come from nowhere, but is often uncannily accurate. There are various theories about how this happens. You could see it as your mind drawing together everything that it knows and coming up with the right answer from your personal, instant-access database.

A psychic might regard intuition as the ability to go beyond individual experience, tapping into much broader sources, similar to plugging into the world-wide web. Like most people, you already have some intuitive ability, but there are positive ways to develop this even further. Many of the exercises in this book – particularly meditation (see page 180) – are specially designed to help you to achieve the concentrated inner focus that will help you to recognize messages from your inner self.

The exercises can also give you more confidence in yourself, and enable you not only to trust your intuition but to act on it. This is particularly helpful if you often doubt your perceptions, and explain away your intuitive insights with "rational" explanations. The best way to overcome this barrier is to take a mental "leap" into the unknown. This means suspending all assumptions, bias and prejudices, and learning to be open to the promptings of your psychic sensitivity. This will open up a whole new resource of vision, and make you much more sure in your judgment; you'll be able to see through surface detail, and make fast, accurate decisions in any situation.

Intuition boosters

Even if you regard yourself as a very analytical person, you can still enhance your intuition.

Instead of dismissing any insights you have about people or events that seem to defy logic, start paying attention to these, and record them in your psychic journal.

If you ever get a sudden sense of danger or threat, never ignore it – trust your intuition.

Learn to identify your sharp, rationalizing "voice". If you hear yourself saying "nonsense" **when you can't explain something that's bothering you, that's when you should listen to your soft, persistent, intuitive "voice".**

If one of your hidden feelings, hunches or predictions is proved right, enjoy the feeling of being "right on" in your judgment, and make a note whenever this happens.

Be playful with your intuition: create harmless "games" – for instance, imagine what someone is about to say, or what they'll wear tomorrow.

Do you have a sixth sense?

If you respond "yes" to a question, check the box next to it. Add up the checks and note your score.

❑ Have you instantly felt that a building was a happy or threatening place?

❑ Do you "know" that you can or can't trust someone?

❑ When the phone rings, do you often know who is calling?

❑ Can you "hear" someone's thoughts and verbalize them?

❑ Have you ever had a physical sensation of someone walking through you?

❑ When looking for a parking space, have you ever followed your instinct to turn down an unfamiliar road, and then found a space?

❑ When you wake up, do you feel something has been revealed to you during the night?

❑ While talking to a person you've never met before, have you ever had a compelling feeling that something unpleasant would happen to him or her? And have you been told later that the person had been in an accident or had become ill?

❑ When you close your eyes do you sometimes see eyes or human faces?

❑ Do the hairs on the back of your neck sometimes bristle, putting you on your guard?

❑ Have you ever made a decision against the advice of friends and family, just because it felt right?

❑ Are you someone who experiences an unusual number of coincidences?

How many questions did you check?

❑ **1–2**
Even if you ticked just one or two boxes, you have some access to your intuitive resources – and these can be developed.

❑ **3–5**
Your intuition is quite active, but you have room to improve. Learn to trust yourself and let your instinct guide you.

❑ **7–9**
You're already well tuned in to your inner sources of wisdom – and with practice, you can use intuition even more precisely.

❑ **10 or over**
Your intuitive abilities are powerfully developed and you have the confidence to trust your innate judgment.

What kind of psychic are you?

You can be psychic in different ways. For instance, intuitive empaths have a great understanding of what is going on with others but may have little sensitivity to atmosphere. Those with shamanic abilities derive a special energy from communicating with nature spirits and are gifted healers – but they may not be drawn to psychic tools such as tarot cards or runes. Mediums have the ability to link with spirits, but unlike channellers, may not be able to connect with higher spiritual forces. Use the questionnaire opposite to discover *your* psychic style.

Identifying your skills

Give the following questions careful thought, then check *only* those to which you have an affirmative response.

❏ 1   Are you generally aware of other people's feelings?

❏ 2   Do you ever get a sense that you are part of the universe?

❏ 3   Do you often know what other people will say before they say it?

❏ 4   While walking outdoors have you sensed something watching you?

❏ 5   Out in open country, have you felt something did not want you there?

❏ 6   Have you been out in a wild space and felt the place protected you?

Assessment

Look at your final total of "yes" answers. Do all, or most of them, fit into one of the following groups of numbers? If so, this will give you a good idea of what kind of psychic you are most likely to be.

1 3 7 8 12
You are an EMPATH

The ability to literally feel for someone else is a finely tuned empathic sense. It gives you the psychic ability to "read" a person's aura, and interpret the information back to him or her (see page 200). It can bring you amazingly close to others; you can sense their true emotional needs with unerring accuracy, and people may be drawn to you like magnets. But avoid absorbing other people's problems, as it's easy to get burned out.

❏ 7 Do you get butterflies in your stomach when you are near someone?

❏ 8 Do you get the same butterfly feeling in a location?

❏ 9 When you walk into a place for the first time can you sense the atmosphere?

❏ 10 Do you really know that the world could be a place of peace and love instead of starvation and wars?

❏ 11 Have you walked into a place and felt a shiver or a sense of a presence?

❏ 12 Do you ever "hear" people's thoughts?

❏ 13 Are there people that you do not like to be physically near?

❏ 14 Have you had an encounter with a spirit of any kind?

❏ 15 Have you woken up to feel a weight on you when nothing physical is there?

❏ 16 Do you get a sense of wonder and love just by being alive?

❏ 17 Do you have vivid dreams that you feel may have really happened?

❏ 18 Do you look into the eyes of someone who is hurting you and see their pain?

❏ 19 At night, do you close your eyes and see eyes, faces or human-like creatures?

❏ 20 Have you felt your body has been on a journey without you moving?

2 10 16 18
You are a CHANNELLER

Accessing information and/or energy from a higher level of consciousness is often called channeLling (see page 326). There is no sense of contact with an individual entity, rather, a connection to higher spiritual forces. Whatever your age, you are viewed by others as "an old soul" and will be sought out for the spiritual insight that you've built up over many lifetimes.

11 14 15 17 19 20
You are a MEDIUM

If you've been aware of an unseen presence, or have seen a ghost, you could be mediumistic (see page 300). You may also have felt the presence of angelic or earthly spirits, which act as guardians to you. You can look into other dimensions such as the astral worlds or the "spirit" world. This vision is a rare gift.

4 5 6 9 13
You are a SHAMAN

As you are vividly aware of nature and the spirit in animals, plants and trees, your style of psychism is shamanistic (see page 298). You derive a highly tuned sense of danger from your instinctive link with wild animals; this is a great asset – your intuition literally saves lives. You can sense impending danger in all situations, whether it's on the pavement, in traffic situations or in the workplace. You may also have natural healing ability – an innate sense of what will harm or help someone who is ill.

Awaken your senses

Psychic sensitivity is not based on some obscure formula known to a few privileged people; on the contrary, you already have every ingredient you need in your five senses. Every second of the day, you're absorbing a changing blend of aromas, flavours, sounds, sights and textures. The process is so automatic it's easy to take it for granted but without your senses you would literally be "dead" to the world. This is the polar opposite of a psychic's experience of life, where everything is vivid, sensuous and alive with meaning.

People who are unusually sensitive can perceive atmospheres, feel invisible presences, see visions, hear messages and experience reality on many different levels. With a little practice, you'll be able to do all this yourself.

A Day of Vision

Ideally, you should choose a day that has a full moon on the same evening (see the exercise opposite). As soon as you wake up, tell yourself out loud: "Today I am going to look closely at everything around me."

Journal notes: **Five sensational days**

- Exploring your senses to their limits takes time, space and imagination. It also requires the ability to focus: a simple way to achieve this is to allot an entire day to discovering a single sense. Then, at the end of that day, write up your experiences in your psychic journal.

- Note down your reactions to any incident, exercise or experiment that gave you positive feedback, and made an active difference to your sensory awareness.

- Pay attention to the exact quality of your reactions; notice whether you felt excited, calmed, aroused, amused, inspired; or frightened, uneasy, curious or repelled.

- Each day's events may also trigger a special chain of association in your mind: for example, a fleeting scent, a fading colour, a grain of wood – any of these can release a flood of memories.

- You may remember people and places that you had long forgotten. Again, write everything down; all these links will lead you towards enhanced psychic awareness.

CANDLE-GAZING

How to enhance your psychic sight.

1 *Choose a quiet, dimly lit place, and light a candle. Place it on a table, and sit down, facing the candle. Get yourself quietly relaxed.*

2 *Gaze into the candle flame, staying relaxed and calm, watching the flame.*

3 *Now, focus your gaze at the place where the blue color of the flame meets with the gold—this is the point where your potential for psychic sight can be developed. Continue gazing at this spot until you feel you have absorbed enough.*

This triggers your visual awareness and prepares your intuition for action. As you go through your day, look at everything with the candid gaze of a child – try to see things just as they are. Look at objects, buildings, colours, people's faces, animals and plants with new eyes. Don't spend time "evaluating" – simply look. This way, you'll take in more visual messages, as you won't be censoring or rejecting anything. At some point in the day, try one of the "gazing" exercises described below.

A Day to Follow Your Nose

The moment you wake up, say out loud: "Today I am going to experience as many different smells as possible." This message will literally put you on the scent; follow your nose through the day, and notice every aroma – starting with the smells of your morning toast and coffee. Be alert to everything – fumes from traffic; smells from coffee shops and restaurants; the waft of perfume from a passer-by. Sniff your newspaper, and breathe in the smell of a leather wallet. This prepares your psychic antennae

MOON-GAZING

See a new vision in the full moon.

1 *Find a quiet place to relax and look up at the full moon; allow your gaze to become completely absorbed by the moon's light.*

2 *Next, close your eyes, and note the intense blue image imprinted on your retina. Draw this blue colour towards you, and use it to visualize yourself.*

3 *If there is no full moon, you could try gazing briefly into a 100 watt light bulb; but you should never look into the full glare of the sun, as this could damage your eyesight.*

for action, as the first hint of an invisible presence may be a certain smell. A faint, old-fashioned scent could be a link with a departed grandmother, and a pungent whiff of tobacco may announce a man who always had a pipe with him when he was alive.

A Day to Listen Closely

Your wake-up message for your listening day says: "Today I'll keep my ears open and hear what the world really sounds like." You may think this is easy; but you're probably unaware of how much sound you automatically block out. This form of "natural selection" is a survival mechanism, helping you to focus on the important signals around you. One of

the first signs of stress is the inability to cope with a constant bombardment of grating and discordant sounds, and censoring these helps you to stay calm and balanced. You can use a consciously selective approach and focus on different sounds, as if they were separate notes in a piece of music. Turn the day into your private musical with tunes made up from varying notes: car horns; doorbells; ringing telephones; hissing coffee machines; clacking cups and saucers; whirring elevators; a slammed door; sudden shrieks; barks; and laughter.

WHAT'S THAT SMELL?

This exercise can be very revealing.

1 *Ask a close friend to make up a "sampler" tray: it could include things like a lemon; furniture polish; starch; stationery; spices; mothballs; a smelly insole; and an overripe piece of cheese.*

2 *Keep your eyes closed or blindfolded, and smell each item individually. Take time to experience each scent – it's just as important to identify what feelings are evoked in you as it is to identify the source of the smell.*

LISTEN TO THE BIRDS

Here's how to follow each part of a symphony of bird song.

1 *Find an outdoor space, where there are plenty of birds – this could be a public park or in your garden.*

2 *Sit quietly relaxed, listening to the medley of birdsong around you. At some point you'll distinguish one song from the others. Focus on this, and spend time listening to it.*

3 *Now let the song of this bird take you to another's, and listen to this for a while. Again, you'll find that you're naturally drawn to the next bird in line. Listen intuitively to each song, sensing the essence within each.*

A Touchy-Feely Day

In the morning, look at yourself in the bathroom mirror and announce: "Today I will live each moment through my hands." Let your fingers tingle in anticipation and start from home: run your hands over the surface of your skin and through your hair; feel your bath towel; touch the cool porcelain of your bath; note the slick sensation of a plastic toy; and feel the bristles of your toothbrush with your fingertips. Throughout the day, make a point of touching as many different textures as possible – smooth, furry, silken, rough, warm, cold – and notice all the different sensations you experience, both positive and negative.

Tasting the Day

If you like eating and drinking, you'll probably enjoy spending an entire day in an extended tasting session. But you should still alert your tastebuds first thing in the morning by saying: "Today I'll pay close attention to everything that I taste." This starts from the moment the flavour of toothpaste floods your mouth; you may follow that with a swirl of mouthwash. What do these flavours evoke? Cool mints? Spicy cloves? Cinnamon? Consider the flavour of everything you put in your mouth. And explore unfamiliar things – for example, if you want to give your tastebuds a real shock, touch the end of your tongue with a metal coin.

A GUIDED TOUR

This journey starts with a simple touch.

1 *Ask someone who knows you well to pick out a distinctively textured object for you.*

2 *Close your eyes and ask your friend to place the item in your hands; as you explore it, talk about the places it evokes. It may take you into a garden from childhood; onto a beach; or somewhere you've never been before.*

3 *Visualize yourself there. Explore your surroundings thoroughly and pay attention to everything that you see. If there are people or animals, how do you feel about them? When you've completely absorbed the feeling of the place, open your eyes.*

DISCRIMINATING TASTE

Use this subtle method to tune your senses and taste the air around you.

1 *Sit in a quiet, airy place and use the breathing method on page 181 to get yourself deeply relaxed.*

2 *Breathe slowly and regularly, then open your mouth slightly. Let the air around you flow into your mouth.*

3 *Focus on the taste of the air, and open yourself completely to whatever you're sensing. You'll be surprised at how much information you'll receive this way.*

Opening up through meditation

If you want to do any form of psychic work, the most important skill to perfect is being able to contact your inner stillness. Whatever your aspirations – to enhance your powers of healing, telepathy or clairvoyance or to learn how you can view auras or connect with the spirit world – you'll first need to know how to meditate.

If you've never meditated before, you may believe that it is a pleasant way of escaping from the world and its problems. Although it does lead to inner stillness, calm, or "the silent place within", meditation is certainly not just about melting into bliss. Rather, it is a powerful tool to help you focus clearly on your physical being. Just as important, it also puts you directly in touch with universal energy or "prana" – the life force that runs though all things. This level of consciousness is precisely what you need to achieve your psychic ambitions; but it improves your life in other ways, too. Meditation sharpens and focuses your mental activity and keeps

Guidelines to meditation

Find a clean, quiet, airy, comfortable, uncluttered place and dedicate this spot to meditation – working in the same area builds up a positive energy.

Unplug the phone before starting and lock the door if you think you might be disturbed.

Wear comfortable, loose, clean clothing.

Bathe or shower, or at least wash your hands.

You may want to use something to focus your meditation; this can be an object such as a candle, flower or picture, a sound such as a mantra, or ambient music.

Sit in a chair or on the floor with your back supported. Place your arms on your legs with your hands in an open position – this puts you in the right posture.

Devote your whole attention to your point of focus; start with five minutes then gradually increase the time to 20, if possible.

Do not force your mind to concentrate. Keep it focused but without effort. When thoughts intrude, don't push them away but let them float by. If your mind wanders, return it to its focus, no matter how often it escapes.

It's a good idea to meditate at the same time every day – many people choose first thing in the morning, as meditation is usually better on an empty stomach. Meditation last thing at night can just cause you to fall asleep, so find a time that suits you to meditate regularly.

you alert at work, at home and in your relationships. It also enhances creativity and self-knowledge.

Most of the psychic development exercises in this book start by asking you to get into a completely relaxed state, and the meditation technique below is one of the most effective ways of doing this. Once you have become completely familiar with it, you'll have the key to opening yourself up to a completely new world of experiences. This way, meditation will dramatically change your life.

BREATHING IN THE LIGHT

This exercise is the key to complete relaxation; it can last as long or as short a time as you wish.

1 *Work in a quiet room where you feel relaxed. You may want to put on some soothing music to help you wind down. When you are completely calm, turn off the music and concentrate.*

2 *Direct your conscious awareness onto your breathing, and listen attentively.*

3 *Tune into the ebb and flow of your breath, and gently focus onto this quiet rhythm, so that your entire being is at one with your breathing. Take your time while doing this – you are entering a deep meditative state.*

4 *Let your breath take you to your inner calm, the "still place within", and consciously breathe that stillness out from the core of your being.*

5 *Visualize your breathing as ripples on a pond, moving outwards in increasingly large circles, or as waves of light radiating from your body.*

6 *Deliberately hold the energy and keep your focus – don't be tempted to "float away". After a while, as you breathe, concentrate on the thought that every living thing breathes. Say to yourself* **"We all breathe in light".** *Now let yourself become completely open to the universal forces of light. Stay with this feeling as long as you like.*

7 *When you're ready, gently lead your consciousness back into your physical body (paying particular attention to keeping your feet on the ground).*

8 *Finally, cross your arms and legs, as an act of closing.*

Your Inner Quest

To find your real self, you must ask: "Who am I?"
Let your mind confront this. At first you'll think of
yourself in terms of your role in life. Keep asking: Is
this really you? If you persist, you will finally arrive
at the core of your true self, which does not change.

If a question is nagging at your mind, the clarity
you achieve during meditation will assist you. Don't
expect an instant answer – it usually comes when
you least expect it. Meanwhile, meditative energy
will have assessed the question through other
perceptions.

If you have an especially active brain, a "Koan" or
paradoxical statement may help. This is a question
that de-intellectualizes the mind by its lack of logic;
the common Zen example is "What is the sound of
one hand clapping?"

Meditation Pathways

You may need to explore several avenues before
you discover the approach to meditation that works
best for you. Each of the pathways described
opposite offers a slightly different resonance. None
is "better" than the others – they are all simply
alternatives. Whatever route you choose, you'll
intuitively recognize when you've arrived at the
unique, calm centre within yourself. This is the
entire point of the journey.

SEEK THE STILL VOICE
*Light, breath, music and mantras are different points of
focus that you can use during meditation. Choose the one
that brings you to the still voice within yourself.*

Breath

Breathing is the simplest focus, and observing its natural rhythms can help to calm the mind. Let each breath enter and leave your body at its normal pace and observe how it moves and reverberates through your body. If you like, you can count the inhalations and exhalations to assist. Inhale to the count of four, pause for a few seconds, then exhale to the count of four.

Music

You may find that special meditative music tapes or certain classical pieces can help to clear the mind of intrusive thoughts. If you've never meditated before, music may be just the pathway you need to help you.

Mantra

The repetition of a single sound, word or phrase produces a powerful force that will block the intrusion of other thoughts. You may wish to focus on a sacred or personally meaningful word. You can say it aloud or repeat it silently. It can be helpful to synchronize your mantra with your breathing, saying it on every out- or in-breath. If your attention wanders, gently bring it back to your mantra.

Light

A lit candle placed in front of you can help work as a point of focus if you prefer to meditate with your eyes open. First close your eyes, then breathe deeply in and out through your nose. Slowly open your eyes and gaze at the flame.

To make you fully equipped for effective psychic action, meditation should become a completely normal activity in your life – as routine as brushing your teeth. However, forcing yourself to do it can be counter-productive – two minutes of complete connection to inner silence is far better than sitting still for 20 minutes without reaching the still voice within. It is quality not quantity that counts.

Mystics believe that meditation is the path to self-enlightenment. Eastern traditions refer to the need to calm the "monkey mind" – the busy, active level of thinking. Deep meditation gives you the power to do this; it enables you to concentrate your thoughts, rather than chasing after every passing notion. Thinking with this level of clarity is the essential ingredient of self-mastery – it is true freedom.

TRANSCENDENTAL MEDITATION

In the 1960s the Maharishi Mahesh Yogi popularized Transcendental Meditation (TM), which uses a sound or mantra to help with focusing during meditation. This might be a single word such as "love", "peace" or "beauty" or the ancient sound "om"; the primary factor is that it resonates both mentally and emotionally. Transcendental Meditation has attracted many followers since, and is still a widely used technique.

AIDS TO MEDITATION
The visual stimulus of a simple object such as a leaf, shell, candle, flower or pebble can help to concentrate your mind during meditation. So, too, can a pleasing fragrance such as incense, or a mandala as shown opposite. Always use what works for you – these are just a few suggestions.

Tuning in to your chakras

A psychic perceives centres of spinning energy, sometimes seen as radiant colours, at seven points along your spinal column. These are chakras, key locations on a pathway of energy flowing from head to toe. This "pranic" energy derives from the highest planes of consciousness, and acts in different ways at each chakra. When your chakras are functioning properly, they allow etheric energy to flow through freely, balancing you in mind, body and spirit and giving you complete harmony.

The chakra centres are an important part of the picture a psychic sees when viewing your aura; they act as focal points for a psychic "scan". A gifted psychic can assess your entire physical, emotional and mental state by "reading" your chakras and aura. As described opposite, each chakra radiates the energy of its colour; starting from the top of the body, these are violet, indigo, blue, green, yellow, orange, and red. They indicate how you interact with the world and experience yourself (see pages 53–71 for more on chakras).

THE CHAKRAS
Positioned at seven centres on your body, your chakras are associated with the lotus, regarded as a sacred flower in India. The unfolding petals correspond to the opening up of a chakra. Each chakra is depicted with a number of petals, starting with the four petals of the base centre, and moving upwards to the crown, which is called the thousand or many-petalled lotus. The functions of the chakras are described on the right.

The Crown Centrer *Sahasrara*
Key energy: "I know"
Set at the top of the head, this chakra represents pure thought. It connects you with infinite consciousness, the highest energy in the universe. By expanding the crown, you can tap into the deepest sources of spiritual wisdom.

The Brow Centre *Ajna*
Key energy: "I see"
This chakra is in the middle of the forehead and acts as the window of the "third eye". Opening this centre gives you vision beyond ordinary sight. It enhances your clairvoyance, enabling you to see past, present and future.

The Heart Centre *Anahata*
Key energy: "I love"
Situated at the centre of your body, this chakra acts as the bridge between the physical and spiritual worlds. Activating it increases your power of love, compassion and empathy with others.

The Throat Centre *Visuddha*
Key energy: "I speak up"
Positioned in the throat, this centre of communication connects with hearing and speech. Activating it inspires you to speak and listen in the spirit of truth. It also promotes spiritual communication and improves psychic hearing ability or clairaudience.

The Solar Plexus Centre *Manipura*
Key energy: "I can"
Based in the stomach area, this chakra represents vitality and will. Opening it puts you in touch with your personal power and transforms your hopes and aspirations into real possibilities.

The Sacral Centre *Svadhisthana*
Key energy: "I feel/want"
The rocket-like energy of this centre is generated from its site at the lower abdomen, between the navel and genitals. Opening it releases your innate creativity and fertility. It propels you into action and fuels your emotions and sexuality.

The Base Centre *Muladhara*
Key energy: "I have"
This chakra is located at the base of the spine. It is always open, linking you to the earth and sheer physical survival. Energizing it grounds you in a healthy desire for the basics of life – food, warmth and shelter.

Your overall sense of well-being depends on the unimpeded flow of etheric energy through your chakras (see preceding pages). If one of these centres is blocked, you may not feel entirely at ease with yourself. This is why it's important to keep this energy moving freely. The breathing exercise (page 189) is an excellent balancing routine that you can do regularly, and you can use the visualization (below) to check for any problems in your chakras.

If you feel that a specific centre needs freeing up, there are simple ways to do this. For instance, to invigorate your base centre, try energetic dancing, jumping up and down, stamping your feet, jogging and kicking out. Anything that gets your hips moving is good for the sacral centre, including pelvic rocking movements. Moving your belly frees up the solar plexus – have fun with a hula-hoop or enjoy a session of belly dancing. To stimulate your heart centre, you need to expand your chest – swimming is effective, also stretching your arms. Ease the throat centre with gentle neck rolls and open your brow centre by rolling your eyes in all directions, stretching them as far as they can go. Finally, to energize your crown centre, stand on your head for a few minutes. By keeping all your chakras open, you'll gain a deeper sense of self.

An experimental journey

There are no right or wrong answers in this exercise. But it will help to free up your mind and identify symbols that you may need in psychic work. It also gives access to your unconscious and any underlying imbalances.

Focus your mind onto each of your chakras, and let yourself be drawn intuitively towards one of them. Now visualize a door in front of you that is the signature colour of that chakra. See yourself opening this door, then entering the room beyond. Now consider these questions:

- ❏ What does the room look like?
- ❏ What is on the walls?
- ❏ What furniture is in the room?
- ❏ Is there a cupboard or drawers? If so, what is inside them?
- ❏ Is there a picture on the wall? If so, describe it.
- ❏ How does the room feel generally?
- ❏ Is anyone else in the room? If so, what is he or she communicating to you?
- ❏ How reluctant are you to leave the room?

Assessment

The way you feel about this room relates to the energy of the chakra you chose. So, if you walk into the yellow room of the solar plexus, you are dealing with your sense of power or helplessness. If you see colours that are strong, vibrant and clear, that's fine; but if they are dark or muddy, you have problems to resolve. Furniture represents encumbrances and anything found inside drawers or cupboards relates to what you need to discard. Also, any picture on the walls is an image of yourself. Psychically, the healthiest state for the room is to be completely empty. If your room is muddled and cluttered, you have a lot of unfinished business connected with the area of yourself that you are exploring here.

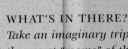

WHAT'S IN THERE?
Take an imaginary trip (see left) into the secret "rooms" of the chakras and discover what's going on inside you.

BALANCING YOUR CHAKRAS BY BREATHING IN COLOUR ENERGY

1 *Focus on your breath as described on page 181, then shift your attention to your base chakra. As you breathe, visualize powerful red energy from the earth's core glowing inside this chakra.*

2 *Now move up to the sacral centre; breathe quietly, and see bright orange flames of fire burning in the chakra.*

3 *Next, breathe bright yellow sunlight into the solar plexus, warming you and filling you with comfort.*

4 *Now absorb the vibrant green of fresh grass into your heart chakra.*

5 *Then focus on the throat: breathe in the pure blue of a summer sky.*

6 *Breathe the radiant indigo of the evening sky into your brow centre. A crystal clear energy cuts through and gives you a higher vision.*

7 *Now breathe violet light into your crown centre, letting in the pure light of divine consciousness. Acknowledge yourself as a spiritual entity.*

8 *Draw pure light down into each centre in a column of pure energy, keeping the flow of your breathing.*

9 *Focus into your heart centre and feel the balance and harmony throughout your centres. Now visualize a circle of golden light around yourself. Finally, concentrate on your feet, and feel a strong root of energy linking them to the earth.*

Use the colour pages 280–95 to aid your meditation.

Understanding your will

An experienced psychic knows that it is possible to exert one's will by energetically focusing his or her thoughts (thoughts and emotions are forms of energy and energy follows thought). Directed thought is a powerful tool in spiritual and healing work, but always remember to use it responsibly. When you send out thought energy, you must know and mean *precisely* what you're implementing. Examine every aspect before following through. And never activate a thought or action against someone's wishes, no matter how loving your intent. You may assume that you're innocent of imposing your will on others, but check the questions opposite, then think about the kinds of will described below. You'll realize that subtle forms such as karmic and divine will are just as important as the more direct styles.

The four types of will

Can you recognize your personal style of implementing your will? Do you go with the flow, or leave nothing to chance? Each has a valuable part to play.

Strong will

You use this will directly, compelling yourself or others to do your bidding. If this results in fine achievements, it is a positive force. But bullying or ignoring other people's needs is harmful.

Skilful will

This wily approach gets you what you want by indirect means. You may manipulate others by open charm or hidden subterfuge. Fox-like, clever, you achieve your ends by stealth.

Karmic will

This is the subtle will of cause and effect – "what goes around, comes around". Your past actions can react on the present with inevitable force, making you reap what you've sown.

Divine will

This is all-powerful, and goes beyond your personal will to the universal level, connecting you with your higher or spiritual self. It unifies heavenly and personal will.

Where there's a will...

Any psychic action needs careful thought; this means adopting the right mental attitude to each situation. If you're a forceful person, you may be tempted to solve a problem using your Strong will. But this could be a mistake – Karmic will may be at work, for example. Or it may be better to employ the indirect Skilful will. Keep an open mind and let your intuition decide what response is needed. Then adapt your will to act in an appropriate manner.

What kind of will do you have?

Read the questions below and check *only* those to which you have an affirmative response.

❑ 1   Do you often wonder why people are negative towards you?

❑ 2   Are you able to fulfil your ambitions effectively?

❑ 3   If you want something, do you take time to work out how to achieve it?

❑ 4   Do you take other people into account when you make decisions?

❑ 5   When you make decisions, do you consider what is for the highest good irrespective of what you yourself feel?

❑ 6   If you want something, do you persist until you get it?

❑ 7   Are you able to accept difficult situations as part of a greater plan?

❑ 8   Are you able to go with the flow of events and find some learning experience in everything that happens?

❑ 9   Are you able to get other people to do what you want without them realizing it?

❑ 10   Do you consider very carefully your actions as ones that are intuitively right?

❑ 11   Do you ever try to persuade people to do something they are unsure of?

❑ 12   Can you keep your mind centered on a question without being distracted?

Assessment

Look at your total of "yes" answers. Do all, or most of them, fit into one of the groups of numbers below? If so, this will give you a good idea of what kind of will you have.

If you had an equal distribution of yes answers, you're well-balanced and exert your will flexibly and positively.

2 6 11
You often implement a STRONG will

Make sure this is not at the expense of others: remember that what you give out will always return. Exertion of your will over others is a form of psychic attack.

3 9 12
Yours is a SKILFUL will

You use skill to achieve what you want. Be careful that it is not used to manipulate others against their own will, as ultimately no good will come from it.

1 4 10
You're aware of KARMIC will

You're a very thoughtful person and respect the natural laws of cause and effect. Therefore, you're more likely to receive positive thoughts and actions from others.

5 7 8
You trust in DIVINE will

You're insightful and altruistic. You are the person most likely to find happiness and contentment, as you are able to perceive an overview to life and a greater meaning in everything.

Using positive thought

Directed thought is the keynote to psychic activity – and each thought has an immensely powerful energy. Knowing this, you can implement concentrated mental force to free yourself from any negative thought patterns. In doing so, you will enhance your self-confidence, deepen your psychic powers, and enjoy a much more productive life.

At first, simply listen to yourself. Do you often start a sentence with a phrase like "I'm afraid", or "I'm sorry"? Have you ever heard yourself saying "Knowing my luck!" If you analyze the thought messages that are being sent out with these words, you'll know exactly why you never *do* have any luck. Shifting old patterns can be hard work. But don't give up; you'll be rewarded.

If you "bad-mouth" someone, that particular energy will come back to you. Everyone has something unique to offer, so use your psychic insight to identify each person's good qualities.

Don't be drawn into negative conversations. If, for instance, a friend regularly becomes involved in disastrous relationships, be sympathetic; then ask the friend what he or she can learn from that pattern to prevent the same thing happening in the future.

While positive thought has many benefits, it can't be used as a panacea for all ills. It should never be a way of hiding or denying pain. If you do have a problem, confront it, then use effective affirmations to change any damaging, fixed patterns of behaviour.

The golden rules

Get yourself into a relaxed, meditative state (see page 181), and ask for an inspirational statement that you can affirm each day to promote your well-being. Use the following guidelines to point the way:

Keep it simple.

Be inventive.

Convert it into a memorable rhyme or catchphrase – no more than four lines.

Say your affirmation out loud at least three times a day, for at least 28 days.

Always refer to the first person in your affirmation – say "I" or "Me".

AFFIRMATIONS

Health	*"My body is the temple of my soul and looks after me perfectly."*
Courage	*"I am one with the universe and safe at all times."*
Employment	*"Perfect work for perfect pay is coming my way."*
Love	*"I love the world and it loves me."*
Success	*"Abundance and success now come to me in endless ways."*
Happiness	*"I am balanced, joyful, happy and radiant and detached from any fear."*
Prosperity	*"The universe is an endless source which pours wealth upon me."*

Exerting mind over matter

You may have used positive thought to change your emotions and behaviour (see preceding pages), but it is a much greater challenge to accept that you can use the same energy to affect objects. This ability is known as psychokinesis or PK. As yet, there is no final answer as to why some people can influence the "heads or tails" fall of coins, stop clocks or stop and start computers. But researchers have identified a specific pattern in the brain waves of people while they are implementing PK. These findings may be the key to this ability – and you, too, can develop the skill. It can give you that vital "edge" over events, and improve your luck on bets with cards or dice. Try the experiments featured on the page opposite and overleaf – they will all help to enhance your psychokinetic aptitude.

Once you've acquired the knack of applying PK energy, you can use it in lots of ways. For instance, during a game of pool or golf, your ball may be poised on the edge of the hole or the pocket. When this happens, try "willing" your ball to drop into place – you'll be amazed how often you will succeed in doing this. Using the same, concentrated thought energy, you may also find that you'll be able to stop or start clocks and computers.

ACTIVATING THOUGHT ENERGY

If you can acquire the knack, this exercise provides direct feedback to boost your PK ability. Suspend your rational self, believe it is possible and "know" you can do it.

1 *Put a candle in a holder, light it, then place it on a table in a quiet, dimly lit room. The air in the room should be as still as possible.*

2 *Sit at the table at least 18 inches in front of the candle. Get yourself completely relaxed (see page 181). Look directly into the heart of the flame, and keep gazing steadily until you feel completely attuned to its movement, rhythm and energy.*

3 *When you're ready, shift your gaze to a spot about 1 inch above the flame. Focus there in a relaxed manner until you feel the flame "pulling" upwards.*

4 *As soon as this happens, direct a sudden charge of concentrated energy into the flame; doing this boosts its upward movement, raising its level.*

5 *Hold the flame there as long as you can, then relax your gaze and allow the flame to drop to its original level.*

BEATING THE ODDS

When you throw a playing card into the air, the odds are 50–50 that it will land face down or up. Can you use your mind to improve the average outcome?

1 *Make yourself completely relaxed (see page 181) and decide in advance whether you want the card to land face down or up.*

2 *Toss a card into the air, and, as it moves, actively "will" it to fall the way you want. Do this 100 times and mark down each result.*

3 *Make a control group of another 100 throws by not trying to target the outcome. Mark down the results – they should be close to the normal 50–50 average distribution.*

4 *Add up your "targeted" score. If you've achieved something like 65 correct "hits," you're showing positive PK ability.*

If you got positive results from basic psychokinetic exercises such as raising a candle flame and making clocks stop (see preceding pages), you'll have experienced the satisfaction of seeing your own thought power at work. But there are even more ways to apply focused mental energy; for example, you may have heard of people who can move objects just by concentrating on them. This is possible, but it's not easy to get results on your own.

The best way to succeed in moving things with applied mental energy is to work with others. If you belong to a psychic development group, you'll already be accustomed to synchronizing your energies. But has your group tried applying its combined thought force to moving inanimate items? Small groups meeting regularly on a relaxed, informal basis have obtained the best results. It's been shown that these PK experimental sessions are a challenging way to sharpen up psychic teamwork skills.

If you're not a member of a psychic group, you could simply ask some friends to join you in the exercise described below. This can be risky, however: even people you know very well might be tempted to "help" a successful outcome to occur, so stay alert.

USING GROUP FORCE

The combined energies of a psychic group can be harnessed to make objects move. Try it and see.

1 *Choose an enclosed unit, preferably made of glass. A glass box with a fitted lid is ideal so you can watch, but not touch, any object inside.*

2 *Place the item you wish to move at the bottom of the container. Use things like sugar or coffee grounds at first and try moving small, solid objects, such as a needle, later. Put the box on a table in full view of the whole group.*

3 *Seat the group around the table. Everyone should now get into a lightly relaxed, meditative state – remember, too much concentration can be counter-productive.*

4 *You can either ask a trusted spirit entity for help, or give a name to the active thought energy of of the group. You could call it "the agency" for instance.*

5 *The group should now quietly concentrate on linking with a spirit or "agency" and ask it to help them move the object in the box.*

6 *If materials such as coffee granules or sugar are being used, the spirit or "agency" can be asked to leave a trail, pattern, or a message. Whatever result the group requires, each person should powerfully visualize this.*

7 *Focus the group's concentration in short bursts – 20 minutes at most. Don't continue this exercise if anyone in the group becomes frightened or senses a sinister energy.*

Sharpen your psychic vision

Have you sometimes noticed an odd shadow out of the corner of your eye, seen a coloured mist around a person or animal, or glimpsed pinpoints of floating light? These are examples of psychic sight – the ability to see energies that are normally invisible to the naked eye. This is an extremely useful skill; it not only adds an extra dimension to your daily awareness of the world about you, it also enables you to focus on someone's aura (see page 200), and enhances clairvoyance (see page 248). You can develop your psychic vision by doing the exercises shown below and on the opposite page. They give you the flexibility to switch your visual focus automatically.

A PERCEPTION-SHIFTING EXERCISE

Not all pictures are what they seem to be at first glance. What do you see when you look at the picture, shown right. A well-known person or a myriad of tiny images with a larger one in the centre? Now try holding the page much further away from you and tilting it slightly. What do you see now?

THIRD-EYE VISION

Ancient Egyptian hieroglyphs often depict the image of the "third eye", an invisible centre of psychic perception located behind the pineal gland in the head. Third-eye vision is a magical art used by priests, priestesses and seers, and takes years, even lifetimes, to mature. It is an immensely powerful tool – giving a complete overview of life, as if you were looking down at events on the ground from an aircraft.

ENHANCING PSYCHIC FOCUS

Improving your abilities to work with observable phenomena will help you see what others may not.

1 *Get yourself thoroughly relaxed (see page 181), and extend your arms out fully in front of your body. Hold your two forefingers upright – about 6 inches apart is fine.*

2 *Concentrate on the space between your fingers, keeping a steady gaze for a few moments.*

3 *Next, gently draw the fingers together until they merge into one. Be aware of how your focus moves to the position of this image. It could be to*

the right or to the left, depending upon which finger receives the greater part of your attention.

4 *Do this repeatedly until you can visualize a third finger without the help of the other two.*

5 *The position of this third finger is where you should look when reading an aura (see page 200) or doing a psychic "scan". Use a relaxed half-focused gaze.*

All living things have a complex electrical field or "aura" surrounding them. Some people are born with the ability to see this with the naked eye, and describe luminous, shimmering bands of rainbow colour radiating from, and encircling, the body. There are various theories about the source of this radiant energy: it is widely believed to emanate from the highest plane of consciousness, entering and leaving your body through your chakras. You can also think of an aura as a powerful electromagnetic field, equipping you with superb sensitivity to external influences, and sending your own energy vibrations into the world.

Recent studies using blindfold tests have shown that people can "sense" when someone is staring at them intently, even if they can't see the person doing it. Researchers believe that this information is picked up within the aura.

The human aura is a complete physical, emotional, mental and spiritual "map" of a person's life and character. It reveals patterns of thought, as well as the ebb and flow of physical and emotional energy, and will show any areas that need healing or energizing. Before you set out to explore the map of someone else's aura, get to know your own first, using the techniques described opposite.

IMAGING THE AURA

The Soviet husband and wife team Semyon and Valentina Kirlian were the first to capture a photographic image of the aura. Technology has progressed rapidly since – the British radiologist Dr Walter Kilner devised special "screens" to view the aura, and, as a result, many psychics have learned how to diagnose and heal illnesses through the aura. You can obtain a colour photograph of your aura at psychic conventions. Kirlian photography is still widely used. A famous example is the Kirlian image of a leaf with half of its area removed. The leaf appears whole in the photograph – the energy radiating from it is not affected.

DISCOVERING YOUR OWN AURA

Use this technique to explore the energy field around your body.

1 *Work in a dimly lit room. Sit in front of a clear area of wall. Relax (see page 181).*

2 *Stretch your arms out in front of you, one hand facing down, the other up.*

3 *Quickly squeeze your hands together. After one or two minutes, reverse hands, and keep squeezing until you feel them pulling.*

4 *Drop your hands down by your sides. Then, slowly raise them with the palms facing. Bring your hands together very slowly until you sense a*

point of resistance. Feel your hands attracting each other like magnets, but don't let your palms touch.

5 *Lightly half-focus your gaze (see page 199) at the area around your hands. You may see a halo of light around them – even a colour. Note this, and feel the energy built up between your hands. You may get a pulsing, tingling feeling – that is your aura.*

AURA CHECK

Your aura reacts to mood, people and places. Using this method, you can take a quick look at its main colour at any time.

1 *It's difficult to see your own aura in its entirety, but you can easily check its current predominant colour.*

2 *Focus closely on the rainbow illustrated here, then gaze at your face in a mirror, backlit with a soft, dim light. Close your eyes and visualize the rainbow over your head.*

3 *Open your eyes quickly and look at the halo of colour(s) above your head. This is your key aura colour at present.*

4 *Use the colour chart on the next pages to interpret the colour or colours you see. And when you check your aura another time, note how the colours have changed.*

Most of us are aware of colour in auras, even though this may be a subliminal insight. Your unconscious vision is reflected in the most casual remarks – for example, you may note that someone is in a "black mood", "browned off", "red with anger", "green with envy", "in the pink", or "feeling blue". These intuitive comments are your response to the predominant colour radiating from someone's aura at any one time – a rapid psychic snapshot. However, it requires a finely tuned sensitivity to decipher each different shade in the rainbow of the aura.

The constant play of colour reflects changing thoughts, impulses and emotions, and it is deeply fascinating to explore the meaning of each shade (see right). Try not to be obsessed with every tiny detail, however – it's equally important to note how the colours make you feel in reaction to the emotional energy they project. What is your response to a particular colour? Is it flowing easily? Or is it sharp and spiky? Most important, is it strong and pure? Dirty, patchy areas are not good news.

You need also to observe how the colours connect. Do they clash? Are they harmonious? When they blend together in an overall flow, this indicates someone who is happy to interact with others. But if colours clash violently with each other, it could mean inner conflict, and an inability to move freely from one level of consciousness to another.

Always remember that the colours of your aura are directly related to your chakras, and the best way to get and keep a balanced, healthy aura is to breathe colour into each chakra centre, as shown on page 189.

Red
Vibrantly active, red reveals physical energy or anger. A deep crimson may mean a high sex drive while scarlet denotes ego. A pure, bright red can restore depleted physical energy.

Pink
Rose pink is a sign of unselfish love and sensitivity. This is the colour of a practicing healer, or may indicate that spiritual healing is currently being implemented.

Green
A clear, fresh green shows balance and growth; a pastel shade, spirituality. Dark green indicates envy and selfishness. Muddy, olive green denotes greed, deceit or depression.

Blue
This can be a deeply healing colour, and indicates an independent spirit. Dark blue areas in the aura show stubbornness or dogmatism – but a deep navy blue is highly protective.

Orange

Bright orange is a sign of healthy sexuality. Muddy shades mean self-indulgence. Reddish orange suggests slyness. If it is "flaming" off the body, it denotes sex running riot.

Yellow

Clear, bright yellow signifies intellect, warmth and compassion. A muddy or dark shade denotes a fearful, resentful, lazy person who thinks the world owes him or her something.

Gold

This truly spiritual colour is rarely seen in the aura – it is the sign of saints or godly beings, as depicted in haloes. Used in healing, gold is an excellent overall aid and protection.

Silver

When surrounded by this colour, the person has erratic mental energy. He or she lives a life of illusion, and may be mentally ill. Silver can also be protective – visualize it around your car.

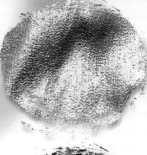

Indigo/Violet

Indigo is the timeless color signature of the priest or priestess, and is emanated by the seeker of truth. A pure violet signifies an intensely spiritual person.

Grey/Black

A band of black or grey over the head shows that a person suffers depressed thoughts. Situated on the solar plexus and lower body, they indicate negative emotions.

Brown

This points to a materialistic person with good business acumen and organizational skills. A muddy brown indicates the need to get what he or she wants immediately.

White

Like gold, this is not a colour that is often seen within the human aura. It always indicates a highly evolved, divinely spiritual being – such as a saint or holy mystic.

Making a complete summary of everything you see within the aura is a subtle art. You'll certainly need to have a clear idea of its structure, and where the different colours are located. This is a vital key to understanding the significance of all the shades of colour that you see there.

To focus your thoughts, look at the illustration on the facing page. It shows that the human aura is made up of seven layers that are powered by the chakras. These subtle layers radiate outwards in bands of colour surrounding the body. The quality of these colours are the major clues to what is happening on each level – when they are bright and pure, that is a good sign; but muddy, dirty, clashing or unharmonious shades indicate problem areas.

If you learn to view the aura clearly, you'll have a privileged insight. You may see great contrasts and extremes of strength and vulnerability. You'll also gain deep knowledge of someone's inner character, feelings, thoughts and psychic gifts.

If you enjoy drawing, try making coloured sketches of the aura – this sharpens your observation and improves your accuracy. If you want to do healing or energizing work on the aura you can consult your sketches to double-check the areas where you found problems.

MAKING AN AURA PORTRAIT

Character, thoughts, feelings, pain, happiness, strength, weakness – they're all visible in the aura.

1 *Assemble some sheets of cream paper and a box of coloured crayons. Ask a friend to sit in front of a white or light-coloured wall, then get relaxed (see page 181).*

2 *Lightly gaze at the area around the edges of your friend's body. Your eyes should be half-focused (see page 199) onto the wall behind him or her.*

3 *Wait until you can see (or sense) the outlines of your friend's energy field. When you see colours, ask your friend to shift position: the colours should move at the same time.*

4 *Now draw the aura. Keep looking and checking; note exactly where the colours are situated, and indicate if they are light or dark. Use the colour references on the preceding pages as a guide to interpreting the colours, but, in the final analysis, always trust your own intuition.*

CHAKRA COLOURS

Each chakra is associated with a particular energy (see page 187) and each energy type manifests itself as a colour.

Red *is the colour of the base, or lowest chakra;*

Orange *the colour of the sacral chakra;*

Yellow *the colour of the solar plexus chakra;*

Green *that of the heart chakra;*

Blue *of the throat chakra;*

Indigo *of the brow chakra and*

Violet *that of the crown chakra.*

A lot can be learned by studying the intensity, clarity and amount of each colour and relating this back to the energy's "meaning".

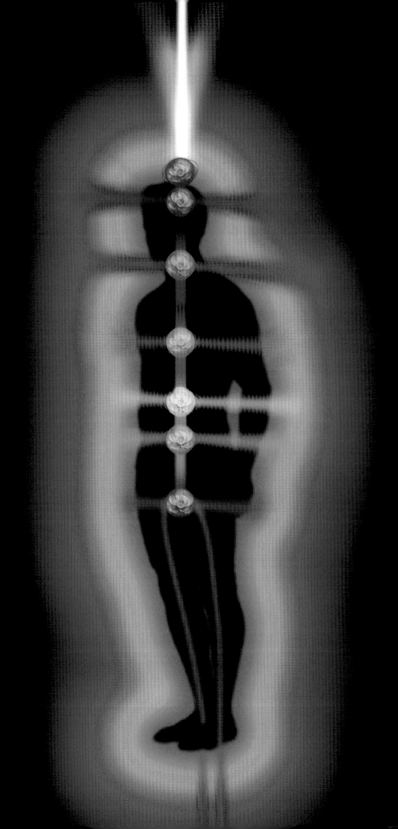

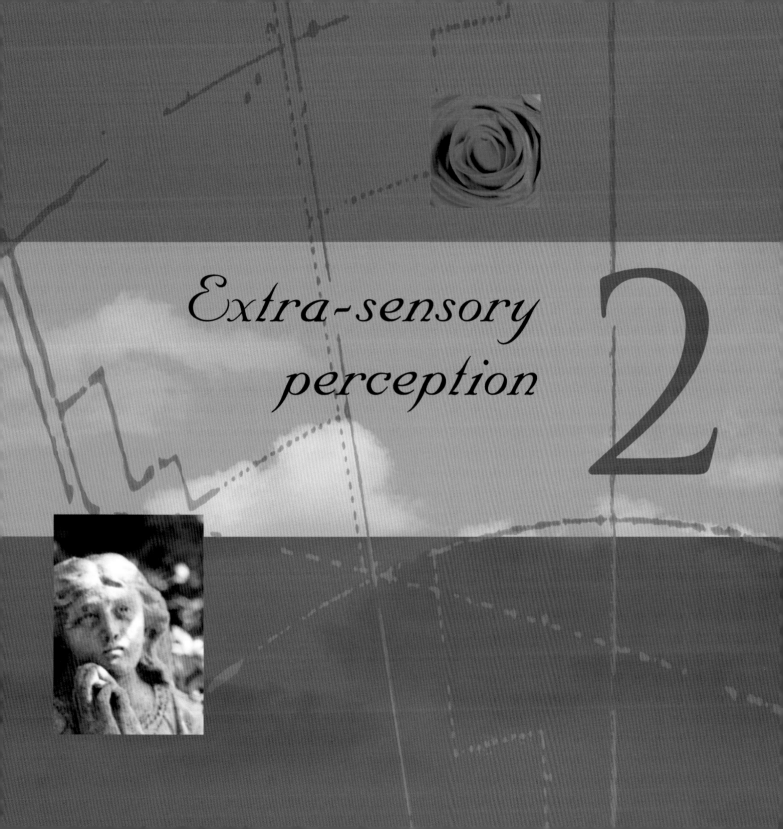

Extra-sensory perception

2

Could you be a mind reader?

Have you known what someone was going to say seconds before he or she verbalized it? If so, you've experienced a form of telepathy – the ability to read minds. This psychic gift is immensely useful; it gives you razor-sharp sensitivity and makes you aware of what others are really thinking. You'll be able to interpret their hidden needs with uncanny accuracy. This is useful in all situations – whether you're trying to work out what your boss really wants from you, or discovering why your friend has suddenly become very reserved.

Telepathic ability has been widely studied by ESP researchers because the data from controlled "mind reading" experiments can be measured against statistical probability. You can improve your own telepathic skills by using well-proven techniques, such as sending and receiving simple images (see below) and by following the information set out on the following pages.

The classic method for testing mind-reading was devised by psychic researcher Karl Zener. He created a series of five cards with simple symbols—a circle, a square, a cross, a star and a set of wavy lines. They have become major tools in psychic research. You can buy these, but it's easy to create your own deck – get 25 plain postcards and make five cards of each symbol. Draw the symbols clearly, but make sure they are not visible through the card.

ZENER TELEPATHY TEST

1 *Working with a friend, decide which of you is to be the "sender" and which the "receiver" of the images, then sit in separate rooms. Both need to be familiar with the images.*

2 *The sender shuffles the 25 cards, then, concentrating on one image for three minutes at a time, mentally "beams" the image to the receiver. The receiver makes a note of the picture he* or she "sees" – generally what appears first. A bell or handclap can be used to signal each new "transmission".

3 *Once the sequence of 25 cards has been tested, check the results and record the scores. There is a 20–25 per cent chance of guessing the correct answer. Consistently correct scores of over 25 per cent indicate a high telepathic ability.*

4 *A quick and easy test can be done by using the grid of Zener images shown on the opposite page. Decide in which direction you'll work – sideways across or top down – then mentally send the images in sequence, spending three minutes concentrating on each. The receiver takes notes as before. How many of the received images were correct?*

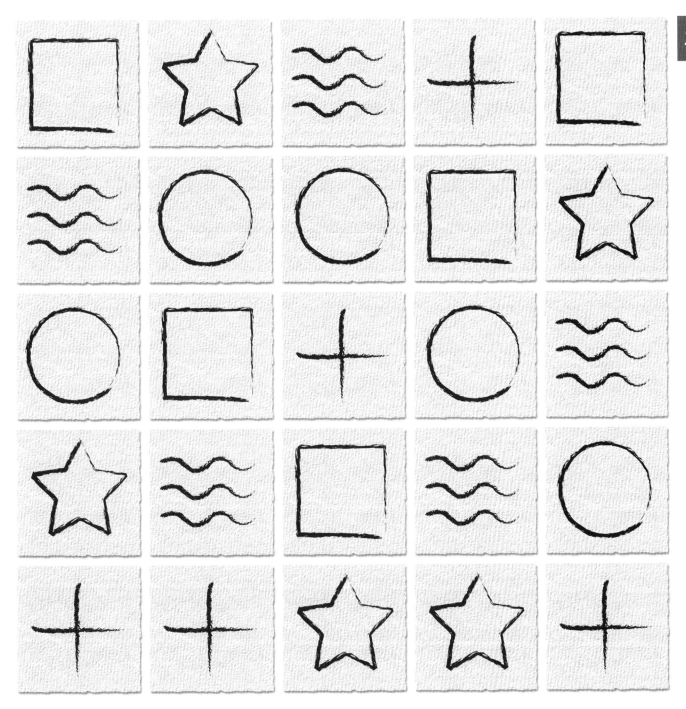

The next stage in improving your telepathy skills is to use completely random images that the "receiver" has not seen previously. This is more difficult than working with Zener cards (see preceding pages), as their simple, graphic images are known to both the sender and the receiver.

It will certainly be helpful if you are mentally and emotionally close to the person with whom you are collaborating. And if it's someone with whom you've already experienced "flashes" of telepathic contact, so much the better. This often happens with people who are related – for instance, the mental bond between twins can be extraordinary.

The exercise and guidelines shown here can help you to achieve an even more advanced psychic state of telepathic sending and receiving. Be open to every sign and impression that you receive, and use your imagination to sense your way through to the image.

RECEIVING UNSEEN IMAGES

Ask a trusted friend to beam you a picture that you've never seen before.

1 *Your friend should choose a random image to send – it could be a postcard or a picture from a book, for example. At first, it is best to use simple, graphic images such as an animal, a tree or a building.*

2 *At a mutually agreed time, your friend concentrates on the picture and actively "beams" it to you.*

3 *Prepare yourself to receive the incoming picture by getting completely relaxed – use the breathing exercise on page 181.*

4 *Let any sensations and impressions come into your mind. As they arrive, simply register them without questioning, and make a mental note of any image you see.*

5 *When you're ready, return to your normal state of consciousness. While the pictures are fresh in your mind either draw the images you saw, or write detailed notes so that you can check the results with your friend.*

Telepathy boosters

Avoid second-guessing what the image might be.

Allow your mind to be as free-ranging as possible.

Don't try to analyze how the choice may have been made by the sender.

As soon as images start coming through, don't dismiss them as ideas from your own mind.

Keep a particular lookout for images and thoughts that seem to come from nowhere – those that just suddenly appear.

When you make notes, describe what you saw in as much detail as you can, but do not invent or exaggerate anything.

Don't be despondent if you didn't receive any images, or if they were inaccurate. Keep trying, you'll eventually get a hit – perhaps much sooner than you imagine.

Alternate between being the sender and the receiver.

GUIDING YOUR PERCEPTION

An image may be of a person, thing, place or situation. As a picture forms in your mind, register its main characteristics and zero in on these.

Are you sensing an outdoor scene?

If so, what is it like? Are you looking up into the sky? Seeing a mountain, a beach, a stretch of ocean – or is it part of a garden? What is the key element in the view? Is it a bird, an aircraft, a balloon, a sculpture? Can you see a large tree? A sail boat? Or a garden seat?

Does the image you're getting suggest a person?

If so, are you sensing a man or a woman? An adult or a child? Is the person doing something? Is he or she sitting or standing? Holding something? Playing a game? Is the person dressed in any special clothes? Or using any tools or equipment?

Do you feel you are looking at a particular item or thing?

Are you in an office or part of a hospital? Or a room in a home? Can you pick out the central focus of the scene? Is it an item or furniture such as a table, chair, fireplace or couch, or some other object such as a bowl of fruit, a vase of flowers, a framed photograph or a birthday cake?

Can you see a place you've never been?

During the dark days of the Cold War, rumours circulated about a new spying technique. Psychic expertise was being used to develop the ability to "see" things from a distance. American surveillance experts trained personnel in the art of remote viewing. This is the ability to tune into a place anywhere on the planet and see what is there – it should be possible to look into any room across the world and take in what is happening inside. Remote viewing can also be used to see a person or object that is some distance away. Remote viewing works similarly to mental telepathy (see page 210) except that information is not transmitted by another but rather, people pick up information without it being "sent".

A Rare Gift

Remote viewing's most exciting aspect is that it literally opens up your world, as you can travel far and wide without leaving home. The psychic Ingo Swann was once given a latitude and longitude position over the telephone by someone he had never met. Immediately he identified a rocky island – there were some buildings there, including an orange structure. He described the coastline and other details. These geographical coordinates marked the island of Kerguelen, where the French had a research base studying the upper atmosphere. Swann had no prior knowledge of this, yet his description was eerily accurate.

As for its practical applications, it would be a great help to those in the creative professions. Novelists and writers could use it to give realistic descriptions of well-known places in their work. Artists, too, could use it to make paintings, backdrops and stage sets of places they themselves are too busy to travel to. On a more every day basis, you're more likely to use it to keep benign track of your loved ones. It's a great way to "accompany" relatives and friends who are away from home. Parents of teenagers, especially, might welcome being kept "informed" of the whereabouts of their youngsters. But always remember to respect an individual's privacy – a loving check is acceptable, obsessive snooping is not.

Testing Proficiency

Professionally, people known to have the gift of remote viewing are often asked to help police find missing persons or remains and to assist with criminal investigations. They can be helpful, for example, in locating the wreckage of aircrafts that crash in mountainous or thickly forested places.

Scientists test for remote viewing abilities by having an outsider pick one photograph from many hundreds. This photograph is subsequently hidden; no person involved in the experiment sees it. The person being assessed is then asked to describe the photograph's contents. An independent panel then assesses the correctness of the description. You can try out your abilities using the exercise opposite.

EXPERIENCING REMOTE VIEWING

For your first efforts, choose a place to "visit" that you've never seen before, but is known to a trusted friend. It could be his or her previous home or workplace, or somewhere that he or she has visited, for example.

1 *Get completely relaxed and close your eyes so you achieve a meditative state. Focus on your breathing, then imaginatively travel to your destination, and slowly enter the site.*

2 *Look around carefully; what do you see? Describe to your friend the colours, textures, furniture, walls, doors, ceilings, pets, people – and take note of anything unusual – any odd detail that catches your attention.*

3 *Once you're satisfied that you've seen enough, take yourself back to your familiar body.*

4 *Check with your friend that you got the details right. Or, if he or she isn't there with you, make sure you record some notes to share with him or her later.*

What can an object tell you?

If you remember ever saying something like "this ring always makes me feel strange when I wear it" or "I don't like the feel of this garment", you may have experienced a form of psychometry. This is the art of sensing energies from inanimate objects. Any object – something small, such as a piece of jewellery or larger, such an item of furniture – can be "read". All objects have their own, unique energy fields and these fields pick up vibrations from the people and places with which they are associated. Even if an object has been in someone's possession for a very short time, it will have absorbed into its energy field that person's particular vibration.

One obvious use for such a gift would be to determine the rightful owner of a found object. It would also be beneficial for healers of all types as clients often withhold information that is germane to their situations or conditions. Reading someone's possession is one way of gaining knowledge without being intrusive.

But as with many psychic abilities, what one gets from such a gift may not be immediately apparent to all – except as a source of wonder. Most psychics believe that information communicated through a sixth sense provides yet another layer through which the world and everything in it can be comprehended. Knowledge is power after all.

READING AN OBJECT'S ENERGIES

Ask the person for whom you are doing a reading to let you hold something belonging to him or her. A ring or watch that has been worn for a long time is a good choice.

1 *Hold the item lightly in your hands and direct your thoughts (and therefore your energy) onto the object. It may help you to concentrate if you close your eyes.*

2 *Visualize yourself sending an arrow of thought to link with the object. Then immediately relax and allow impressions to float into your mind. In doing this, the energy you are using is both active and receptive. You need both kinds when doing psychic work.*

3 *Note exactly what you are receiving, whether it is an image, sensation, thought, or any kind of impression. Discount nothing; even the faintest feeling may be an indication. On the other hand, psychometry can be very physical and you may experience quite distinct sensations such as an object turning hot or cold.*

4 *Try not to be deterred by the notion that these thoughts and impressions are "just in the mind". Simply accept that all information has to travel through your mind. You may receive familiar images, but this does not mean they are unimportant.*

5 *Tell the person exactly what you see; don't omit or embellish anything. Avoid projecting your judgments and experiences onto what you are seeing.*

Insider info PSYCHOMETRY

The most immediate perceptions *are images of what the owner of the object you are reading has been thinking, feeling and doing over the last 24–48 hours.*

Strongly-held thoughts *and feelings or emotionally charged actions will persist in an object's vibrations for years. Those that are fleeting, however, produce similar short-lived energies.*

How much you can tell about past owners *depends on the object's history. If you tune into an object inherited by a daughter whose mother died 20 years previously, you may not receive much information about her mother. However, if the daughter is still very affected by her mother's death, you may receive more of a picture of the original owner.*

Can you sense things that others can't?

Some people have an exceptional gift for sensing things that are out of the range of ordinary perception. This is known as clairsentience, a form of intuition that deals with infinitely fragile, subtle energies, which are accessed in seemingly inexplicable ways. One way of developing a heightened sensitivity is by connecting with the benign energy of living plants (see below). This can imbue you with a vibrant sense of well-being. Positive energy will then emanate back from you to the plant, creating a dynamic, beneficial cycle. By establishing an active psychic relationship with nature, your senses will become alive to everything around you and you will acquire information beyond others' knowing.

GETTING IN TOUCH WITH NATURE

All flowers, plants and trees generate beneficial energy, which can be comprehended as their "guardian spirits". To tune into this positive force, visit a favourite outdoor spot and let yourself be drawn to a particular tree, plant or flower.

1 *Sit under or close by your chosen plant so you move inside its aura.*

2 *Once you're in a serene, meditative state, spend some time connecting to your breath (see page 181); then, when you are centered, focus your breath into your heart centre.*

3 *Literally open your heart and wait. Nature energies are on a different frequency to yours, so, if you have never tried this before, you may need plenty of time to tune yourself in.*

4 *Receive the energy from the plant, and quietly ask its guardian spirit to communicate with you.*

5 *Your sense of smell is a good route into the plant's energy, so be aware of the scents surrounding you. If you make a good link, you may sense the breath of the spirit. It feels as if you are being stroked by butterfly wings.*

6 *Be open to any impressions you receive, and cherish this privileged contact with nature.*

UNDERSTANDING THE LANGUAGE OF FLOWERS

Although connecting with the "spirit" of a flower may provide you with insights that surpass any ordinary knowing, you can also learn a great deal about a person from looking at the colour, shape and aspect of his or her favourite flower.

Primary or pastel? *The shade of the bloom can tell you a lot about the person. Bright yellow flowers, for example, suit someone with a keen intellect, while red flowers are associated with fiery natures.*

Flower away from or close to its leaves? *If the flower stands apart from other parts of the plant, this indicates independence and/or ambition. Proximity signals dependence.*

Single or multiple blooms? *If the former, the person may be a bit of a loner. Lots of blooms and leaves on the stem points to someone sociable who loves having people around.*

Straight, twisted, long or short stems? *Stems show a person's path in life. Are they straight or twisty, long or short? The lower section describes the past or youth, the middle the present or adulthood, the top the future or old age.*

Strong and healthy flower? *If so, this should be mirrored in the character of the person who chose it.*

What the Flowers Say

For hundreds of years flowers have been used to carry hidden messages – particularly between lovers. Traditionally, each bloom is characterized by a special meaning. Because they can pick up your own personal energy, you can use flowers to convey your thoughts or feelings. Again, by linking with a flower (see page 216), you can infuse it with your intent so, when the recipient receives your gift of a flower, it may communicate a larger vocabulary of coded meanings. Made up into a posy or bouquet, the message in each flower effectively adds up to a living document. So, next time you give someone a bunch of flowers or even a single bloom, think about the meaning you want to communicate, and see if the recipient picks up the special message that your gift conveys. To help you choose the most appropriate flowers, some well-documented meanings are set out opposite.

Anemone
Estrangement. "Your charms no longer appeal to me."

Apple Blossom
Beauty and goodness. "You are the epitome of loveliness."

Arbutus
Love. "You alone I love."

Aster
Afterthoughts. "I regret my impetuosity."

Begonia
Warning. "We are being watched."

Bell-flower
Morning. "Meet me tomorrow before noon."

Bindweed
Persistence. "You"ll never be rid of me."

Blackthorn Obstacles. "Some one is coming between us."

Bluebell
Constancy. "I am faithful."

Broom
Devotion. "I am your faithful admirer."

Buttercup
Radiance. "Golden beauty is yours."

Camellia
Loveliness. "How radiantly lovely you are."

Camomile
Fortitude. "I admire your courage in adversity."

Carnation
An indication of feelings –
pink: Encouragement needed.
red: Passionate love.
white: Pure affection.

Cherry blossom
Increase. "To the ripening of our friendship."

Chrysanthemum
The state of a relationship –
bronze: Friendship.
red: Reciprocated love.
yellow: Discouragement.

Cornflower
Delicacy. "Your feet barely touch the ground."

Crocus
Joy of youth. "I delight in your freshness."

Cyclamen
Indifference. "Your protestations leave me unmoved."

Daffodil
Refusal. "I do not return your affections."

Daisy
Temperance. "I will give you an answer in a few days – I might learn to love you."

Dandelion
Absurdity. "Your pretensions are ridiculous."

Evening Primrose
Mute devotion. "Humbly I adore you."

Forget-me-not
Remembrance. "Think of me during my absence."

Foxglove
Shallowness. "You are not really in love."

Fritillary
Doubt. "Can I trust you?"

Fuchsia
Warning. "Beware! your lover is false."

Gardenia
Sweetness. "You are agreeable to the senses."

Geranium
What's happening? –
pink: Doubt. "Explain your actions."
scarlet: Duplicity. "I do not trust you."
white: Indecision. "I have not made up my mind."

Gladiolus
Pain. "Your words have wounded me."

Hawthorn
Hope. "I shall strive to win your love."

Honesty
Frankness. "I'm not certain about my feelings."

Honeysuckle
Plighted troth. "You have my heart."

Hyacinth
Expression of feelings –
blue: devotion.
white: admiration.

Hydrangea
Changeable. "Why are you so fickle?"

Iris
Ardor. "I am passionate about you."

Ivy
Bonds. "I feel connected to you."

Jasmine
Elegance. "You have the most marvellous taste in everything."

Lavender
Negation. "I like you very much but it is not love."

Lilac
Newness –
purple: First love.
white: Innocence.

Lily of the valley
Maidenly modesty. "Friendship is sweet."

Lobelia
Negativity –
blue: Dislike.
white: Rebuff.

Magnolia
Fortitude. "Be not discouraged, better days are coming."

Marigold
Unattractiveness–
African: Boorishness.
French: Jealousy.

Mimosa
Sensitiveness. "You are too brusque."

Narcissus
Self-love. "You love no one better than yourself."

Orange Blossom
Purity. "You are my first lover."

Orchid
Luxury. "You deserve all the riches I can lay at your feet."

Pansy
You are in my mind –
purple: Souvenirs.
white: Thoughts of love.
yellow: Remembrance.

Peony
Contrition. "I beg forgiveness."

Petunia
Proximity. "I like to be near you."

Poppy
Holding back –
red: Moderation.
white: Temporization. "I have not made up my mind."

Primrose
Dawning love. "I might learn to love you."

Rose
Expression of love –
red: Passionate love.
white: Refusal. "I don't love you."
yellow: Misplaced affection.

Rosemary
Remembrance. "Please keep me in your heart."

Snapdragon
Refusal. "Please don't trouble me anymore."

Snowdrop
Renewed attentions. "I find that I can't forget you."

Sunflower
Ostentation. "You're an absolute knock-out!"

Tigerlily
Passion. "My love knows no bounds."

Tulip
Avowal. "By this token I declare my passion."

Violet
Modesty. "Your lack of pretentiousness is pleasing."

Wallflower
Constancy. "I am yours till the end of time."

Do you know what's going to happen?

Some people have a startling, uncanny ability to predict exactly what is about to occur; the knowledge of future events literally seems to come to them out of the blue.

Presentiment, also often known as precognition, is this strong sense that something is going to happen. This sensation is often non-specific – you may have an excited tingle of anticipation, or an uneasy feeling of apprehension. You have these feelings because your intuition is on the alert before your conscious awareness has come into play. But it's not difficult to develop and encourage the gift of precognition in yourself. The quiz below should reveal if you have known things in advance – which, if you had, may come as quite a surprise. Check those questions that have been true for you.

Enhancing Precognition

Knowing things in advance gives you that extra "edge" in all kinds of situations – whether it's dealing

A sense of things to come

If you respond "yes" to a question, check the box next to it. Add up the checks and note your score.

- ❏ Have you been in a situation where you suddenly sensed danger? Did the hairs on the back of your neck stand up?
- ❏ Has a letter made you feel happy even before you knew what it contained?
- ❏ Have you overheard people talking and had a sense of foreboding without knowing the background to their discussion?
- ❏ Have you ever had a compelling feeling that something was wrong while a friend was telling you about someone he or she had just met?
- ❏ On your way to an arranged meeting, have you ever had an uneasy sense that you should not be going there?

- ❏ After taking a test, have you been certain that you had passed/failed?
- ❏ While listening to someone talking about a future date, have you had an overwhelming sense that you would be in a specific place at that time?
- ❏ Have you "known" that something would occur that actually happened to you later?
- ❏ When you were a child did your parents or friends suggest a possible career? And did you "know" that you would do something completely different?
- ❏ Have you ever bought a raffle ticket and been sure that you were going to win before you did?

with people, or assessing events. So, once you've learned to trust your hunches and inner signals, you'll gain a positive boost to your confidence.

How do you enhance this amazing ability? Firstly, whenever you have a feeling that something will happen, always regard it as a "pay attention" alert. And in particular, if you ever sense danger or threat, trust your intuition – never ignore it.

It helps a lot if you can put these feelings into words and say them out loud. Then visualize the outcome in graphic detail, as if it has already happened. Once you've got the full picture, write it in your psychic diary – and keep regular notes of every "hunch" you have about people, or events. Check later whether these were accurate.

Another good intuition-sharpening technique is to do ESP exercises in telepathy (see page 208). Eventually, you'll be able to listen to your inner voice without devaluing your ability to reason.

How many questions did you check?

❏ **1–3**

If you answered "yes" to even a few questions, you're already equipped with the basic ability to experience precognition.

❏ **4–6**

Learn to trust your hunches and feelings – you've more than average sensitivity to useful "out of the blue" information.

❏ **6–10**

Perhaps you should consider taking psychic development classes, as you are in touch with extra-sensory skills that could be successfully developed.

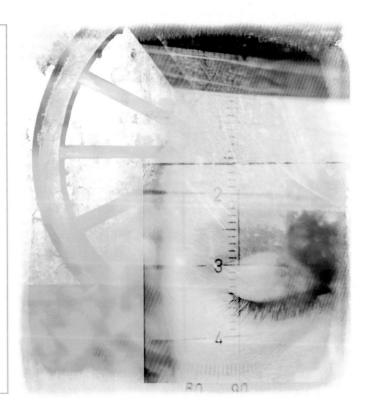

Exploring the collective unconscious

The psychologist Carl Jung believed that getting in touch with powerful universal images helps your inner self to function harmoniously with your conscious mind, while keeping you in tune with the cosmic world. This is a profoundly healthy state for anyone to be in, not only if you want to become an accomplished psychic but also if you want to be happier and more insightful at all times.

Jung found that various mythical and archetypal figures appeared in his patients' dreams and waking fantasies. He also knew that these feature in myths and legends around the globe. These figures can be equated with the major arcana cards of the tarot (see page 242). He suggested that archetypes emerge from a vast "data base" of human knowledge and called this the "collective unconscious". This is a very powerful resource as it serves as a connection among people of the world.

Jung's experience of working with such images persuaded him that using archetypes can trigger intuitive insights that surpass reasoned analysis; this then allows us to better understand the actions and motives of others. His method of "active imagination" described below stimulates this creative process.

WALKING WITH ARCHETYPES

The imaginary journey featured here is a good example of Jung's technique. Done on your own, it is a highly effective way of boosting your intuitive powers by walking you through archetypal situations and encounters. However, if you ask others to do it as well, you'll be able to compare your "experiences" with theirs. Check your experiences with the interpretation of images on page 223. It is also a good idea to record your experiences on your journey in your psychic journal.

1 Once in a highly relaxed, meditative state (see page 181), imagine that you have woken up on a bright sunny morning – and that you have the whole day to yourself. Suddenly, you find yourself on a road.

2 Start walking along the road until you come to a stretch of meadow. Relax and walk about here, feel the grass under your feet, the air on your face, the smells, sights and sounds around you.

3 When you are ready, return to the road and start walking along it again. You gradually become aware that the road is becoming steeper, and that you are climbing up a mountain. Observe what the journey feels like, and when you arrive at the peak, take some time to look down from the top of the mountain to the landscape below.

Images in your journey

Pictures in visualizations and dreams are attempts by your unconscious to speak simply. They are not intended to mislead – often the obvious meaning is the most accurate, and a series of archetypal settings act as a gateway to your mind.

Meadow *This represents nature in her beneficent aspects, the positive creative basis of life and the life of the inner child.*

Mountain *Obstacles are challenges to prove yourself. The way you climb shows you how to develop your psychic freedom.*

Forest *The crowding trees show your dark, fearful side. Walking in the forest lets you reconcile these difficult aspects of yourself.*

Chapel *This symbolizes the intimate aspects of your soul; it also shows you some possibilities for psychic transformation.*

4 *When you leave, and you walk along the road again, you realize that the trees seem to be closing in and are becoming increasingly dense. Now you discover that you are right in the middle of a forest. What does this look like and how do you react to it?*

5 *After a while the light gets stronger and brighter and the road leads you out of the forest. Further along you see a building; as you get nearer, you realize it is some kind of chapel. You decide to go inside. While you're there, pay attention to your experiences and impressions. Leave the chapel when you are ready.*

6 *Outside, the sun is shining, and you start the journey home, back to your own world. What do you see on the way, and how do you feel about yourself and your surroundings? And how do you feel when you're finally back in your own home?*

What do your dreams tell you?

Your dreams can bring you an amazing fund of insights about your inner thoughts and feelings. Researchers in sleep behaviour now believe that we need to dream in order to maintain equilibrium in mind and body. Some dreams either replay the events of the previous day or enact your expectations of the next. This is your mind's way of sorting and assimilating data – rather like filing documents on your computer. Researchers know that the most vivid dreams occur three or four times a night during REM sleep (a phase marked by rapid eye movement). If you are deprived of REM sleep, your body makes up the deficit, as it depends on regular amounts for overall health. So, in addition to what dreams "mean", they also help to reduce stress, tidy mental clutter, and keep you healthy and calm.

DREAM TEMPLES

People from ancient cultures used sleep and dream interpretation for healing. They built temples with sacred sleeping chambers attended by priests and priestesses trained in dream interpretation. Each patient was given a purifying bath, massaged with sacred oils, and taken to the dream chamber. The following morning, the person described his or her dreams to the priest or priestess who analyzed and explained them in great detail. This process was repeated until the patient felt restored to health.

Journal notes: Discovering your inner vision

- A dream diary will give you great insight into your unconscious life. Keep a special notebook and pen by your bedside and use it to record your significant dreams.

- You won't remember every dream you have, but note all those that are in your waking consciousness. These dreams will act as a "database" of your inner world.

- As soon as you wake up, outline your dream in detail in your diary. Concentrate on the main images; and if there were people you know in the dream, think about what they mean to you.

- As your dream diary builds up, you will begin to notice a link between your dreams – the same ones may recur, or there may be persistent images, colours and symbols.

- Make regular summaries: group dreams under major themes, noting their subjects, storylines, places, colours and images.

- Your dreams will make sense over time. A friend who was undergoing therapy for fear of flying had terrifying dreams about air travel. As therapy progressed, the dreams became more benign; flying became fun rather than a source of fear.

Aspects of interpretation

Have you ever had a dream which left you completely puzzled? What did it mean? If you ask the experts, you'll find that there are several classic lines of thought – so how do you decide which interpretation is right for you? For instance, you dream that you are drowning in the sea...

*A **behaviourist** could view the dream as an aspect of your personality. Drowning may mean that you don't feel in control – you might be "drowning" under work demands, for example.*

*A **pragmatist** would ask what you did the night before. Did you see a TV programme on disasters at sea? It is likely that a vivid image is lodged in your memory.*

*A **Freudian** would link the dream to sexual wish fulfilment. Drowning is symbolic of being overwhelmed by sexual passion.*

*A **Jungian** regards the sea as an image of the collective unconscious. A drowning dream would indicate that you are in touch with the world at a spiritual level.*

Who is right? Don't dismiss a viewpoint without giving it some thought. These approaches all have an internal logic, so keep an open mind. As a final arbiter, use your intuition to discover what your dream is saying. When you reach the "right" meaning you will feel an "Aha!" sense of recognition.

You probably have experienced various kinds of predictive symbols in your dreams. Possibly, in your family, there are images that have particular recognized meanings. For example, if a member of the household dreams of a picture falling off the wall, it may be commonly assumed by the relatives that someone will be leaving home. But the next door neighbours may interpret this as the impending death of a family member.

Some people dream of an event just before it occurs – many individuals claimed they had "seen" President Kennedy's assassination in a dream a day or two before it happened. It is as if the shock waves of a traumatic event reverberate through time, giving a glimpse of the future. But don't assume that every bad dream is going to come true.

Use common sense when interpreting dreams: some of the meanings of the dream symbols given here may be unfamiliar to you, but they reflect the experiences of psychic interpreters. Use them simply as guidelines. For instance, if you dream of a road, look at what is going on. If the road is open, free and easy to travel, your life journey will be unimpeded. But if it is full of obstacles, you will have difficulties. Also pay attention to the overall atmosphere: clean, clear and bright elements suggest positive outcomes while dirty, broken or decaying features point to negative situations.

Accident *A confusing situation requiring thought and discretion.*

Aircraft *Ambition and courage.*

Anchor *Resolution of present worries.*

Angels *A fortunate omen.*

Animals –
domestic: *Happiness.*
wild: *Treachery and cruelty.*

Ants *Increased industry, prosperity and expansion of business.*

Baby *New beginnings.*

Bath –
warm water: *Failure through laziness.*
cold water: *Success and prosperity.*
empty: *Warning against decisions made in anger.*

Blood *Hard but rewarding work.*

Boat *Change of residence or a journey.*

Book *Discoveries.*

Bridge *An indication of change.*

Cage –
full of birds: *Good omen.*
empty: *Loss of opportunity through carelessness.*

Cave *Rumours.*

Church –
outside: *A good omen.*
inside: *Impending trouble.*

Clock *Business worries.*

Cross *Hardwon joy and triumph.*

Crown *Accolades and honours.*

Cut finger *Recent damage.*

Dagger *Strife, enmity.*

Dancing *Joyful anticipation.*

Death *News of a birth.*

Devil *Approaching danger and temptation.*

Dove *Peace and prosperity.*

Dragon *Change of residence.*

Eagle *Realized ambitions.*

Eating *Strife between friends.*

Eggs *Innovative ideas.*

Elephant *New and influential friends.*

Eyes *Anticipated true love.*

Face A reflection of yourself.

Fire Impending trouble.

Fish Fertility.

Flowers A surprise (see pages 218–19 for specific flowers).

Forest Shadows and fears.

Fruits Abundance.

Garden A happy marriage.

Giant Very lucky omen.

Grass Success and fertility.

Grave Health for the sick.

Hair Good health.

Head Misfortune.

Hill Realization of ambitions.

Horse True friendship.

House Domestic comfort.

Ice Failure in business or the end of a romance.

Journey There will be a journey in real life.

Jumping Triumph over obstacles.

Key –
single key: Love.
many keys: Prosperity without affection.

King Assistance from a rich and powerful friend.

Knife Illness, loss of money, or quarrels with relations.

Ladder Success.

Lake Comfort and freedom.

Letter A letter or message needs sending.

Lightning Inspiration or spiritual awareness.

Lion Power.

Medal Timidity and weakness on your part.

Money Fortunate omen, especially for those engaged in lawsuits.

Moon Happiness in love.

Mouse Interference by others in your affairs. Are you a man or a ...?

Mouth Expected wealth.

Nest Domestic happiness.

Nut Warning of extravagance.

Oak Very good omen. Calm and untroubled life.

Ocean –
rough: Disturbance.
calm: Reconciliation between two friends.

Owl Wisdom.

Parents Joy.

Pictures An image of you.

Prison Freedom.

Pyramid A very lucky omen.

Queen Profit and prosperity as a result of hard work.

Rain Domestic trouble.

Rainbow Health and wealth.

Rat Secret and powerful enemies.

Ring An important new friendship.

Road Your life's journey.

Shield Honour and fame.

Skeleton Comfort from unexpected quarters.

Snow Good news and gain.

Spider A lucky escape from an accident.

Stones Visit from a relative.

Sun Advancement and success.

Swan Happiness and psychic ability.

Sword Unhealthy situation that could affect you adversely.

Table Domestic happiness.

Teeth Sign of major changes, particularly if extracted or falling out.

Tiger Warning of someone with harmful intent.

Tower Great gains or great losses.

Uniform A journey full of adventure.

Valley A meeting with an old friend.

Veil Revelation of a secret.

Wall Obstacles and danger.

War Peace and success.

Wasp Envious enemies.

Watch Dependency.

Window Reconciliation after a quarrel.

Zoo Profitable change of employment.

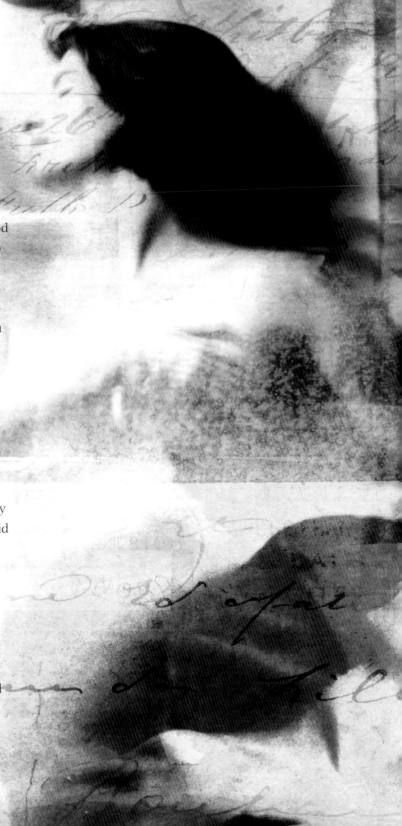

Can you control your dreams?

When you don't know what to do about a problem, you may decide to "sleep on it". This phrase is a good example of how ancient wisdom has percolated into common speech. It has long been known that the answer to a baffling question may occur during sleep. A variant of this is known as lucid dreaming: when this happens you are perfectly aware that you are dreaming, and can deliberately alter details that occur in your dream. For instance, if you are dreaming about an aggressive Rotweiler, you could turn it into a pacific Chihuahua.

Primitive peoples regarded lucid dreams as an important route into the spirit world. Individuals who were able to access this dream state were often chosen to be the shamans of a tribe.

Scientists at Stanford University's sleep laboratory have offered various clues about how and when lucid dreaming occurs. The dreamer often becomes lucid while in the middle of a dream. Perhaps because something extraordinary happens, the person suddenly recognizes that he or she is in a dream. Another common trigger is returning to REM sleep after being woken up in the middle of an episode taking place in a vivid dream. Test subjects gave prearranged signals (such as fist clenching) to signal that they were in a lucid dream.

DREAM WORKS

Sleep can be a source of dazzling inspiration – many breakthroughs happen during dreams.

- *Tartini, a violinist in eighteenth-century Italy, was reputed to have made a pact with Satan; he dreamed that he was visited by the devil and played a piece "more ravishing than anything he had ever heard". The following morning he wrote out the complex sonata of his dream and called it* The Devil's Trill.

- *Robert Louis Stevenson used a lucid dreaming technique to literally "dream up" his exciting adventure stories.*

- *The poet Coleridge claimed that his poem* Kubla Khan *was a "vision in a dream".*

DIRECTING YOUR DREAMS

People vary in how vividly they dream and how successfully they can redirect a dream's story line. With practice you can learn the technique of lucid dreaming.

1 *In the morning, start planning your dream in dramatic, colourful detail.*

2 *Return to your dream story at frequent intervals during the day and go over its details repeatedly, until the entire sequence is fixed in your consciousness.*

3 *Just before you go to sleep, relax, then replay your dream in your mind. Tell yourself with complete conviction that you intend to be conscious while you are dreaming.*

4 *If this disturbs your sleep try the following. As soon as you wake up in the morning and are in a half doze, "will" yourself to have a lucid dream, then go back to sleep.*

Insider info LUCID DREAMING

Use it to enhance mood and supply the thrill of adventure. *One of the most popular, playful activities in a lucid dream is that of flying. The sense of release, freedom, and pleasure this gives is unforgettable. Lucid dreaming can also help you to dispel nightmares. You redirect the "plot" of your nightmare so that the horror is confronted and transformed into something harmless. This is a great way of conquering fear and boosting confidence.*

If you have trouble making decisions, *lucid dreaming can help you visualize what a job, holiday or new home could have in store. It will enable you to experience working somewhere or being in a new location. You will react to these various situations in your dreams – are you happy, frightened, worried?*

The effects of positive visualization on body and mind *are well established. Lucid dreaming can be used to overcome stress, phobias and grief, and also to facilitate physical healing. Some enthusiasts have spotted the potential for helping stroke victims recover neuromuscular function through lucid dream imagery in which they "see" themselves moving, walking and talking normally.*

Travel to other worlds in your dreams

Psychics can be highly aware of the astral body, the invisible subtle structure that acts as a bridge between the physical world and the world of spirit. When you are awake the astral body is superimposed onto your physical form; however, as you fall asleep, the astral body loosens and separates an inch or two away from your physical body.

During sleep, the astral body of a living person is sometimes able to cross into the spirit world – this is called an astral dream and feels so "real" it becomes super-real. Here, you may meet a loved one who has died; you have a powerful feeling that he or she is physically present. You can literally hear, see, smell and even taste during the dream. On waking you will probably feel profoundly comforted and will remember this experience very clearly.

Insider info ASTRAL TRAVEL

You might encounter other beings – *people report meetings with wise teachers. These beings may reveal the deeper aspects of your life, or long-forgotten wisdom.*

Things are experienced differently *on the astral plane; energy follows thought with unusual speed – you only have to think of a place and you're there. And any image that enters your mind will materialize instantly.*

It can change your life. *The sensation of being outside your body gives you a sweeping, panoramic perspective – this can be liberating and calming, providing you with a wider perspective. Visiting the astral worlds during sleep gives you a good idea of what the spirit world is about and reassures you of the continuity of life.*

ATTEMPTING ASTRAL TRAVEL

1 *When in a completely relaxed state (see page 181), focus carefully on where you want to go and what you want to achieve, and why. Make sure you're in a safe place and lock the door. You'll also want to be psychically protected from any negative experiences, and you can do this by calling upon a spirit guide or guardian to assist you in your astral journey. Project a positive message asking for the highest, greatest good. Make your request clear and concise.*

2 *Close your eyes. Concentrate on a repetitive sound – a mantra, rhythmic drumming or chanting. You should be relaxed but mentally alert. Visualize a trap door some distance away and hurl yourself against it. The door represents the pineal door of the third eye.*

3 *If you succeed in "escaping", you will be surrounded with golden light and, as long as you don't fall into a deep sleep, you can step out of your physical body as easily as if you were*

climbing out of bed. You will be aware that your mind is awake but your body still sleeps.

4 *Once you are on the astral plane just let yourself go to wherever the spirit guides you. It will take some time to acclimatize yourself, so just accept what happens.*

5 *You will automatically return to your normal state when ready. Immediately note down your travel experiences in your dream diary.*

Is your pet psychic?

Domestic pets often have an uncanny psychic ability to anticipate their owners' thoughts, moods and actions. The most common example is the family dog that goes to the front door just before its owner arrives and sits expectantly, tail wagging. This even happens when the owner has deliberately varied his or her arrival time in order to "test" a pet's ESP. Cats have similar predictive talents, and many riders say their horses know when they are approaching the stable. Cage birds, too, often hop up and down on their perches in excitement just before their owner comes home. Your own pet may have similar abilities – have a look at the quiz on page 233 to find out more.

In addition to possible psychic powers, it's now well recognized that pets also have positive health benefits. Domestic animals can make good therapists. People who find they can't talk to other humans about their problems, often find it easier to confide in a pet. There's great comfort in their loving, non-judgmental attention.

Animal owners generally enjoy better health than non-owners. Heart patients are known to live longer when they have a pet, and tests have shown that high blood pressure drops to a healthy level when a pet is around. Caring for animals calms stress, and just being with them reduces anxiety. That is why dentists often have fish tanks in their waiting rooms.

Incredible journeys

Nowadays families move home frequently; some people think it is best to find a new home for a pet rather than upsetting it by taking it far away from its familiar territory. Most pets settle down, but others have different ideas, and travel hundreds of miles in search of their owner.

This happened to a New York veterinarian who got a new job 2,000 miles across the USA in California. He decided to give his cat to his friends and set off to establish his West Coast

practice. Six months after he'd arrived, his cat walked in through the door. There was no mistaking the identity of this particular creature; he quickly checked it for a slight deformation on its tail – it was there, as he expected. He had treated the injury (the result of a bite) when the cat was a tiny kitten.

Although no one really knows how animals can track owners with such accuracy, some parapsychologists regard this ability as a form of "remote viewing" (see page 212).

Rate your pet's ESP

❑ 1   Does your pet seem to understand your moods and feelings?

❑ 2   When you have made an appointment to take it to the vet, does it disappear?

❑ 3   Has it spent hours looking at a wall, seemingly watching something that isn't there?

❑ 4   Does it howl or hide during a seance or other psychic happening?

❑ 5   Is it always at the door to meet you, whatever time you return home?

❑ 6   Does it becomes more affectionate when you're in a bad mood?

❑ 7   When someone it knows calls, does your pet nuzzle the phone?

❑ 8   Just as you think about taking the dog for a walk, does it get excited?

If you answered "yes" to numbers

1 6 7
Your pet may have healing skills.

2 5 8
Telepathy is your pet's speciality.

3 4
This shows that your pet is sensitive to spirit presences.

Psychic
tools

3

Would you recognize true love?

Astrologers believe that the stars have a strong impact on your life. This correlates with the psychic's understanding that all matter is linked by a unifying energy. If you're looking for true love, you may have explored astrology to find out the star sign that is most compatible with yours. While there's no way that complex relationships can be generalized into twelve categories of attraction and suitability, don't give up on the zodiac completely. It may prove to be a surprisingly good psychic matchmaker.

Your birth chart provides the key: as well as defining your character, it also spotlights the qualities in others that attract and complement yours. The saying, "men are from Mars and women are from Venus" has true astrological validity; their positions in your birth chart are highly significant to your love life.

YOUR IDEAL PARTNER

Mars and Venus will appear in particular zodiac signs in your birth chart. If you're a woman, check where Mars is located and if you're a man, look for Venus in your chart. Refer to the table (right) for the qualities you would expect to find in a male or female of the particular sign. Each sign is affiliated to one of four elements: Earth, Fire, Air or Water. You're mostly at ease around those with the same energy influences, but opposite elements can be harmonious, too. Air and Fire signs feel comfortable with each other, as do Earth and Water.

Earth signs

TAURUS
Tactile, sensual, loyal, relaxed, easygoing, patient, practical. Likes to be invited and feel wanted.

VIRGO
Focused, skilful, intelligent, clean, discerning, sincere. Wishes to be heard, respected and trusted.

CAPRICORN
Ambitious, wise, understanding, responsible, disciplined. Needs respect and to be allowed to organize.

Fire signs

ARIES
Active, assertive, independent, leading, expressive, energetic. Needs self-expression and independence.

LEO
Playful, creative, fun, hearty, passionate. Demands to be loved and appreciated.

SAGITTARIUS
Adventurous, honest, knowledgeable. Requires honesty in others and benefits from adventures.

Air signs

GEMINI
Intellectually curious, communicative, light, spontaneous, playful, witty. Needs to communicate and be regarded as interesting.

LIBRA
Charming, diplomatic, romantic, polite, considerate. Wants romance and caring consideration.

AQUARIUS
Exciting, different, rebellious, friendly, compassionate. Demands the freedom to be him/herself.

Water signs

CANCER
Caring, affectionate, loving, sensitive, protective. Craves affection and needs leeway to be moody.

SCORPIO
Passionate, feeling, deep, loving, loyal, empathetic. Must be deeply emotionally expressive.

PISCES
Trusting, intuitive, sensitive, mediumistic, peaceful, imaginative. Asks for trust in return and to be given space.

Insider info BIRTH CHARTS

Each person's chart is unique *and provides information that no other source can. Although fairly easy to construct, their complex interweaving energies are much harder to interpret. Charts are available by mail order or on the internet; you'll need to know the place, date and time of your birth.*

To assess the Venus/Mars influence, *you'll need to find the position of Venus or Mars in your birth chart (depending on whether you're a man or a woman) then, refer to the keywords under the relevant sign to discover what qualities you should seek in a partner. Think about your important relationships. Did partners you were happiest with exhibit a large number of these qualities? Did failed relationships, or difficult ones, lack the qualities indicated as necessary for a good relationship?*

A person's rising sign or ascendant is important. *It governs the way we express ourselves. Therefore, if you know when your partner was born, check his or her rising sign, or ascendant, as it will be a major influence on him or her.*

Attraction is not always automatic. *Although the sign occupied by Venus or Mars is a good indicator for happy relationships, it does not necessarily mean that people born under that sign will be your best match. It merely says that the qualities of that sign will need to be present.*

The I Ching, a profound psychic tool that has been in use for over 3,000 years, imparts celestial wisdom from the ancient spirits of heaven and earth. The more you use the I Ching for your intuitive development, the more you'll appreciate its profound subtlety. You'll find that it gives you unusual insights, not just about complex areas of self-growth but also practical, day-to-day problems.

The I Ching's messages are relayed through 64 hexagrams, configurations that hold an entire system of thought based on the Chinese concept of yin and yang. It teaches that the aim of life is to achieve and keep a balance. Yin and yang represent core male and female principles: the male or active energy of yang inspires you to have an idea, impose your will and take action; the female receptive energy of yin enables you to go with the flow and adapt to events.

BUILDING YOUR HEXAGRAMS

Use the following method to construct your six-lined figure; then you can interpret its meaning.

1 *Formulate your question clearly in your mind. If you're not happy in your job, for example, you may want to know if you are in the right one or if another would make you happier. Think of it as you sit at a table or other flat surface with a notebook and pencil ready for use.*

2 *Choose three coins of similar size and shape with clearly defined heads and tails. Heads represent the yang or unbroken line (——) and tails signify a yin or broken line (— —).*

3 *Focus on your question and throw the coins onto the table six times in succession. A majority of heads makes a yang line; mostly tails a yin line.*

4 *Write down each line, starting from the bottom up. Repeat the procedure until you have a stack of six lines. This is your hexagram – the I Ching's response to your question.*

5 *Look up your hexagram and its meaning from the list on the following pages and keep a note of the questions and answers in your psychic journal.*

6 *If you asked whether you should change your job, and you threw 63 Fording Now or 5 Caution, the former would be affirmative, the latter negative. Other answers, like 50 The Vessel may be less immediately obvious. Use your intuition to connect the given meaning with your own thoughts and instincts.*

1 Creative action *You are confronted with many obstacles – it is a time to take action. Use persuasion rather than force.*

2 Letting go *Join with others but don't shirk responsibilities. Quietly accept, cherish everything and help it grow.*

3 Gestation *Allow matters to evolve. Chaos precedes a new venture. New ideas are beginning to form.*

4 Growth *Your understanding is dull and clouded through youthful folly. Wait and learn.*

5 Caution *A time for waiting – there could be danger ahead. Go slowly, especially in love. Watch for the right time.*

6 Arguing *This is not a harmonious time, it is full of contrary people and ideas. Compromise if necessary.*

7 Discipline *A time to put things in order. Seek people of experience and authority.*

8 Alliance *Mutual support. Discard old ideas and find new ways to regroup your affairs. Change must come now.*

9 Gradual accumulation *Adapt to whatever comes along. Take the long view on life. Be flexible and adaptable.*

10 Treading *Find and make your own way. Persevere in your efforts to create a profound change.*

11 Pervading *Great abundance and harmony. Stay resolute within and adaptable with others. Peace is at hand.*

12 Obstruction *Blocked communications and obstacles. Stagnation. A dead-end situation and a period of isolation. It is not your fault.*

13 Harmony *A communal life with common causes or shared interests with those who combine their talents and efforts.*

14 Abundance *You have great power to achieve success. Concentrate your inner force to create joy.*

15 Humbling *Abandon pride and arrogance. Keep your words and actions simple. Taking lower positions will bring success.*

16 Awareness *Be ready to respond. Build up your strength and resources to prepare for whatever the future will bring.*

17 Following *Go with the flow. Be guided by the way life is moving. Everything has its season.*

18 Corruption *Decay and hidden poison. Slovenliness, laziness and weakness must be fought against. Prepare carefully for changes.*

19 Arrival of the new *A situation that is evolving and progressing. Possible promotion or advancement.*

20 Vigilance *See other's true motivations and show your own. Contemplate – let everything come into view.*

21 Biting through *Confront your problems. Be tenacious – know you have made the right decision and stick to it.*

22 Grace *Show your true self. External forms are ephemeral and illusory.*

23 Splitting apart *Tear up old ideas and eliminate what is unusable. An unavoidable period of collapse, misfortune and destruction.*

24 Returning *Renewal, rebirth and new hope. Stir things up and work with this energy. A new age is beginning.*

25 Innocence *Disentangle yourself, be spontaneous, free from ulterior motives. Trust your instinct and follow your conscience.*

26 Power of the great *Focus on the highest ideas – this is a time for great effort and achievement. Learn through experience.*

27 Nourishment *Feed both your earthly and spiritual body for complete well-being.*

28 Excess *Hold onto your ideals. A plan will bring profit and insight. Do not be afraid to act alone.*

29 Abyss *Unavoidable danger. Take the plunge and face your fear. Now is the time to concentrate and take risks.*

30 Radiance *Light, warmth and spreading awareness. Combine high values, noble principles and intellect, logic and good sound ideas.*

31 Conjoining *Stimulation and excitement. A good time to marry. Accept and submit to the female – yin brings birth and renewal.*

32 Persevering *Endurance is the way to acquire a powerful character. Act in the long term to attain objectives.*

33 Retiring *Withdraw and conceal yourself. Deal with the situation from a distance – the surrounding circumstances are not favourable.*

34 Strength *Power must be implemented gently and with moderation. Renounce violence.*

35 Prospering *Progress in a changing situation. Take a new view of yourself.*

36 Hidden brightness *Protect yourself and accept a difficult task. Conflicts must be faced even if you cannot solve them.*

37 Family *Nourish and support the family – this will bring illumination. Use clear language to connect with your relatives.*

38 Discord *Make an effort to eliminate conflict. Avoid people and situations that clash and react against each other.*

39 Difficulties *Confront obstacles – they will point out the course to take so that you can progress and be free from troubles.*

40 Loosening *Resolve a difficulty by disentangling problems one by one. This will bring relief or deliverance.*

41 Diminishing *Something will be revealed showing that sacrifice is needed. Tone things down and show restraint and moderation.*

42 Augmenting *A rewarding situation overflowing with abundance and possibilities. Increase without limits.*

43 Breakthrough *Face disorder with speed and resolution, while controlling your passions. Use firmness, adaptability, and kindness.*

44 Coupling *The opening influence of yin. Sexual intercourse and marriage. For true union respect social rules and principles.*

45 Clustering *A large number of people can work together with the same objective and motivation, but they must be organized.*

46 Ascending *Lift yourself to a higher level through your own efforts. Amass small things to achieve the great.*

47 Oppression *You are cut off – this is a moment of truth. Turn inwards and find a way to open communication.*

48 The well *Interact with others. A situation of potentially inexhaustible resources and possibilities is open to all.*

49 Renewal *Another layer or facade is removed as part of a natural process. For improvements, revolution must occur.*

50 The vessel *Discover your inner qualities and the correct way to use them for spiritual and material transformation. Exercise free will.*

51 Shake *Wake up! Start all over again – spring has come. It will bring storms but they will clear the air and enable new beginnings.*

52 Stillness *The calm of the mountain. Seek stability by surrendering your desires, fears, speculations and fantasies.*

53 Gradual advance *Progress must be slow, so learn to proceed step by step, without angst.*

54 Converting the maiden *Realize your hidden potential for passion or desire. Marriage of a younger sister or daughter.*

55 Plenty *A time of affluence, profusion and generosity. Use this advantage sparingly so that it lasts.*

56 Exile *Wandering far away from home. A restless situation is uncertain, but there may also be wonderful potential.*

57 Gently penetrating *Be supple and flexible. Let yourself be shaped by events. Don't impose your will but never lose sight of your purpose.*

58 Joy *Good humour and a positive attitude bring pleasure to life. Be sympathetic to all through communication and self-expression.*

59 Dispersing *Clear the decks. Now is the time to start a new project or found an enterprise – but keep things fluid.*

60 Limitation *Learn to walk the middle path to give your life a measured form. Play by the rules now.*

61 The centre *This is the power of a free heart without prejudice or judgment. Inner truth is always within – just listen.*

62 Small scale *A time of subtle transition resulting in the triumph of the soul. Whatever the moment forces you to do is right for now.*

63 Fording now *Everything is ready for you to proceed. Be vigilant at all times and pay attention to detail to avoid mistakes.*

64 Not yet fording *Important change is imminent – gather your energy for the right moment. Be objective and don't be blinded by enthusiasm.*

Reading the tarot

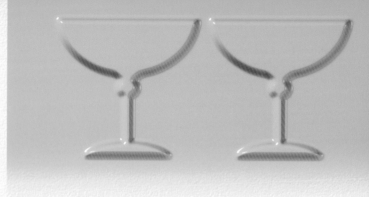

The tarot pack opens up a miniature, mysterious world, full of portentous symbols with significant meanings. The reader lays out the cards in different combinations to explore the past, present and future. A tarot pack has 78 cards. 56 of the cards are the minor arcana; these are similar to ordinary playing cards and consist of four suits with court cards. 22 of the cards are the major arcana; they feature archetypal images that illustrate various stages of spiritual growth.

If you want to get the best from the tarot, take time to examine various decks, and let your intuition tell you which is right for you. There also are many reference books with "interpretations" of the cards – again, you'll discover those that resonate with your own sense of their meanings (not surprising as the tarot symbols are tied into the collective unconscious, see page 222). But follow your own hunches even if they contradict received wisdom; this is an example of your intuition at work.

THE MINOR ARCANA CARDS
Whether you're reading for yourself or someone else, the person asking a question of the tarot is called "the inquirer". Take plenty of time to study the cards and their network of associations. Meditate on each one, and use them in simple spreads at first (see right). Let the interplay between images inspire your intuition as you build your interpretation. But never use the tarot when you are upset or traumatized – your negative vibrations will almost certainly give you an incorrect reading.

Cups

ISSUES	*Emotions and love issues*
TIME	*Spring/days*
ELEMENT	*Water*

KING, QUEEN, KNIGHT AND PAGE OF CUPS
These cards represent a blond, warm-hearted person full of good intentions. It may be the man or woman the inquirer loves.

ASTROLOGICAL SIGNS
Cancer, Scorpio or Pisces.

Swords

ISSUES	*Illness or difficulties*
TIME	*Summer/months*
ELEMENT	*Air*

KING, QUEEN, KNIGHT AND PAGE OF SWORDS
These indicate a person with dark brown colouring who has power over people – possibly a manipulator who is not always honest.

ASTROLOGICAL SIGNS
Gemini, Libra or Aquarius.

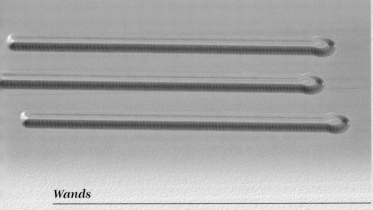

Wands

ISSUES *Family and business concerns*

TIME *Autumn/weeks*

ELEMENT *Fire*

KING, QUEEN, KNIGHT AND PAGE OF WANDS

If you choose one of these cards, it signifies a fair-haired, friendly, sympathetic, family centered person who can help you.

ASTROLOGICAL SIGNS

Aries, Leo or Sagittarius.

Pentacles

ISSUES *Money or material matters*

TIME *Winter/years*

ELEMENT *Earth*

KING, QUEEN, KNIGHT AND PAGE OF PENTACLES

This may point to someone wealthy with dark hair and eyes who can materially help the inquirer.

ASTROLOGICAL SIGNS

Taurus, Virgo or Capricorn.

A SIMPLE TAROT SPREAD

1 *Use only the minor arcana cards and pick out a court card that matches the inquirer. For instance, a blond woman from a water sign would choose the Queen of Cups. This is the significator, the centre of the spread.*

2 *The inquirer shuffles the cards for a few minutes then cuts them with the left hand. Seven cards are set out left to right, with the fourth card on top of the significator.*

3 *The first three cards relate to the past; the fourth, lying on the significator, relates to present circumstances; and the last three indicate the outcome and future possibilities.*

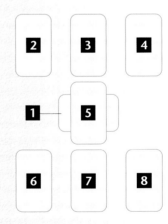

The next step in using the tarot is to include the 22 major arcana cards in your spreads. These are believed to hold a powerful code of occult wisdom dating back over 3,000 years to the sacred rituals of ancient Egyptian priests. The images of the major arcana are "archetypes" (see page 222), and help you to connect with the deeper meaning underlying events and people in your life.

0 The Fool
Listen to all: everything has meaning and everyone is your guide.

1 The Magician
This reminds you that your thoughts have power. Monitor your ideas and think positively.

2 The High Priestess
The nature of life is change: accept this and trust your own intuition. Do not be afraid of hidden secrets.

3 The Empress
The archetypal woman – let her understanding stabilize and guide you. Look at your female aspects. Are they happily balanced?

4 The Emperor
The man of authority, strength, courage and will. Examine your male aspects and balance them with your inner female side.

5 The Hierophant or Pope
Listen to your inner voice for divine inspiration, wisdom and truth.

6 The Lovers
You are connected to the inspirational and spiritual forces of love.

7 The Chariot
Take the reins of your life and start to control its true direction.

8 Justice
The laws of cause and effect are eternal – nobody is exempt.

9 The Hermit
After a period of retreat to contemplate inner illumination, understanding and truth must be shared with others.

10 The Wheel
Without movement life stagnates. Let go of the past and look to the future: everything is part of an endless learning process.

ASK YOUR ARCHETYPE
If you are troubled, shuffle the major arcana cards, silently asking for the archetype that will help you. When the cards feel warm in your hands, cut them into two piles. Take the card on the top of the lower pile. Meditate on this image; let it come alive and bring you insight, wisdom and calm.

11 Strength

No one faces anything that they can't handle. Hardships build up your spiritual muscle.

12 The Hanged Man

Is your sacrifice really necessary, or is it simply an excuse not to be responsible for your life? Be brave and follow your inner truth.

13 Death

In death there is also birth. And on the higher levels there is no death, only movement and change.

14 Temperance

Wisdom and restraint are needed. The flowing healing waters of time will nourish you, supplementing your deficiencies.

15 The Devil

Instead of listening to the quiet, still voice of love you hear the voice of fear. Look the devil directly in the eye. Only then will he vanish.

16 The Tower

A brilliant flash of lightning reveals the problems that you have ignored. Search for a more balanced, healthy existence.

17 The Star

Life is exacting and will give you the lessons you need in no uncertain terms. Illumination is the outcome but hope is always present.

18 The Moon

Only a fool would say they are never wrong. Know and forgive yourself as you really are and walk on.

19 The Sun

True success comes with application. Everything on the material plane is transitory – only your inner being is immortal.

20 Judgment

Like the phoenix rising from the ashes, you will emerge triumphant.

21 The World

When all energies are aligned, everything becomes possible. At the same time, you realize that all your needs are met and you want for nothing.

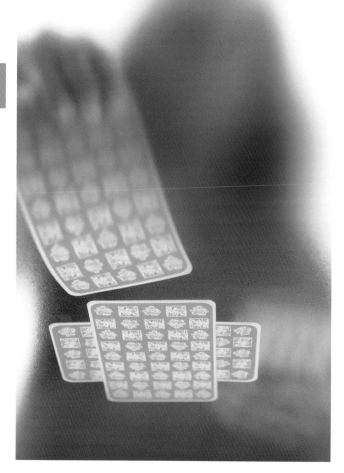

The simplest way to read the cards is to pay heed to their surface meanings – try asking what the symbols suggest to you. Or, you can study the arrangement of the cards and see how action might develop – what is going to happen over the course of the next year. Lastly, in looking at a layout, you begin to become aware of insights never before experienced – you suddenly realize your life has followed a particular pattern – you've never had a satisfactory relationship with anyone and now you can see why.

As your confidence builds, you should develop a sense of dynamic psychic connection with the cards and begin to try more complex spreads. The Celtic Cross (see right), is a helpful example. If you find that you have a natural empathy with the tarot, make good use of it. A psychic tool that resonates in close harmony with your intuition and imagination is immensely helpful in all areas of your life – from your emotional relationships to professional and leisure pursuits.

Improving your tarot reading skills

The "inquirer" is the person seeking answers – whether you're reading for yourself or someone else, study each card and talk through your responses and impressions.

If the majority of the cards are from the major arcana, powerful outside forces may be at work.

If several court cards appear, this suggests that many people are involved.

If the tenth card is a court card, the outcome will depend on someone else's influence.

If you feel that the last card does not make sense, remove it and go through the whole process again, using this card as the significator.

Use the outcome card in your meditations and thoughts, especially before going to sleep, and ask for enlightenment about your question.

If you draw the major arcana card "the Moon" in the first position, put the cards away – you will not get an effective spread now. Try again in 24–48 hours.

THE CELTIC CROSS

This is a wonderful method of thinking about and feeling through a puzzling situation such as how should you react to a crisis arising at work or in a personal relationship.

1 *Choose a significator (card 1) to represent you as inquirer (see pages 242–3) and position it as shown below.*

2 *Shuffle the cards until they feel warm in your hands. Cut with the left hand and set out as shown here.*

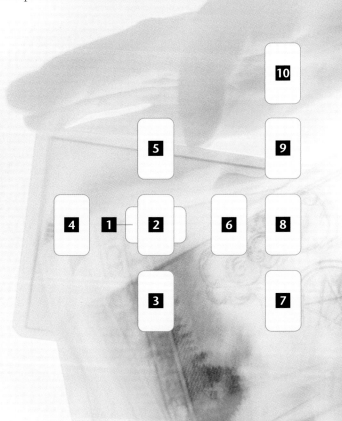

1 This covers the inquirer, relating to the general situation and influences.

2 This crosses the inquirer, warning of any opposing forces whether they are positive or negative.

3 This is beneath the inquirer; it is the basis of the matter, showing something that may have come to light.

4 This is behind the inquirer, pointing to what has just occurred or is beginning to pass away.

5 This crowns the inquirer, representing a possible influence that may or may not come about.

6 This is before the inquirer, revealing the influences that will operate in the near future.

7 This explores fears and any negative feelings around the situation.

8 This uncovers the opinions and influences of friends and family.

9 This reveals the inquirer's own hopes and ideas on the subject.

10 This suggests a possible outcome, drawn from the influences of the other cards.

Developing clairvoyant vision

If you've ever consulted a traditional clairvoyant, he or she may have described various images seen while gazing into a crystal ball. This shining object is the tool of the professional seer or scryer – ancient names for a clairvoyant – a person who "sees clearly". The psychic art of seeing images of past, present and future events can be yours, too; learning it gives you a special insight into what's happening in your world, and a picture of how events will turn out for you and others.

If you want to develop your clairvoyant skills, you don't need go to the trouble and expense of buying a crystal ball. People have been scrying for thousands of years, using all sorts of reflective surfaces including dark pools of water or ink, clear or coloured marbles, pieces of coal, jet or onyx, polished metal – in fact just about anything that helps to focus and attune psychic vision. Pure quartz crystal is known to intensify psychic energies and makes a particularly good scrying tool.

Scrying requires enormous patience and an exact level of relaxation. The surface you use acts as a doorway into time and space, and gazing into it produces a light hypnotic trance. This allows you to "see" information arriving in the form of pictures, symbols, letters, impressions and sensations, which appear generally in answer to a question that you or another puts forward.

Guidelines to clarity

The symbol you see may mean different things depending on circumstance. A cat may mean good luck in one situation (you'll land on your feet) and act as a warning in another (you're thinking about someone who may or may not be a friend). As you gain in experience, recording your visions and what comes to pass, you'll learn to combine your intuition with an observant and open mind.

Your character and the issues that interest you will strongly affect the meaning of any images. For example, the symbol of scales may appear. This could mean that you are involved in some kind of legal process. On the other hand, if you are doing research, it might refer to your judgment of the data. If you ask a question about spiritual matters, the scales may represent divine justice.

USING A SCRYING TOOL

1 *Work in a dimly lit spot and sit with your back to the light source. When you're scrying for someone else, he or she should sit at least an arm's length away from you.*

2 *If your scrying tool is transparent, put a small square of black velvet or other dark fabric underneath it, to help focus your vision.*

3 *Make yourself deeply relaxed, stay perfectly silent and concentrate your gaze right into the heart of your scrying surface. If nothing happens the first time, take a break. Try again in short bursts of up to 20 minutes.*

4 *You'll know when images are starting to form – the inner surface stops reflecting external pictures. It turns a milky colour and this will swiftly turn black. At this point, shapes emerge.*

5 *Two kinds of images appear, and you'll need to use your intuition to interpret them. Those with direct messages reveal a scene or incident played out in front of you, as if you were watching a film. These represent actual happenings, past, present or future. At first you'll find it difficult to determine in what time scale the images shown are happening, but trust your hunches. With practice, you'll get better at identifying this.*

6 *Other images are indirect or symbolic. They are similar to those in dreams, and you can use dream symbols as guidelines (see page 224). Again, practice and dedication will give you the confidence to interpret them accurately.*

What can you see in the tea leaves?

If you've never tried divination before, the simple act of drinking a cup of tea may bring surprising revelations. You don't have to have any particular psychic ability to do it – anyone who has the patience to study symbols and their meanings can become proficient. But as with any method of divination, you shouldn't use it too often – read the leaves once or twice a week at most. Some symbols will stand out immediately; the larger the symbol, the more important and relevant it will be.

Check to see if any of the symbols are connected. If you see a human face, for example, is there an initial letter next to it that may give you a clue as to who it might be?

THE AREAS OF THE CUP
The cup's "regions" act as a psychic map for the questioner. The pictures created by the leaves are interpreted according to where they are situated.

Opposite the handle
This is the site concerning work and business.

Handle *This area represents you, your home and close family.*

The sides and bottom of the cup *These denote time scales: if a symbol is close to the rim, it refers to something happening soon. Images on the side of the cup are not so immediate in their impact and those on the bottom represent events a long way into the future.*

THE TEA RITUAL

For a good, clear reading, buy a leaf tea that has large leaves – China tea is ideal but other Oriental varieties are suitable too.

1 *Put a tablespoon of tea in a pot and cover with boiling water. Serve it in a cup and saucer – use a plain white or light coloured cup with a wide mouth.*

2 *Drink from the tea until about one teaspoonful is left in the cup.*

3 *Hold the cup in your left hand and swirl it three times in a circular*

anti-clockwise motion. As you do this, focus your mind on your question. Be very specific if you want good results.

4 *Invert the cup onto the saucer and leave it for at least a minute, until the liquid has drained away.*

5 *Now turn the cup over and examine the leaves, as described.*

Should I move house now?

Here's how the leaves answered the question. The bat shape at the top of the cup over the handle covers the area concerning the home. A bat may seem ominous, but it can mean that your fears of the unknown will be banished in the light of day. A female figure at the base carries a broom. It could indicate a completely new start.

Positive symbols
Acorn, amulet, anchor, angel, ark, bees, birds, boot, bridge, bull, circle, clover, corn, cow, crown, dove, duck, eagle, elephant, fig, fish, flowers, horseshoe, ship, swan

Negative symbols
Alligator, arc, arrow, bat, black flag, coffin, cross, dagger, drum, hour glass, monkey, mouse, rat, scythe, skeleton, square, stake, sword, wreck

What can a person's hands tell you?

Classically trained palm readers study the lines, shapes and marks on hands in remarkable detail. You may not be an expert in this sense, but you can certainly use your psychic skills to "read" hands. When someone puts his or her hand in yours, take plenty of time to psychically tune yourself into the particular energy you feel. This will be your main source of insight about that person. Any patterns and lines you see act as focal points, triggers for your intuition rather than a blueprint.

Left or Right?

There are two main opinions about the significance of the left and right hands. The traditional view is that the passive hand (left for a right-handed person and right for someone who is left-handed) is a miniature profile of innate character and potential. The features of this hand are believed to remain constant over the years, while the lines on the dominant hand change and evolve to reveal what has been achieved with any inborn aptitudes.

Modern palm readers say that the lines on both hands change, and that the hands are "cross wired" to the right and left sides of the brain, which affects the changes. The right hand shows reasoning, analytical and logical ability, and the left reveals emotional, intuitive and creative aspects.

Again, your intuition is your best ally here; whichever hand that you're holding, listen to the psychic messages that you pick up and trust them.

WHAT'S YOUR HAND SHAPE?

A quick glance at the shape of someone's hands can tell you a lot. There are seven major types – can you recognize which one is yours?

Square
Fingertips are flat across the top and the palm appears as high as it is broad.

You're a steady, matter-of-fact person who reaps the benefits of your own efforts.

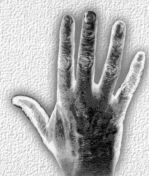

Spatulate or active
Thickish fingers with flat tops that are short compared with the palm.

You're bold and daring, a courageous pioneer seeking to improve the lot of others.

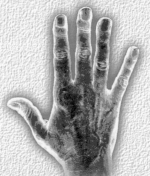

Conical or temperamental
Slender, tapering fingers slightly shorter than the palm.

Impetuous and impulsive, your mood fluctuates quickly – you get depressed about trivia.

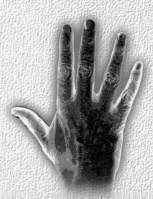

MAIN LINES

Heart, head, fate and life lines are the key indicators. Strong, unbroken lines signify positive aspects.

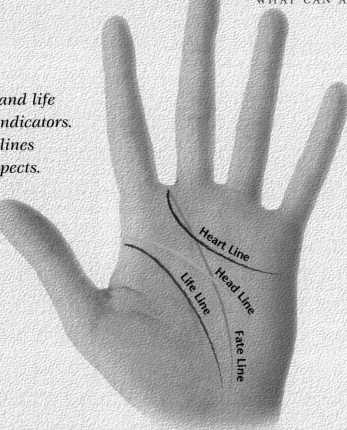

Heart Line

Head Line

Life Line

Fate Line

KEY MARKS

Any of the marks below may occur along the main lines. Pay attention to these though they may relate only to one period of time and tend to come and go.

Crosses *Shock and worries*

Squares *Restriction*

Triangles *Talent*

Star *Luck with money*

Grills and grids *Illness*

Islands *Hardships*

Chains *A line full of chains shows confusion*

Non-specific dots and pitting *Usually occur at the end of a line and indicates illness or weakness – usually temporary*

Knotty or philosophical	**Pointed or idealistic**	**Elemental**	**Mixed**
Shortish, uneven fingers combined with a tall, slender palm.	*Very long, smooth, tapering fingers with a tall, thin palm.*	*Short, wide fingers and palm.*	*Equal-length fingers and palm.*
You're an intellectual; you love analysis using methodical, reasoning.	*A lover of art and beauty, you're an idealist but rather impractical.*	*You're practical, not intellectual. In exceptional circumstances you can be a great leader.*	*Adaptable and versatile, you're a jack-of-all trades. You may be a gifted inventor.*

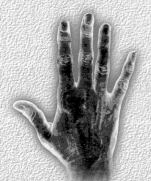

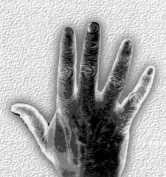

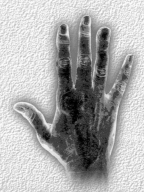

What can you learn from the runes?

Those gifted with rune magic are said to get their powers from Odin, the one-eyed god of the occult. If you discover that you have psychic affinity with this Scandinavian oracle, you'll derive great benefit from his mysterious powers. A single rune can be meditated upon when thinking about the answer to a problem, such as "Is now a good time to break up with my present partner?" More information, however, is gained from drawing several runes and judging how they work together. Can they point out the direction you should take in achieving your goal – when to suggest and how to manage a separation in the least painful way, for example.

Carved stone or wood runes are widely available. To make your own, collect 25 1-inch diameter round, flat pebbles. Use a marker pen, paint or nail polish to create the symbols shown below. Take plenty of time to meditate on the meaning of each rune as you decorate it; this way you will reinforce the energy within the stones. Keep runes in a roomy drawstring bag. Every time you use the runes, their vibrations become even more powerful.

The Self
Rectification comes before progress. A time of change and growth.

Partnership, a gift
True union can only occur when both parties are strong.

The Messenger
Observe what is around you. Everything has meaning for self-growth.

Retreat, inheritance
You gain through abandoning the past. Submission is required.

Strength *Just as trees drop their leaves you must give up something to allow new growth.*

Initiation, secrets
Surprises. For spiritual transformation, set aside external matters

Constraint, pain
Fears and struggles. You have restricted yourself. Pay off debts to progress.

Fertility *You can complete what you have begun. Birth is often painful – persevere.*

Defence *Delays. Be patient, relax and wait. Quietly put your house in order.*

Protection *Don't let emotion prevail. Reason and action are the only true protection.*

SIMPLE RUNE DIVINATION

1 *Hold the bag of runes in your hand and concentrate on a question. Keep it very simple. As you do this, gently shake the runes in the bag.*

2 *When you feel you'll get an answer open the bag and put one hand inside,*

moving the runes around until one stone seems to stick to your fingers. This is the one that will give you the answer to your question. See below for an interpretation of each rune's meaning.

3 *If you need a broader view, follow the same procedure but choose three runes and lay them out left to right.*

4 *The first relates to the situation, the second to any action required, and the third to the outcome or new situation.*

Possessions *The laws of cause and effect are clues to success. Share with others.*

Joy, light *New energy, clarity. A realigned self brings fulfilment and renewal.*

Harvest *Be patient – this is no time for speed. Know that whatever the outcome, all is well.*

Opening *Be free to receive and let light pour into your life. Don't be afraid.*

Warrior energy *The spiritual warrior uses will without attachment to the outcome.*

Growth *To accomplish the work modesty, patience and kindness are required.*

Movement *You have made steady progress and gained security and self-confidence.*

Flow *Relax when the water is gentle and take action when it is choppy.*

Disruption *Things will not go to plan now. Power comes from inner strength.*

Union *This is the soul's journey, linking spirit and matter. Discard illusions.*

Gateway *A time for reflection. Look at the past and what you have gained. Now move on.*

Breakthrough *Darkness is behind you and everything is transformed for ever.*

Standstill *A cold atmosphere. Find what keeps you on ice and let it go to thaw out.*

Wholeness *You realize that you already possess what you seek within yourself.*

The Unknowable *A blank. Courage is needed. Inner change means emancipation.*

Using a divining rod

We don't really know how a piece of wood or metal can detect the presence of underground water, oil and minerals, but people have been dowsing for thousands of years. There are various theories as to how dowsing works: one view is that humans retain some primitive tracking instinct for water that is normally dormant, but may become activated. Then there is the possibility that the divining rod emits waves of energy that are bounced back once the dowser has made a "hit". Another idea is that the dowser psychically tunes in to the energy field of hidden materials, using the divining rod to trigger the process. Whatever the explanation, it is an exciting experience for the novice psychic to feel the reaction of the dowsing tool as it responds – you feel profoundly close to living energy sources.

Today, dowsing is used as a tool by people interested in environmental health; it can help locate underground sources of water that may cause degenerative disease in the people living above.

MAKING YOUR OWN DIVINING ROD

Traditionally the divining rod is made out of a forked hazel or willow twig, but a shaped piece of metal works just as well.

1 *Find a metal coat hanger, untwist it and make it straight. Then split it into two pieces.*

2 *Bend each piece into an L shape: these are your divining rods. Now get two empty disposable ballpoint pen tubes and place one rod inside each.*

When you hold these upright the rods should have room to move freely.

3 *If you want a traditional rod, and have plenty of trees nearby, look for a hazel or willow branch that has grown into the shape of a wishbone. This makes a fine divining tool.*

NARROWING THE SEARCH

Dowsers are asked to identify many different kinds of underground materials in addition to water. They may be looking for oil or valuable minerals; seams of gold, silver, platinum and other precious metals, or rock formations that hold diamonds and other gems. Each of these produces a slightly different reaction from the rod, so some practitioners use an ingenious method to improve their accuracy. They "pre-tune" their rods to the precise vibrations of the material they are seeking. For instance, if a dowser is searching for gold, he or she assesses the rod's reactions to a sample of gold ore. If the rod has exactly the same reaction on site, the chances of finding gold are greatly improved.

DOWSING FOR WATER

Water may be hidden deep below a piece of parched earth – can you find it?

1 *Concentrate, but remain relaxed, walk slowly and purposefully around the designated area and silently ask where you can find water.*

2 *If you're using metal rods, you'll know when there is water below the ground because the rods will move together to form a cross.*

3 *If you are dowsing with hazel or willow, hold the two wishbone sides lightly between your fingertips and walk with the single end pointing up. This end will suddenly "pull" and point downward with a strong force when you have detected underground water.*

4 *At the spot where the metal rods crossed or the wooden stick pointed down, you should make an exploratory dig for the water source.*

What can you do with a pendulum?

Psychics and mediums are frequently asked to find missing people and objects. Some use a dowsing tool such as a pendulum to focus their impressions. You can learn how to use one yourself, especially if you had success with a divining rod (see preceding pages). If you're lucky, you may discover that you have a real gift for dowsing.

So how do you get a pendulum? It's easy; you can make one yourself – it's simply a weighted object suspended on a length of thread, string or a thin metal chain. You can use almost anything: some people prefer objects they wear all the time such as a plain wedding band suspended from a favourite gold chain. You could even use a small metal key. If you're buying a pendulum, there are beautifully carved wooden examples, or you might be attracted to a shaped crystal. Choose what feels right for you.

Once you've got your pendulum, put your own energy vibrations into it; handle it frequently and keep it with you constantly. You can "charge" it with healing energy and use it to detect health problems by dowsing your own or someone else's body. Explore what's happening by asking the pendulum detailed questions, then "beam" healing energy from it onto the affected spot.

You also can use the pendulum to locate and heal disturbed spirits or negative energies in sites and buildings that have a troubled spiritual atmosphere.

Insider info DOWSING

It is a great tool for helping you to choose things – *from recommended courses to remedies of different types. You will need pictorial representations of your choices. If, for example, you want to know whether you'd find it more beneficial to take a scuba diving or sewing course, put your finger on the image of each in turn and ask the pendulum if this one will be helpful to you.*

Using it with a map can help you locate something or someone. *Position the pendulum over a map and see whether it is more active over a particular area. This may be where to find missing persons, or ancient sacred sites, hidden caves, water or mineral deposits.*

It also can be used to identify problems. *If you feel you may have a food allergy, line up some possible suspects such as dairy or wheat foods and dip a finger into each in turn. Ask your pendulum if this particular food is bad for you. Keep checking right through the list – there may be more than one food that is causing a problem.*

PROGRAMMING YOUR PENDULUM

1 *You need to programme positive/negative responses into your pendulum. To do this, hold its cord between your thumb and fingertip and suspend the pendulum over a flat surface. Wait until it is completely still.*

2 *Gently swing the pendulum diagonally in front of you; concentrate your thoughts and say out loud: "This is yes". Repeat this several times.*

3 *Now swing it gently in the opposite direction and say: "This is no". Again, do this repeatedly.*

4 *Now check the pendulum for accuracy. Say your name out loud and ask it: "Is this my name?" It should react with a "yes" response. Then say a completely different name and ask the same question again. This time you should get a "no" reply.*

HOW TO FIND LOST OBJECTS

1 *If you've lost something, your pendulum can help to find it. First check out the general location – ask the pendulum a series of questions to confirm whether the lost object is in the office, your home, in the car or the garden.*

2 *Once you've got a positive answer, be more specific. If the object is somewhere in your home, ask which room it is in. Is it in the bedroom, bathroom or kitchen?*

3 *When you've got a "yes" answer to one of these questions, take your pendulum to the specified room and turn around slowly, asking the pendulum which direction to follow. It should point you straight there.*

Who's got your number?

How can your name have a hidden meaning? And in what way does it define your essential character and destiny? The answer is the powerful link between letters and numbers. The ancient Egyptians attributed magic numbers to particular letters and used them to foretell the future. But the science of numbers (numerology) originated in Greek and Hebrew cultures. The Hebraic system known as the Cabbala attributed a specific number to each of the 22 letters of the Hebrew alphabet. So any word can be reduced to an arithmetical figure, and holds a secret meaning.

This explains why the original name your parents chose for you is so significant. It was created by the natural laws of universal attraction at your birth, and is more important than any other name you'll acquire, including your married surname.

When you discover your personal numbers of destiny (below) and explore their meanings (see opposite) you may discover surprising new insights into your character.

Your birthdate produces your life number, which is fixed and unchanging and represents your special characteristics and attributes and innermost nature. Your name number is the way you express yourself outwardly, your personality. Your two numbers can work in harmony or be antithetical. In the latter case, this may explain why you feel that deep-seated needs that you have are not being expressed.

PRIMARY VIBRATIONS

Here's how you can calculate your two personal numbers of destiny.

1	2	3	4	5	6	7	8	9
A	B	C	D	E	F	G	H	I
J	K	L	M	N	O	P	Q	R
S	T	U	V	W	X	Y	Z	

The first number is based on your date of birth

1 *To formulate this, write out your full birth date: for instance,* **December 2, 1958** *becomes* **12/2/1958**.

2 *Now add up each number:*

1 + 2 + 2 + 1 + 9 + 5 + 8 = 28;

then add both final digits to achieve a single figure:

2 + 8 = 10, *which reduces to a final figure of* **1**.

So: **12/2/1958 = 1**

THE NUMBERS AND THEIR MEANINGS

Remember, each number has its positive and negative aspects – how you use them is up to you.

1 *Independent, self-reliant, tenacious, single-minded. Intolerant, conceited, narrow, stubborn.*

2 *Placid, just, unselfish, harmonious, sociable. Irresolute, indifferent, unable to take responsibility, weak-willed.*

3 *Freedom-seeking, brave, adventurous, exuberant, brilliant. Indifferent, impatient, over-confident, lacking in stamina.*

4 *Stolid, loyal, imperturbable, honest, strong-willed, practical. Clumsy, dull, conservative, inflexible.*

5 *Adventurous, vivacious, courageous, healthy, sympathetic. Rash, irresponsible, inconstant, unreliable, thoughtless.*

6 *Idealistic, selfless, honest, charitable, faithful, responsible. Superior, weak, impractical, submissive.*

7 *Wise, discerning, philosophical, enduring, deep, contemplative. Morbid, hypercritical, inactive, antisocial.*

8 *Practical, powerful, business-like, decisive, controlling, constant. Unimaginative, blunt, self-sufficient.*

9 *Intelligent, understanding, discreet, artistic, brilliant, lofty. Dreamy, lethargic, lacking in concentration, aimless.*

Note: traditionally the numbers 11 and 22 should not be broken down to single figures.

11 *This is the number of the super intellect or genius, also regarded as a lucky person. Transformation.*

22 *Because of its great power this number may result in outstanding ascendancy or disastrous downfall.*

The next significant formula is the one derived from analyzing your given name

3 *To reduce your name to a final figure, check the graph opposite for the number corresponding to your name.*

My first name is:
J = 1 U = 3 L = 3 I = 9 E = 5

This adds up to **21**; *broken down to single figures* **2 + 1 = 3**

My family name is:
S = 1 O = 6 S = 1 K = 2 I = 9 N = 5

This adds up to **24**; *then, broken down to single figures*
2 + 4 = 6

So, added together, both my names, Julie and Soskin total **9**.

4 *Your birthday and name numbers are unique to you— check their meanings from the list above.*

Psychic healing 4

Did you know that you unknowingly implement some form of healing every day? You give a stranger a smile, take time to listen to a colleague, send out a kindly thought to a far-away relative, feel compassion for someone you read about and call a friend when you sense that he or she is feeling sad. When you've hurt your own hand, you instinctively rub it to make it feel better. Whenever you make these ordinary expressions of love and concern, you are sending out healing energies.

Distant Healing

You can make these actions even more effective by learning how to enhance your natural healing energies. This may take the form of distant healing, whereby you "send" powerful, beneficial thoughts to someone in need. For example, when I was very young I joined a psychic development group. We were asked to think of someone who would benefit from absent healing. A friend was going through a difficult emotional patch, so I put her name into the healing energy. I went to visit her the following Sunday; she told me that on the previous Thursday evening she had suddenly experienced a powerful wave of feeling sweeping over her. She also had been swept by a reassuring sense that everything would be fine. This had happened around 7:45pm, the time when our group had met and held the healing session. My friend had no idea about my psychic interests and certainly didn't know about the group.

Guidelines for psychic healing

If you find that you're a "natural" healer, it can be flattering to your ego – but don't get carried away.

Know that any "hands-on" work you do is one part of a much wider healing process. You are simply a channel for healing energies. Healing energy (often called prana) comes from a universal source, not from you.

Remember, you are the instrument or channel for healing energy, therefore self-awareness and spiritual development will greatly assist you.

Don't diagnose or play doctor and never contradict medical advice given by a professional to another person.

A Channel for Healing

You can also work on getting in touch with your inner sources of regenerative energy (see opposite page) and use this to promote well-being in others. Although all people have the ability to promote healing, some can do so more directly (see box on opposite page). If you "test" empathetic, for example, people may begin to feel better just by being near you. If you are shamanistic, you should have an innate sense of what will harm or help someone who is ill. If you have true psychic healing ability, others will benefit directly from your healing touch. If your healing ability appears more spiritual, then you may serve as a channeller for healing by higher powers.

FINDING THE POWER WITHIN

*In order for yourself or others to gain positive benefit,
learn to access your inner sources of regenerative energy.*

1 *Sit in a relaxed position and place both hands onto your solar plexus.*

2 *Close your eyes and focus your entire awareness onto your hands. Gradually they will become warmer from the prana energy stored in your solar plexus.*

3 *Now place your fingers very gently onto your forehead. This will make them tingle and feel alive with energy.*

4 *Let the streams of prana energy flow into your head; notice the vivid sensations this causes.*

5 *When the tingling stops, take your fingers away and shake your hands energetically for a few moments.*

6 *Finally, return your hands to your solar plexus. Let them rest there for a few moments. They should now feel alive and "glowing" with energy.*

What kind of healer are you?

❏ **1** Are you a good listener?

❏ **2** Do you make others feel at ease?

❏ **3** Can you feel a connection with the earth and nature?

❏ **4** Do people confide in you?

❏ **5** Can you "shake off" a headache?

❏ **6** Do you want to make the world a better place?

❏ **7** Have you ever felt the presence of an angelic or healing guide?

❏ **8** Do you have an intuitive link with animals?

❏ **9** Do you often feel completely at one with the world?

❏ **10** Do you feel other people's pain?

❏ **11** After you've visited or phoned, do your friends feel better?

❏ **12** Could you "decide" not to be unwell?

If you answered yes to

1 2 4
You are empathetic.

3 8 10
You are shamanistic.

5 11 12
Your gift is psychic healing.

6 7 9
You have spiritual healing ability.

(See opposite page)

Healing yourself first

If you discover that you have an effective healing ability, it's only natural to feel proud of yourself. But you also would be getting the wrong message. Always remember that the only *personal* healing skill that you can honestly claim is the ability to heal yourself. In all other instances, you merely act as a channel for life-force energy or prana. That is what promotes healing in others.

Once you have understood this, you'll also realize that, in order to become an effective healer, you will need to sort out your own health first. This means resolving both emotional and physical problems – healing yourself demands great self-awareness and acceptance. It also means giving up any long-held grudges, resentments and other negative feelings, however justified they may have seemed until now.

You shouldn't be too hard on yourself, though; never underestimate how much self-healing you can achieve simply by not thinking too much about the past or the future. Live and enjoy your life as it is today: you're the sum total of all your experiences and whatever is left unresolved from your past will manifest itself in the here and now. Observe, acknowledge and confront what is in your life, and you'll activate a vibrant, flowing, energy through which you can prosper and grow.

Natural Powers

The exercises on the opposite page are designed to help you emulate and access the abilities of other common creatures. Butterfly breathing is all about becoming "powerful" quickly – just as the butterfly gains its beauty and final form in short order, while we all recognize the short, sharp sting of the bee.

Insider info   HEALING OR PRANA ENERGY

Healing energy is present inside all of us. *People are born with this prana energy and it links you with everything in the universe – all forms of matter, both animate and inanimate.*

The stores of this energy can be increased. *You can boost your levels of prana by linking with universal energy during meditation (see page 181), by making positive affirmations (see page 192), and by balancing your chakras (see page 189).*

There are special sources of this energy. *Prana flows through everything, but it seems to be particularly concentrated in water and earth. Activities such as sailing, swimming and gardening are effective and pleasurable ways of boosting your prana energy.*

BREATHE LIKE A BUTTERFLY...

Draw powerful healing forces quickly into your body along with your breath.

1 *Place your hands on your heart and take a really deep breath. As you do this, push your arms and hands up straight towards the sky. Mentally link yourself with the boundless sources of prana or universal energy.*

2 *As you breathe out, let your arms and hands fall to your sides.*

3 *Repeat this up to ten times, drawing increasing amounts of prana energy into and around your body.*

...STING LIKE A BEE

Use your powers of visualization to zap cold and flu viruses, and other enemies of your immune system.

1 *Make yourself completely relaxed (see page 181) and mentally scan your entire body from top to toe, sensing any areas of your body that are affected.*

2 *Focus your concentration onto these areas and visualize armies of strong "soldier" cells marching out to search and destroy the invasive virus.*

3 *Be as graphic and detailed with your imagery as possible – give your soldier cells incredibly powerful weapons to make them truly effective.*

4 *Watch your "troops" destroying the virus – the more imaginative energy you put into this the better it will work.*

Healing your garden

Many psychic healers have flourishing, healthy plants in their gardens. This is not at all surprising: energy directed into plants through benign human contact can makes a dramatic difference to their health. Experiments have shown that plants that are regularly touched and stroked do noticeably better than their neglected companions. These discoveries by plant researchers make complete sense to a practicing psychic – loving communication automatically promotes healing and well-being, and positive focus onto the aura of living things can produce highly beneficial outcomes.

Each plant has its unique spirit counterpart – you often see them illustrated as fairies, gnomes or pixies. It is no coincidence that people put statues of these in their gardens – they are instinctively acknowledging the hidden world of the earth spirits and unconsciously asking them to help.

If you want to make your plants blissfully healthy and happy, focus your psychic energies on your gardening skills. For a start, you should learn to communicate with the spirits of the plants in your garden (see page 216). By doing so, you will enable them to grow stronger and live longer.

THREE-STEP RESCUE REMEDY

Even if a plant seems to be on its last legs, you can give it a chance to flourish.

1 *If parts of the plant are already dead, remove these and clear the soil around it. Now connect with the plant and ask it what's wrong? Is it is too dry, waterlogged or in the wrong soil? Trust your intuition.*

2 *Correct any imbalances you've sensed – repotting the plant may be necessary if the soil is unsuitable – then focus healing energy into the plant, from the roots upwards.*

3 *Visualize a bright life-line of energy going from you, down into the plant's roots, up through its leaves and back to you again in a continuous cycle. Do this until you intuitively feel that the plant has absorbed enough healing.*

TOP TIPS FOR PSYCHIC GARDENING

Make your garden grow beautifully by using all your psychic skills. Project nourishment into the soil, discourage pests, draw in nature's helpers, and generate positive energy for your plants.

Nourishment *Enriched soil means healthy plants: feed it with homemade organic compost (a good gardening book will tell you how to make it). As you dig in the compost, visualize your garden full of glossy-leaved flourishing plants.*

Water *Many psychic gardeners like to "power" water before using it on their plants. Pour it alternately from one container to another to infuse it with prana or life energy, or use a crystal (see page 270) to beam healing energy into it.*

Pest protection *Offer a sacrifice to slugs, snails and bugs. For instance, you can make a bargain with the spirits of snails. Agree that they can have a certain number of your fruit and vegetables, leaving the rest free for your own use.*

Helpful creatures *Give a warm welcome to useful creatures such as ladybirds and frogs by invoking their aid. They will keep down destructive pests and help you to maintain your garden in a dynamic, healthy balance.*

Mood *Make everything in your garden feel loved and appreciated by walking around regularly and checking that all is well. If you choose a special place in the garden for your meditation, the positive energies will be greatly enhanced.*

Healing with crystals

If you've ever had a strong attraction to a crystal or gemstone, don't ignore that feeling. You may have found an ideal psychic healing partner. Each stone carries the energy of its time spent deep in the earth; it not only acts as a powerful focus for healing work, but will actively enhance the process.

There are many kinds of crystals available in specialist mineral, new age or museum shops, and it's easy to feel overwhelmed by so much choice. For practical purposes, however, an effective psychic healer needs just one gemstone, programmed and dedicated for this particular task. A piece of clear, unblemished rock quartz with one, well-defined, pointed end, is excellent for most healing work; choose one that fits comfortably in your hand. Alternatively, raw amethyst is another wonderfully effective healing stone.

Once you've chosen your crystal, you can prepare it for healing work by linking it up with your own energy (see right). Your crystal is then ready for action; to implement healing, use the simple but effective technique described on the page opposite. This restores energy levels that have been sapped by pain and illness; at the same time, it triggers the healing resources that are already present in the person you're helping.

Whatever crystal you choose, take good care of your stone and keep it in a safe place. You should cleanse it regularly (see right) to remove any negative energy it may have absorbed.

Cleansing guidelines

Crystals retain and magnify energy more than any other material, so regular cleansing is crucial. Here are a few simple methods:

Hold the crystal for a few minutes under clear, running water.

Place the crystal on a clean, non-plastic plate (china is best) and put it in direct sunlight for at least a couple of hours.

Visualize a ray of clear, bright light thoroughly cleansing the stone.

POWERING YOUR CRYSTAL

Before using your crystal for healing work, you need to activate its latent energies.

1 Wash your crystal under clear running water for a few moments. Dry it, then keep it close to your body for a few days to align its vibrations as closely as possible with your own. You might like to keep it under your pillow at night while you're asleep.

2 When you're ready to charge the crystal, sit in a quiet place and relax completely, holding it gently in your hands. Focus your concentration onto the crystal.

3 Look deep into the crystal; at the same time, invoking the highest good or other spiritual guardian, mentally direct a sustained pulse of healing energy into the crystal, from the base to its apex.

4 You'll feel the crystal "throbbing" in your hand; when you sense that it is fully programmed, wrap it in a clean piece of white cotton or linen and store it in a safe place.

HEALING WITH A CRYSTAL

This method is excellent for general healing work – it is both safe and effective.

1 Make sure that the person who is receiving healing is comfortable and relaxed – he or she may prefer to lie down, or lean back in a reclining chair – and that the room is calm and quiet.

2 Take your crystal in your right hand, and mentally link with its vibrations until you feel a "throbbing" sensation in your hand.

3 Angle the point of the crystal at a spot about 12 inches over the head of the person you're treating, and slowly move the crystal clockwise around his or her body. As you do this, visualize a "laser" beam of energy pulsing from your crystal. Repeat this

several times until you have completely surrounded the person's body with a healing force field.

4 If you sense that an area needs specific healing, direct the crystal's pointed end at that site for a few moments. Target energy onto it until you feel ready to move on.

5 You will know instinctively when you have done enough. At this point, transfer the crystal into your left hand, and visualize the crystal's energy flowing gently back into itself. There are no guarantees of success, as with all healing, but practice will increase your abilities.

Once you're confident about using a crystal for healing, you may want to extend your range, and explore other kinds of gemstones. Again, these are widely available from specialist mineral and museum shops or by mail order. Most new-age magazines contain advertisements from gemstone suppliers.

If you feel attracted to gemstone healing, you'll find it leads you to the chakra centres of the body. These actively respond to the vibrations from different gemstones, and, if you choose the right ones, you can use them to energize and heal, as described on the page opposite. The chakras play a key part in every aspect of your well-being – physical, mental and spiritual – and have a direct influence on the health of your aura. Each chakra has its own signature colour, so it's important to choose the right stone for healing at these centres. When choosing your chakra crystals, let your intuition guide you, and spend time exploring, touching, sensing and assessing the vibrations from all the different kinds on display. At some point, one stone will feel just right. You'll know this by instinct – it is almost as if it is saying: "Choose me!"

The Crown Centre

A suitable gem for this centre could be a piece of clear quartz, a deep violet amethyst, or a rich purple sugalite. Hold the crystal on the top of the head.

Healing benefits *Calms feelings of constant anxiety, insecurity and alienation from others.*

The Throat Centre

Choose from blue gems such as sapphire, turquoise, lapis lazuli, aquamarine and blue lace agate. Cradle the crystal in the hollow of the throat.

Healing benefits *Sore throats, coughs and swollen glands can all be eased.*

The Solar Plexus Centre

Go for golden gems such as citrine, amber, yellow topaz and citrine, and place the crystal you chose just above the navel.

Healing benefits *Helps with food disorders such as anorexia and bulimia; and calms any stress centered in the gut.*

The Base Centre

Choose the earthy colours of red jasper, or a red-brown tiger's eye. You can also use a plain black pebble. Rest your chosen crystal at the base of the spine.

Healing benefits *Use for aching bones, stress and irritable bowel syndrome.*

The Brow Centre

The deep indigo shade of sodalite works well on this chakra. Balance the crystal on the spot between the eyes.

Healing benefits *Good for "fuzzy" headaches, blurred vision, disturbed sleep and general nervousness.*

The Heart Centre

Look for green gems such as malachite, moss agate or jade. Alternatively, you can use a pink stone such as rose quartz or rhodonite. Position your crystal at the centre of the chest area.

Healing benefits *Alleviates bronchitis, asthma, chest infections, heart problems and violent emotional reactions.*

The Sacral Centre

Use stimulating orange from coloured gems such as amber, carnelian, orange agate and orange pebbles. Put the crystal on the genital area.

Healing benefits *Good for problems with menstruation, PMT, infertility and impotence.*

Using sound to heal

A mother cradles her child, singing a familiar lullaby, and murmurs soothing, loving words. The baby has already become attuned to her voice in the womb, and responds with cooing, gurgling sounds, completing the loop of intimate harmony. This ordinary event is just one aspect of the power of sound.

This force has been known from the dawn of time: "In the beginning was the Word". This single phrase from the Bible (St John 1:1) signifies the release of an astounding energy, through which the entire world was created.

Music, too, has profound psychic power; some traditions hold that every musical note represents a spirit being. The Indian musician Ravi Shankar believes that sound is God; and he regards music as a spiritual path, leading to divine peace and bliss.

When you psychically attune yourself to sound, you can direct its healing forces inside yourself. Using music for meditation can help restore and revive yourself in mind, while stimulating your chakras with sound can help to correct any imbalances that are causing ill-health or disease.

THE HEART OF MUSIC

Meet the healing spirits in music through this simple meditation.

1 *Choose a piece of music that always makes you peaceful and reflective, and play it as you enter a calm, meditative state (see page 181). Now focus on the music, and let it take you to the highest spiritual level.*

2 *As you go deeper into meditation and contemplation, feel yourself completely united with the cosmos.*

3 *Let the sound of the music play into your consciousness, so that it becomes part of your own rhythm. Attune your entire being to the dance of the song, and now connect with the spirits within the music.*

4 *At this point, ask the spirits of the music to bring you healing and open yourself to them. Do this until you feel restored and revived, then return to your normal state.*

SING TO YOUR CHAKRAS

1 *Concentrate on your breath as shown on page 181, then close your eyes. Visualize the red, spinning disk of your base chakra, focusing at its centre. Listen attentively. You will hear the sonic pitch of the chakra intuitively (the lower centres have deep notes, which become higher as you progress up the body).*

2 *Sing out the note you hear, pitching its sound to the exact vibration you feel at the base chakra. This is a strong note, with the sound "OO".*

3 *Next, focus on the orange disk of the sacral chakra; tune into its sound vibration as before, then sing out its note to the sound "OR".*

4 *Now imagine the brilliant yellow core of the solar plexus chakra; listen for its special note, then sing it out to the sound "AH".*

5 *Move on to the green centre of the heart chakra next; wait for its note, then sing it as the open sound "ARE".*

6 *Next, focus onto the clear sky blue of the throat chakra. Tune into its note, and sing it as a short clipped "A" sound (as in apple).*

7 *Conjure up the deep indigo depths of the brow chakra; focus onto its sonic pitch, and sing it to the sound "E" (as in even).*

8 *Now visualize the pure violet colour of your crown chakra. Listen intently until you hear its note, then sing it to the sound "E-OO".*

9 *Finally, focus your concentration back to the heart centre, and hum softly to yourself until you feel completely in tune throughout your body.*

Healing yourself with colour

Did you know that colour is so powerful, it can influence your breathing rhythms? Exposure to a red light alerts your mind, raises your blood pressure, arouses your emotions and spurs you into action. Conversely, all these reactions will be reversed by using the calming effect of blue.

You can use the therapeutic power of colour in various ways – but the best place to start is in your own home. Whether you have a tiny flat or a spacious family dwelling, a sensitive choice of colour can transform your living environment into a positive healing zone.

When you're planning to decorate a space in your home, consult the chart (right) to see what psychic impact each colour makes. To help you to sleep better, for example, you could bring the calming action of soft green to your bedroom. Conversely, the bright, joyful energy of red is best for action spots such as children's play rooms, while inspiring sunshine yellow is perfect for a study or work room.

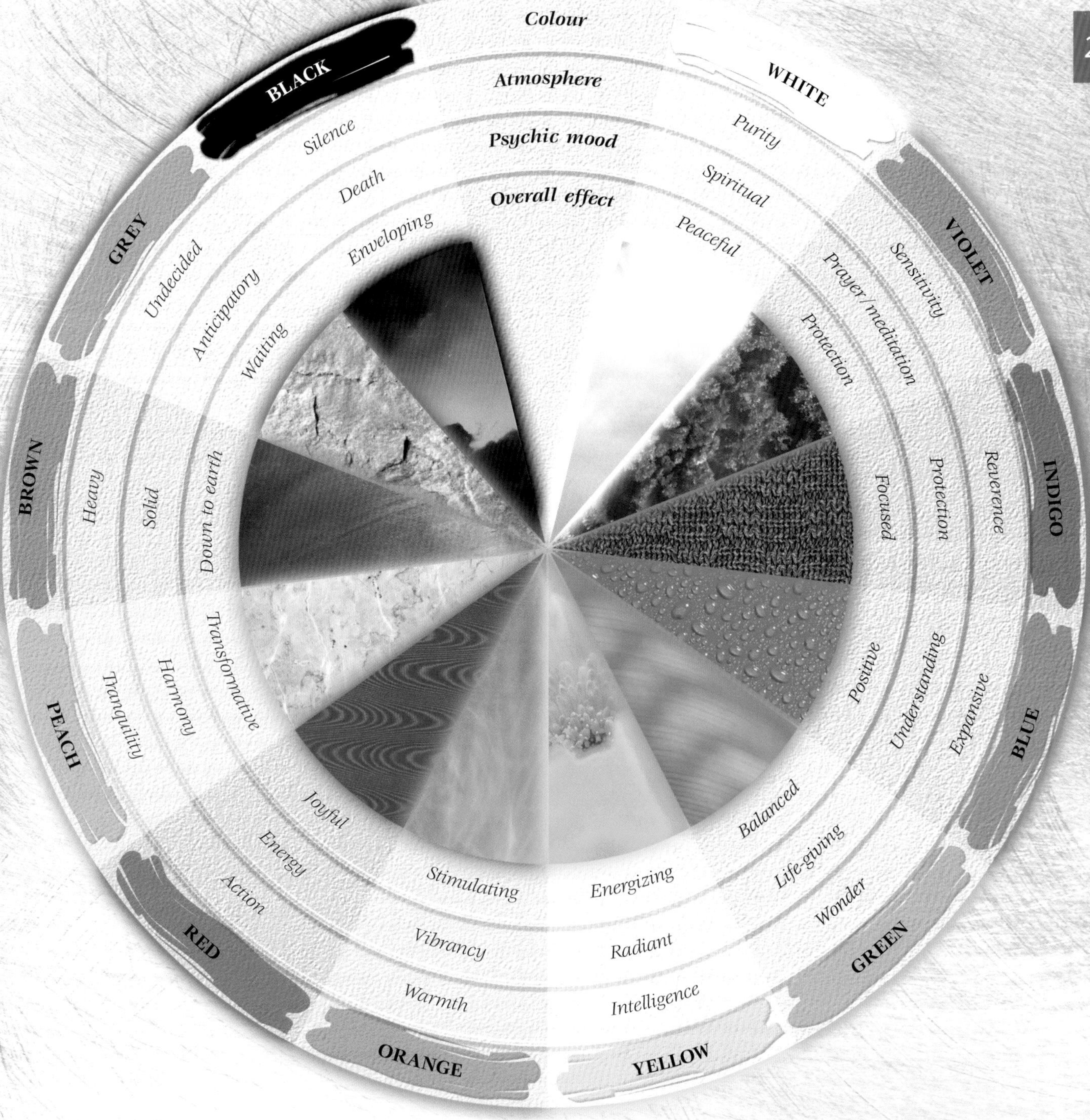

Colour

Atmosphere

Psychic mood

Overall effect

BLACK

WHITE

Silence

Purity

Death

Spiritual

Enveloping

Peaceful

GREY

VIOLET

Undecided

Prayer/meditation

Anticipatory

Protection

Waiting

Sensitivity

BROWN

Heavy

Protection

Solid

Reverence

Down to earth

Focused

INDIGO

Transformative

Positive

PEACH

Tranquility

Understanding

Harmony

Expansive

BLUE

Joyful

Balanced

Energy

Life-giving

Action

Wonder

RED

Stimulating

Energizing

GREEN

Vibrancy

Radiant

Warmth

Intelligence

ORANGE

YELLOW

Colour energy is already active at the very core of your being, at the "grass roots" of your chakra centres. The best way to keep yourself in peak mental, emotional and spiritual balance is to breathe colour into your chakras as described on page 189. Do this exercise regularly, using the colour pages that follow on pages 280–95, and you'll also maintain a balanced, healthy aura.

However, at certain times you may want to use colour in a more direct way, to target specific problems. For instance, you can enclose yourself in a circle of therapeutic colour (right), or channel coloured light into your body, as shown opposite. Each colour has particular healing properties, and these techniques help you to "zero in" on a range of ailments, such as arthritis, raised blood pressure, nervous exhaustion and anxiety.

HOW COLOURS HEAL

The time each colour needs to take effect varies. Follow these guidelines, and don't exceed the recommended times.

Red **7 minutes**	**Orange** **10 minutes**	**Yellow** **12 minutes**
Energizes, improves circulation, raises blood pressure. Use for sciatica. Do not use it if you suffer from hypertension.	*Helps digestion and improves your metabolism. Good for rheumatism, cramps, spasms and asthma.*	*Stimulates the nervous system, liver, pancreas and kidneys. Use it to treat constipation and arthritis.*

A HEALING CIRCLE OF COLOUR

Surround yourself with therapeutic colour to relieve a health problem.

1 *Read the list of colours and their healing properties (below), and choose the one best suited to your problem. If you're feeling stressed, for instance, green may help.*

2 *Lie down comfortably, with your arms at your sides, and use the breathing exercise on page 181 to relax you completely.*

3 *Visualize yourself enclosed in a glowing circle of your chosen colour, and focus on your heart centre. Breathe the colour into this centre and visualize it circulating throughout your aura for a few minutes.*

4 *If you find this gives relief, increase the time spent circulating the colour – 10–20 minutes should be enough.*

RADIANT COLOUR THERAPY

Use coloured light to beam healing energy into your body.

1 *Check the list of colours for their healing action (below), and choose the one you need. If you have digestive trouble, for example, orange can help.*

2 *Fix an appropriately coloured light bulb into an adjustable desk lamp, or*

tape a translucent sheet of the appropriately coloured paper across the bottom of the shade. Put the lamp on the floor and switch it on.

3 *Take off your shoes and socks, and sit on the floor with your legs out*

straight. Your feet should be about 18 inches away from the lamp. Direct the light beam onto the centre of the sole of one foot – this is a natural route for colour energy to flow into your body.

4 *For balanced healing, treat both feet; check the colours (below) for advice on how much time you need.*

Green 15 minutes	**Turquoise** 15 minutes	**Blue** 15 minutes	**Violet** 15 minutes
Brings mental and physical equilibrium, and is excellent for stress. Use as directed to avoid over-stimulating the heart.	*Refreshing and restful, it strengthens both the immune and nervous systems. Soothes inflammation and eczema.*	*An excellent all-purpose healing colour. Reduces blood pressure, and promotes the healthy growth of cells and body tissue.*	*Improves mental stability, helps to purify the body and raises self-esteem. It is also excellent to treat shock.*

Dynamic red

The warm, life-affirming potency of red influences you at primal levels. Its energy courses through your body in your blood, and also activates your Base chakra, the psychic centre that links to the inner core of the planet. Deep within the earth is where a fierce, glowing energy can be found – and this is what gives you your basic appetite for life. This is why red lifts your spirits and stimulates your blood; it can also generate great emotional intensity, ranging from a fierce protectiveness, passion and aggression to sudden violence.

Shades of Red

You can absorb red in its brightest, purest form but its colour differs depending on what is happening to you. Your aura will reflect this: a light red shows your spontaneous, playful side, while deep, rich shades indicate courage, endurance and strong emotions. If the colour is noticeably dark or muddy, however, this signals dangerously blocked, frustrated energy.

Restoring the Balance

An imbalance of red in your system is reflected not only in your aura but you may be "red in the face" with frustration or anger. Should you suffer a shock, defeat or trauma, your core reserves of life energy will be seriously depleted. Correct these extremes by using the chakra balancing exercise described on page 189. Visualize your Base chakra glowing with a pure red energy – and use the image on the facing page for inspiration.

Healing with Red

Psychic healers use red to boost blood circulation, stimulate energy and to ease aching joints and muscles. If stress has severely overtaxed your adrenal glands, so that you're completely exhausted and run down, red can bring you back to life again.

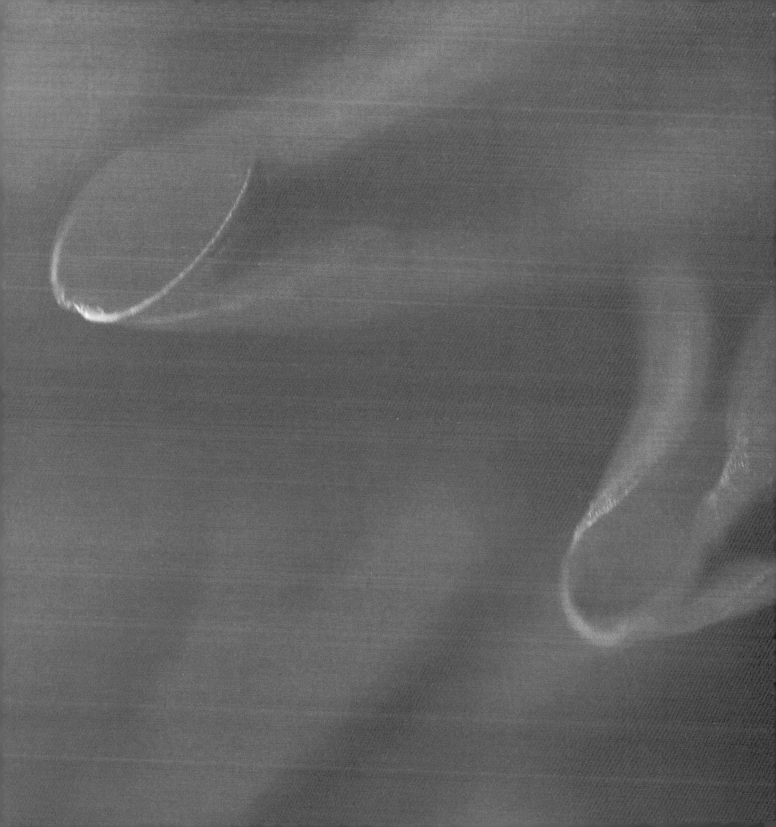

Joyful orange

The warming glow at the heart of a flame is the perfect representation of orange's cheerful energy. This is what activates your Sacral chakra, and is expressed in joyful, instinctive love of life. Orange energy stimulates your pleasure in food, music, dance and sex, while nourishing a deep sense of well-being, happiness and abundance.

Shades of Orange

A pure, clear orange in your aura is a positive sign of energy, optimism, imagination, focus and purpose, but various shades may appear, depending on what is going on in your life. For instance, a light, orange-yellow tint indicates highly creative mental activity, while at the opposite end of the scale, a reddish-orange can reflect confusion, ambivalence, cunning and repressed emotions. A very dark or muddy shade warns of uncontrolled self-indulgence.

Restoring the Balance

If orange is severely out of balance in your system, this will be reflected in the shades of the colour in your aura, but it will show in your external behaviour also. Too much and you're never satisfied, seeking endless gratification from food, possessions, sex or money. Too little and your joy in life may have been depleted by extreme deprivation of some kind, and this may result in lack of vitality and depression. To restore your aura to health, balance your chakras as shown on page 189 – and use the image on the facing page to inspire you.

Healing with Orange

Orange is a superb tonic for the reproductive system and it recharges your batteries when you are tired, stressed or ill. In the right proportions, it also acts as a natural corrective agent, enabling you to know when "enough is enough", and restoring you to health and vitality.

Illuminating yellow

The signature colour of the Solar Plexus chakra – the centre that generates your sense of personal power, self-worth and achievement – yellow is also the colour of the sun, with its positive qualities of radiance, openness, clarity and warmth. The power of yellow in your life is twofold: on the physical level it enables you to be comfortable with yourself; intellectually, it promotes clear thinking, open communication, analysis, logic, judgment and intelligence. Yellow can give you the supreme self-confidence to realize your ideas, but it may also overwhelm and confuse you with too many possibilities.

Shades of Yellow

A bright, vibrant yellow in your aura reflects the sunny side of your personality. A very light yellow shade indicates areas of mystical thought, while a dull yellow points to confused, ill-defined or unimaginative ideas. It could also reveal secretiveness and dishonesty.

Restoring the Balance

If many negative aspects of yellow are reflected in your aura, your self-esteem is probably at a low ebb. Your confidence, courage, sense of intrinsic value and sense of humour may be lost. You can restore harmony to your system by balancing your chakras as described on page 189. Breathe the clean, clear energy of pure yellow into your Solar Plexus chakra, using the image facing this page for inspiration.

Healing with Yellow

Psychic healers use yellow to improve digestion and to eliminate toxins from the liver and gall bladder; its gently stimulating effects can also strengthen and calm an exhausted nervous system, and this helps to promote clear, effective thinking. On an emotional level, it is used to restore self-esteem and pleasure in life.

Life-giving green

The soothing, power of green brings tranquillity and harmony to the very core of your being. It is the colour energy that radiates from your Heart chakra, where it governs your ability to give and receive love, empathize with others, and find peace within yourself. Nature's own colour, green brings you into a relaxed, healing contact with the world around you; but, as in nature, it can also stagnate and decay, leading to festering emotions such as jealousy and resentment.

Shades of Green

A clear, bright, green in the aura is a wholesome sign of fine judgment, adaptability and balance, while a very light shade denotes spirituality, the ability to heal and an intensely sympathetic nature. On the other hand, if someone is "green with envy", this would be indicated by a dark or olive green shade. A muddy or dull green points to cunning, deceit, emotional deprivation and secretiveness, a yellow-green to possessiveness and a grey-green to depression.

Restoring the Balance

If you don't have a healthy balance of green in your aura, you may literally look "green around the gills". But however stale or sluggish you're feeling, you can use the power of pure, fresh, green to detoxify your system. Do this by balancing your chakras as described on page 189, and use the image on the facing page for inspiration while you breathe the invigorating energy of green into your Heart chakra.

Healing with Green

Green has a powerful restorative energy that regulates the heart and blood pressure, heals the lungs and chest and also removes toxins from the system. As green is the most relaxing of all colours, it soothes your frazzled nerves when you've been under pressure; it also assists the circulatory system and aids balance and harmony.

Inspirational blue

The cool, calm power of blue connects you with the infinite vistas of the sky and ocean, evoking spirituality, devotion and a sense of the sacred. Blue is also the colour of your Throat chakra, your centre of communication. When activated, this chakra inspires you to speak in the spirit of truth. Blue is an immensely far-reaching force that can be expressed through an independent personality, an aloof idealist and, at the other extreme, a deeply emotional person who often feels overwhelmed by powerful feelings.

Shades of Blue

A clear sky-blue in your aura indicates self-confidence and mental clarity; turquoise signifies a tranquil attitude; and a soft, light hue indicates devotion to an ideal. If the blue is very pale, this points to superficial thoughts. Deeper shades may mean that you're "feeling blue" due to a phase of sadness, or a more long-term, serious depression. But some dark blues are very positive – midnight blue is a sign of enhanced intuition, while navy blue reflects a protective energy at work.

Restoring the Balance

When your system has been affected by the negative aspects of blue, your faith in life can be undermined, and you may lose perspective. You can correct these problems by doing the chakra balancing exercise described on page 189. Using the facing page, restore the effectiveness of your Throat chakra by breathing in the brilliant energy of pure blue.

Healing with Blue

Blue is an excellent pain-reliever. Psychic healers also use it to trigger the body's own healing resources – its cooling properties are useful in the treatment of thyroid, mouth and throat problems, and fever. Blue is also used to heal spiritual and emotional trauma, restoring a sense of peace and calm.

Visionary indigo

The hypnotic, midnight blue of indigo has a transformative effect on your body and soul. It is the sign of a true mystic and is also the colour of the Brow chakra. This psychic centre enhances clairvoyance and expands your psychic vision so that you are able to see past, present and future as a unified picture. Because indigo stimulates the right side of your brain, it triggers your creative imagination, deepens your intuition, and gives you a serene, inner confidence that you know the truth. But these same qualities may also make you a remote and isolated figure, who finds it difficult to communicate with others.

Shades of Indigo

Indigo often shades into purple and violet tones in the aura, and these colours all connect you with higher levels of consciousness, promoting a wonderful sense of peace and spiritual harmony. But a pronounced level of indigo in your aura may also cause you problems. People with mystical qualities are often misunderstood, and this may result in exclusion and loneliness.

Restoring the Balance

You may be absorbed in psychic visions, but if this leads to isolation and remoteness, these are warning signs that should be heeded. By doing the chakra balancing exercise described on page 189, you can bring yourself down to earth without losing contact with your higher self. Using the image on the facing page for inspiration, integrate indigo into your entire being, and stay in touch with the joy of ordinary life.

Healing with Indigo

Indigo has a powerful sedative action and can act as a light anaesthetic. Psychic healers use it to treat mental disturbance, as it helps to clear the head. If your nerves have been frayed to the point of breakdown, indigo will come to your rescue, and restore your inner balance.

Mystical violet

The gem-like radiance of pure violet heralds a transcendent level of consciousness, informed by the desire to know eternal truth. It signifies enlightened thought and a profound connection with the spiritual world. Known as the colour of kings, violet is worn by royalty, bishops or popes to indicate power beyond the temporal. It is also the colour of the Crown chakra, the psychic centre that links you with knowledge from the deepest sources of spiritual wisdom.

Shades of Violet

When you see violet in the aura, it is usually bold and bright, and has no negative aspects. Even when the colour is dark, this is not a problem – on the contrary, it signifies a near perfect connection with the divine. You may feel magnetically attracted to violet, as it has a strong psychic influence; this is fine, as long as you don't use it to fuel a fantasy of yourself as a superior spirit in a bid to escape the demands of daily life.

Restoring the Balance

It is highly unusual to see a preponderance of violet in the aura – in fact some people have very little. This may result in a "deadened" feeling that life has no meaning beyond the purely physical. By doing the chakra balancing exercise described on page 189, you can integrate a healthy level of violet into your aura. Using the image on the facing page for inspiration, breathe violet into your Crown centre, to help you stay in harmonious contact with your higher self.

Healing with Violet

Violet calms the brain and nervous system and helps dispel irrational obsessions and neuroses. It is used by psychic healers to treat shock trauma or emotional distubance. Violet has a cooling effect on rashes and sunburn, the pineal gland and the eyes, and balances your metabolism. It is used also to provide effective psychic protection.

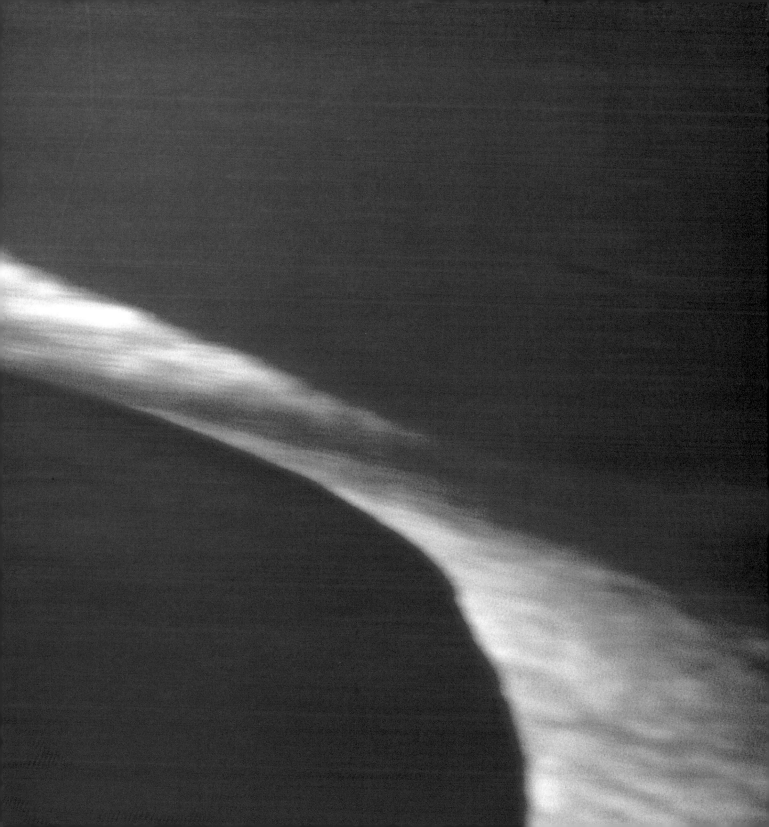

Purifying white

The quiet grace of newly fallen snow is the perfect image of both the beauty and silence of white, the colour that represents the fully awakened spirit. Its pure, clean energy expands your mind into a luminous stream of white light, connecting you to the highest levels of consciousness through your Crown chakra. This experience brings profound spiritual relief and release, and an immensely peaceful sense of distance from all emotional confusion and mental clutter.

Shades of White

White is very rarely seen in the aura, as it signifies a fully enlightened being. If white *is* present, it will usually emanate from the crown of the head, and is a sign that the person is receiving inspiration from a high spiritual source. When this happens, pure light is drawn in from the cosmos and filters throughout the aura, enhancing its radiance.

Restoring the Balance

Connecting with white is a perfect way to cleanse yourself in mind, body and spirit. Focus your breathing as described on page 189, then imaginatively link yourself with the highest source of spiritual energy. Using the picture opposite for inspiration, visualize white light flowing into your Crown centre, and travelling through all your chakras in a shining beam of energy. With each breath, expand this white light into every part of your aura. Finally, seal the energy within yourself by visualizing a band of gold around your entire aura.

Healing with White

When you are in complete despair, white can exert a powerful, healing force. It purifies your thoughts, promotes calm reflection and helps to restore you to a wider, healthier, spiritual perspective. This means that you can accept events that you cannot control, and have faith that they can't destroy your spirit.

Encountering spirits

5

Could you be a shaman?

Great healers and clairvoyants, shamans are found in many cultures, including Native American and Australian aboriginal groups. Most shamans pass through a gateway to the "other world" of spirits. Here, they can talk to their ancestors and get help from them. Shamans enter a sacred space where they go into a trance, meditate and plug directly into the planet's energy.

If you have an unusually close affinity with plants and animals, you may feel a natural empathy with shamanism. Being close to the natural world can make you better able to help the people close to you. You'll "know" what's good for them and what's bad. You can strengthen this bond with nature by making regular links with plant spirits as shown on page 216. You also can create your own version of a sacred space (see below). Going inside this sanctuary may be your first experience of meeting your "real" self, with a new sense of connection with the world around you. Shamanism is as much about drawing on the reservoir of ancient wisdom as it is about reaching out to help others.

A SACRED SPACE

To experience what it's like being a shaman, create your own sacred space. From this "home base" you can contact the essence of your secret inner world, using all your senses.

1 *Focus on your breathing as described on page 181. Invoke the image of an outdoor space where you feel completely secure and at peace with yourself – it could be a beach, a woodland, a river bank or a favourite spot in your garden.*

2 *As you meditate, visualize yourself right there in your safe place. Feel the ground beneath your feet, and sense the air around you. Open all your senses and explore the landscape – there may be trees, flowers, sand, rocks, glittering sea spray or a river flowing between grassy banks.*

3 *Take time to absorb the spirit of this unique place, letting its atmosphere soak through your skin.*

4 *Using your breath as a focus, breathe in and hold the picture steady. Then, on the out breath, let the picture grow in intensity and movement, and watch as mists form and billow.*

5 *When you feel completely at one with this vision, hold the image, then allow yourself to dissolve into the mist. When you're ready, return to your everyday world.*

6 *Repeat this connection frequently until it becomes as easy as stepping outside your own front door. In time, your sacred place will develop a life of its own – you'll be able to watch flowers and trees growing and see all the natural cycles of life taking place.*

THE SPIRAL PATH

A shaman has to walk the "Spiral Path", a psychic initiation that gives insight into the mysteries of the inner and outer worlds. Labyrinth walking can be done in a similar spirit in order to gain personal knowledge.

The journey to the centre
The inward path, winding towards the centre or heart, is the path of the self. On the way, the individual tries to conquer and overcome fears and pain, promotes hope and joy and faces the shadow or dark sides of human nature. Only then is complete self-acceptance possible.

Going to the outer edge
The corresponding path leads outwards into the world. This is where the shaman or individual gets in touch with the planet. The goal is to meet the secret spirits in all living things, and see the entire "web of being" linked by a stream of endless energy.

Complete union
If you complete this psychic journey, you probably would have met dark aspects of the self and possibly encountered strange spirit creatures. The reward for completing this psychic journey is the experience of "falling into wonder" – a unity with the endless, vibrating energies of the universe.

Contact with departed spirits

When you're fully absorbed in your daily life, you may not have much time and space to think deeply about other levels of existence. But all that can change when someone close to you dies; this is the moment when you may start to wonder what happens to the human spirit after death. Most psychics believe that the souls of people who have died enter the astral or spirit worlds. You may already have visited these realms during an astral dream, or when astral travelling (see page 230), and met the spirit of someone you've loved. Some people also claim to do so during "near death" experiences.

A visit to the spirit world is not always a one-way journey – a departed spirit may decide to come and visit you. In fact, some psychics believe that it is not possible to "command" the spirit of a person to return against his or her will, it is the spirit who decides to make contact with you. Many people report experiencing visits from loved ones shortly after their deaths. If this happens, you might simply accept it as a natural event, without feeling the need to explore the matter further.

On the other hand, it may make you very curious about what happens after death – you may even feel

Insider info MEDIUMS

The role of a medium *is to contact the spirits of people who have died and are now in the astral or spirit world. The medium usually does this on behalf of people who have lost someone close to them.*

Contact between loved ones *can be very comforting. For instance, the person who died may have been too ill to express his or her feelings or to say "goodbye" and the relatives also may not have had an opportunity for a final exchange. It is a good chance for both to tie up loose ends and resolve any outstanding questions.*

Mediums link with spirits *mainly through spirit guides that they know and trust. The guides establish contact – but only if the spirits wish to be in communication.*

The spirit of someone who has died *may appear vividly alive to the medium, as if he or she is in the same room; or the medium may sense the person so completely that he/she is able to give a realistic description of the person. The medium also can have two-way conversations with the spirit.*

a compelling desire to be in contact with spirits on the astral level. In this case, it's most important to seek expert guidance. Even if you have an inborn gift for contacting spirits, you can be drawn into subtle, nebulous areas that can create illusions and delusions. Do plenty of research first, and consult a highly recommended spiritualist association, a trained medium or a reputable psychic development group.

Steps to Mastering Mediumship

A development group under the supervision of a competent medium or teacher is the place in which to work on any innate abilities. Silence and meditational exercises will be used in order to make individuals more receptive to the currents in the spirit world. The teacher will work with you to help develop your gifts of clairvoyance (see page 248), clairaudience (hearing voices), and clairsentience (see page 216) – all of which come into play when you make yourself a channel for spirits to communicate through.

THE OUIJA BOARD

Many people try to contact departed spirits with the help of a ouija board – this has letters and numbers on it and a sliding pointer that spells out messages in response to questions. It can be used by one person or a group. Though it is generally regarded as an entertaining psychic "game", the ouija is a frightening experience for some because it tends to attract lower spirit entities. These have been known to tease and scare people by spelling out worrying messages – including warnings of death or injury. The safest way to use the board is to invoke only the highest and most benevolent spirits before you ask your questions. Prayerful meditation before beginning can create the best atmosphere.

If you've ever wondered whether it's possible for you to initiate communication with a being from the spirit world, the answer is "yes" – but it is often easier to receive help from a spirit guide. Unfortunately, you can easily be led astray in your quest. While Native American chieftains, cosmic brothers from distant galaxies, or famous people from history have all been hailed as the only true spirit guides, the reassuring truth is that a spirit guide or mentor does not have to project a distinct identity. In fact, the most effective ones are the least "personalized", and don't even have names. Essentially, the absence of personality in a guide is the sign of a truly genuine force. Authentic spirit mentors never interfere or intervene in anyone's daily life. No benevolent being would tell you what to do. Your guide's role is to unconditionally advise you. They can also assist you to make contact with the spirit world, directing you wisely and safely.

You can safely link up with a spirit guide as described opposite, as long as you invoke this guidance with trust and goodwill. Alternatively, if you think you'd feel more comfortable doing this with other people, always choose a highly reputable psychic development group.

Are your messages real?

A quick way to check whether you're dealing with an "authentic" spirit is to see whether you agree with the following statements.

There is a distinct feeling of love and wisdom.

Taken out of context, the messages have a general meaning.

The information you received was inspirational and thought-provoking.

If, on the other hand, the list of statements below more accurately reflects your experiences, then you shouldn't take this source seriously.

When messages come through, they refer to personal matters.

The guide has an impressive sounding name.

The guide tells you what to do.

He or she has told you that you were special.

The guide says that its message is vital to save the world.

RECEIVING SPIRIT MESSAGES

Perform the following exercise to connect with the spirit world. Ask a reliable friend to tape the words you receive.

1 *Use the exercise on page 181 to become deeply relaxed, and breathe steadily until you feel fully balanced.*

2 *Powerfully invoke your desire to be linked to the highest forces of good through prayerful meditation. Ask for help to make a clear connection with your guiding spirit.*

3 *Visualize the top of your crown centre (see page 187) opening out like a funnel of pure light, and take your consciousness as high as you can. Now take it a little higher, and then raise it even further upwards.*

4 *Visualize yourself enveloped from head to toe in a column of pure light. You may be aware that words are filling your head out of nowhere.*

5 *Speak these words out loud as they come to you. If you notice that your attention is wandering, you have broken the link. You can either guide yourself back into communication, or stop and try again some other time.*

6 *Return to your regular state of awareness by visualizing a taproot of energy leading down into the inner core of the earth.*

7 *Draw on that energy, feeling deep security and pleasure in your physical existence.*

Messages from beyond

In times of acute crisis or trauma, you may have uttered a desperate but unconscious cry into the universe, begging for an answer to your dilemma. Sometimes, these calls for help trigger a response; it may arrive in the form of a dream, or through some event that turns out to be a "heaven-sent" solution. This is because you have unwittingly achieved a form of pure communication to the higher powers.

You don't necessarily require faith to appeal to them; the ability to be true to your inner self, and remain open to all sources of help, is just as important. Moreover, sheer inspiration can get to the heart of many difficulties, though it often means changing your perspective.

When you're struggling with a dilemma that tests you to your limits, every nerve in your body can feel wired. Ironically, such tension may also make you less receptive to the subtle ways in which messages are delivered. Try and keep part of your mind relaxed and open, so you have the mental space to sense the hidden meaning behind odd words or phrases that arrive "out of the blue". Answers tend to sneak into your mind when you're involved in mundane tasks such as brushing your teeth or driving your car. You can often be more open to inspiration when you're physically occupied. Once you learn to keep an open mind, you'll recognize signals promptly and trust what you receive.

JUST ASK!

When seeking divine guidance, always make sure you know exactly what you want.

1 *Concentrate on the essence of your question, and formulate the simplest way of expressing it. This helps to generate a positive result.*

2 *If possible, choose a night when the moon is waxing (half way between a new and full moon). Look deep into the night sky, then send your question to the guiding forces of the heavens.*

3 *If you have a dream that night, and recall it when you wake up, write its details in your psychic journal. This could be your answer.*

4 *Otherwise, note any unusual insights that arrive; they will certainly come from a higher source of intuition. Accept these messages without analyzing them too much, even if they don't immediately make sense. In time, their meaning will become clear.*

HOW TO LISTEN

Messages arrive from beyond in a variety of ways. The following are just a few examples.

Key words

You gradually become aware that a single word seems to pop up all the time – in a newspaper headline, on a poster, in a television ad, on a road sign, even on a food wrapper. As soon as you've realized this, the meaning of that word will be clear.

Images

As with word messages, you'll suddenly notice yourself seeing the same image over and over. This may be something as simple as an arrow pointing in one direction. The moment you acknowledge this, you'll know what the message is saying.

Inspiration

You may feel compelled to take an intuitive leap in the dark and reach for a particular item among many – a fortune cookie, a rune, or a playing or tarot card. Whatever you discover, there is your answer.

Coincidence

Sometimes the message seems to drop in front of you out of the sky – as you're walking along, you see something on the pavement. It may be a bird's feather, a coin or a discarded flower. As soon as you pick the object up, your mind recognizes the message that is being sent.

You are surrounded by countless angelic beings who act as messengers between earth and heaven, and link you with the highest good. The most familiar of these is your guardian angel, the protective being that presides over your life from the moment of your birth (see page 318). However, an array of different angels are responsible for delivering the life-changing messages that act as torchlights in darkness and provide higher guidance, healing and protection.

You may have been living from day to day without a particular sense of purpose, unaware of these mighty angels who are particularly concerned about your personal destiny. They can see the path you need to follow for your ultimate spiritual fulfilment; moreover, if you know how to "ask", they will help you to find your way, and restore you to your spiritual roots.

Angels are known to prefer quiet, spiritual atmospheres; with this in mind, reserve a special place in your home, and introduce some of the elements described below. Ideally, this will also be the place where you meditate regularly.

Angels always act in a spirit of unconditional love – they will unfailingly point you towards your true destination, stimulating your mind and imagination, sharpening your perception of the world and supporting your instinct to do good. They can also bring you dazzling insights – and a sense of true enlightenment that will enhance your psychic creativity.

A WELCOMING ATMOSPHERE

The qualities that most appeal to angels include:

Calm
Regular meditation brings you inner quiet and peace, and this permeates the space around you.

Candlelight
Light a candle every day – its steady flame will attract quiet, gentle illumination into your life.

Cleanliness
Always keeping your meditation space tidy and dirt free.

Simplicity
Keep your space clear and uncluttered.

Joy
What makes you happy? Is it music, a picture or an exquisite shell? Use and enjoy these in your meditation space – angels love happiness and are said to dance on the vibrations of your laughter.

Many people have actually seen angels – usually at times of great crisis. One of the most famous sightings was witnessed by soldiers on the battlefield at Mons, in France, during the 1914–18 war. In the midst of the slaughter, a huge, radiant being appeared, giving comfort and love to the wounded and dying; it was the legendary Angel of Mons.

There are several common factors in eyewitness descriptions of angels: the overwhelming impact is that of a tall, shining presence that is so bright, it dazzles the eye. The streams of light that emanate from these androgenous beings appear to be wing-like forms, and the emotional projection is one of great strength, reassurance and profound love. Angelic forces rarely speak in words, but the messages they bring penetrate directly into human consciousness, and are clearly understood.

At any time of your life, you can appeal to the archangels for guidance, even though you may never see one. You must know how to ask, however, and this means being clear about what is going wrong in your life. You may feel adrift in your career, or in your relationships, or you may have no sense of inner peace. Take some time to focus these concerns around the different strengths offered by each archangel – they are the messengers who will respond most directly to your problems. Clear your mind and compose your thoughts in your psychic journal; and trust your intuition to lead you to the angel that can help you most at this point in your life. Then, approach your chosen angel through the avenues suggested here – those of meditation and prayer.

THE ARCHANGELS

Gabriel

The messenger of divine comfort, Gabriel represents female power. Gabriel announced the coming of Christ and is thought to be the messenger who dictated the Koran. This is the angel to invoke to help with fertility problems; the archangel also brings news.

Metatron

This heavenly scribe has many eyes and records everything that happens; his key task is to reunite male and female principles. His name means "mentor", and he is the angel to invoke when you seek spiritual teaching and guidance.

Michael

With his mighty sword of truth, Michael stands for justice, and springs to the defence of the weak and downtrodden. When you're at your lowest ebb, ask for his courage, fortitude and integrity. He will help you to defeat any terrifying elements that haunt your life.

Raphael

Turn to Raphael when you are feeling ill; he will bring you a deeply regenerative energy that can restore you to health.

Raquel

The angel of ethical procedure, Raquel monitors all aspects of behaviour. Invoke him when you are seeking justice and the right course of action – he will help you to make those difficult choices in your life.

Saraquel

This is the teacher of Moses – a fallen angel who then repented. If you feel that you've done wrong and seek forgiveness, turn to him to restore you to your peace of mind.

Uriel

The angel of enlightenment and the upholder of moral teaching, Uriel misses nothing and is a steadfast doorkeeper. His energy is uncompromising, he will always "tell it like it is". Appeal to him when you feel mentally overwhelmed and confused.

ANGELIC MEDITATION

Let your chosen archangel bring you messages in the stillness of meditation.

1 *Focus on your breathing as described on page 181, and let yourself become perfectly serene and still inside. If you wish, you can hold a picture of the archangel you have chosen, or a card inscribed with the angel's name.*

2 *Now shift your attention to your heart centre, and open yourself completely and trustingly to the archangel's loving presence.*

3 *Allow any form of communication from the angel to enter your consciousness freely; accept, trust and absorb what you are given in the spirit of truth.*

4 *Remain in quiet contact with the angel until you feel that you have thoroughly absorbed its guidance at every level of your being; then return to your normal state of awareness.*

REACH OUT TO YOUR ANGEL

Talk to your angel in simple words spoken from the heart.

1 *Choose the angel who can help you most – for instance, if you're feeling bullied and intimidated by more forceful people, Michael can help you. Think how you would talk to a trusted friend when asking for advice, then imagine that you are addressing Michael in the same way. Write your words down in the form of a brief letter.*

2 *For example, you could say, "Dear Michael, I'm so frightened, and uncertain all the time. I let people walk all over me, and I've lost all confidence in myself. Please help me to find my inner strength, and protect me from all my fears. Thank you for*

knowing what I'm going through, and for standing up for people like me who have lost their courage. The feeling that you're always on my side is a true comfort."

3 *At bedtime, calm your thoughts and trust that your angel is ready to come to you. Then either read your prayer silently or say it out loud, knowing that your words are being heard and understood.*

4 *A good night's sleep, after which you awaken rested and confident, may be a sign your prayer was heard. Or you can always "ask" for a more concrete response (see above).*

Can you identify different spirits?

Have you ever met a ghost? Those who've had first-hand experience describe remarkably similar sensations: the sudden feeling of extreme cold, an unpleasant odour and an unsettling sense that something is very amiss. A ghostly form is simply a non-physical manifestation of someone who is dead. Many old houses claim to have a ghost-in-residence. One example might be a spectral presence that walks on the staircase at certain times. Beings such as these are earthbound spirits; they have failed to move on to the astral or spirit world because, for some reason, they are unable to leave their familiar home ground. There is some evidence that they can be helped to move on (see below).

A poltergeist, or "noisy spirit", is quite a different matter. It gets up to all sorts of mischief, moving objects around, breaking things and making violent, loud noises. It certainly wants to be noticed, whereas ghosts are usually shy and elusive.

The latest evidence suggests that, far from being a spirit presence, a poltergeist may manifest from the disturbed energy of a living person. One often appears in the home of a young person who is emotionally disturbed; he or she may be completely unaware of having any connection with the mysterious noises and activity. Fortunately, once any hidden problems are acknowledged and treated, the poltergeist usually goes away.

FREEING A GHOST

Rescuing an earthbound being demands great love and freedom from fear.

1 *Using your breath as a focus, meditate on the unity of all life, as described on page 181. Know that, as you breathe, everything else breathes.*

2 *Now focus on your heart centre, and visualize it opening out like a giant blossom, basking in sunlight. With each in-breath, take the sun's warmth and healing energy deep into your cells, to the core of your being.*

3 *With each out-breath, share this warmth with everything around you, without exception.*

4 *Now ask the angelic forces of love to come to you, and welcome them inside your heart. Feel them repairing and healing your aura, wrapping you inside a powerful energy field of protection and strength.*

5 *At this point you can communicate with the ghost or spirit energy; if you feel the time is right, lovingly suggest that it moves into the realms of light.*

6 *The spirit will only respond positively to being liberated when you are completely free of fear yourself. If you have the smallest doubt, do not intervene; you should never approach a spirit alone, and without strengthening yourself in advance.*

What spirit is there?

If you're not certain of the nature of the spirit you've encountered, look at the statements below. If you agree with the first three:

❏ Objects get thrown around or move on their own;
❏ There are sudden thuds or other unexplained noises;
❏ The spirit seems to know how to make you angry;

This would indicate poltergeist activity, so you should check whether someone in the house is suffering from a hidden psychological disturbance.

If, on the other hand, the following statements are more indicative of the spirit's behaviour:

❏ The presence always appears at the same time;
❏ The activity is always in the same place;
❏ The spirit is apparently unaware of your presence;
❏ You feel that you vaguely recognize the being;
❏ The atmosphere suddenly becomes very cold;

Then the presence is most likely to be a ghost. If the ghost is upsetting your life, and you want it to leave, you might try to set it free yourself. But this should only be attempted when you are psychically strong; if you have any doubt, ask for help from a trained medium recommended by a spiritualist group, or a priest trained in exorcism.

*Psychic
protection* 6

How strong is your aura?

When you balance your chakras as described on page 189, you strengthen your aura by activating levels of pure energy deep inside yourself. As a result, the harmony restored to your mind, body and spirit is reflected in a strong, clear, shining aura. This shows that you have the psychic energy to live your life to the full, and you radiate an almost tangible glow of inner security and confidence. Sadly, however, this strength won't last if you haven't corrected the more negative traits and imbalances in your character – your aura will inevitably revert back to its weaker, unhealthier state.

Psychic healing and enhanced intuition can certainly transform your life – but only if you help the process along. Do this by building up your store of self-knowledge; keep regular notes in your psychic journal, acknowledging and accepting your particular weaknesses and strengths with candour and good humour. Try to correct your negative habits, but most important of all, reach out for any

How strong are you?

Look at the questions below and tick the ones that relate to you.

When you have a disagreement with anyone, do you drop any negative feelings:
- ❏ **a**   Within minutes.
- ❏ **b**   24 hours.
- ❏ **c**   Several days or even weeks.

When you're talking to someone who is in a bad mood or distressed, do you:
- ❏ **a**   Maintain your own equilibrium.
- ❏ **b**   Let that person's pain affect you.
- ❏ **c**   Feel drained afterwards.

When you visit a friend who is sick or in the hospital do you:
- ❏ **a**   Know you can bring a positive atmosphere with you.
- ❏ **b**   Feel slightly uneasy around anyone who's ill.
- ❏ **c**   Become unwell yourself.

When someone compliments you, do you:
- ❏ **a**   Say "Thank you!" but pay little attention.
- ❏ **b**   Feel embarrassed and turn the compliment back.
- ❏ **c**   Glow with pleasure and tell everyone.

If you someone criticizes you, do you:
- ❏ **a**   Acknowledge that there is some truth in it, and try to adjust any imbalances to your character accordingly.
- ❏ **b**   Fire back some negative words.
- ❏ **c**   Spend days, or even weeks, brooding about it.

opportunities to change your life for the better, rather than pretending that you don't have any problems.

However, much as you try to bolster your aura with healing, visualization and balancing work, any persistent weak spots will be revealed there. You can identify some of these by answering the questions below; don't be discouraged – you'll discover your positive qualities there as well.

If you answered...

❏ Mostly a's

You are very centered in your own energy – this is a good basis for maintaining your psychic health.

❏ Mostly b's

You respond naturally to the input around you and are highly sympathetic, but you need to develop a stronger sense of autonomy. Use visualization and meditation to help with this.

❏ Mostly c's

Faced with other people's opinions and moods you are easily shaken and put off-balance. Seek help and skilled healing to restore your inner balance.

Emergency action

However robust you are normally, situations can suddenly overwhelm your inner resources. Here are three examples of how to get yourself out of trouble:

When talking to a distressed friend, you may realize that, while he or she is obviously feeling better by the minute, you are becoming totally exhausted. This is easy to rectify: simply fold your arms across your solar plexus – this prevents you from "bleeding" psychic energy.

You may suddenly find yourself in a threatening situation, for instance, when you're walking alone at night. If this happens, visualize a powerful golden light all around you. This often has the effect of making you invisible to others.

If you're having a lot of trouble with someone – parent, child or colleague, for example – visualize yourself in a clear bubble of white light. Spend several moments just being comfortable and happy inside. Then, conjure up an image of the person with whom you are having problems. Now imagine that person in his or her own separate bubble of light. Draw a figure of eight between them, then visualize cutting apart the two bubbles and watch the other person's bubble gently float away. Implement this exercise in a detatched manner. Performed correctly this is a powerful healing tool.

Amulets and talismans

Do you have a special mascot that makes you feel safe and strong, or always brings you luck? If so, you're part of a psychic tradition that is as old as humanity itself; this recognizes that certain objects either have powerful qualities in themselves, or can be endowed for a particular purpose.

These potent items fall into two groups – amulets and talismans – but they equip you with extra psychic strength in different ways. An amulet is protective in its action and diverts evil influences from the owner; its traditional purpose is to ward off the "evil eye", the common phrase used when someone is directing negative energy at you.

Amulets may repel danger, but they don't necessarily attract luck. This is the role of the talisman – a special charm with the power to bring you good fortune. Charm bracelets remain a popular item today. They enable the wearer to amass a collection of tiny objects, some acting as amulets.

The best way to protect yourself from negative energies is to keep your aura strong and healthy as described on page 314. But if you are intuitively drawn to an object because it makes you feel particularly good, follow your instincts. Keep your mascot close to you at all times; you could wear it on a chain around your neck, on a key-ring, hang it in your car, or keep it safely hidden away in your purse or wallet. Its presence will reassure you and give you a sense of extra good fortune and protection.

"Abracadabra" *Used by magicians all over the world, this is one of the oldest magic formulas and means "Speak the blessing". Written on a piece of silk and worn around the neck, it wards off disease.*

Beads *Glass eye-beads represent the "all seeing" deity that averts danger.*

Cat *The ancient Egyptians believed cats were sacred, and represented the moon. Black cats are thought to be lucky, but some people fear them. Only you will know whether a cat mascot will benefit you, so trust your intuition.*

Coin *This is traditionally silver, but if it's the right coin for you, the humble penny will bring you health and wealth.*

**Crosses –
Ankh or key cross** *This originated in Egypt and symbolizes life and immortality.*

Greek cross, or the cross of St Benedict *Both these crosses send off evil spirits with the commanding message "Get thee behind me Satan!"*

Roman cross *This was a powerful protective amulet long before Christianity.*
St Andrew's cross *Traditionally worn as a potent amulet against bad influences.*
Tau cross *Shaped like a "T" and worn to protect against diseases such as epilepsy. It is symbolic of eternal life and is also used to guard the spirit.*

Dragon *Usually used to enhance peace and felicity, dragons also help the wearer to conquer enemies in war – you must choose how to use its power.*

Fish *The symbol of early Christianity, fish charms attract abundance and riches, and represent creation and fertility.*

Four-leafed clover or shamrock *These are very lucky plants, renowned for bringing you luck, whether it's in money, gambling or love.*

Frog *A talisman for wealth, fertility, health and long life, frog charms should be worn by lovers to ensure a happy relationship, blessed with mutual ardour and constancy.*

Garment *Any piece of clothing can bring the wearer luck – especially in competitive sports. Football players often have "lucky" socks, and some tennis players wear the same shirt throughout a tournament.*

Hand of Fatima *A powerful amulet, this is very popular in the Middle East. It is a hand of benediction, and is mainly used on the doors or walls of the house to protect all within.*

Heart *This is usually worn to attract love and joy. At one time, however, a heart amulet was used to prevent evil spells being used on the wearer.*

Horseshoe *The ancient Greeks and Romans used these to bring wealth and happiness to the home. To make it effective, the horseshoe must be nailed onto the door of the house pointing upward.*

Key *Worn by the Greeks and Romans to bring luck, enhance foresight and improve judgment, keys represented the god Janus, keeper of the gate of heaven and guardian of all doors. Janus was two-headed, and this enabled him to look into the future as well as the past. The Japanese use a key charm to bring wealth, love and happiness.*

Lamb *The Christian emblem of the Redeemer, a lamb carrying a cross and flag is worn as a protection against accidents, storms and diseases.*

Lizard *Painted on the outside of houses, a lizard brings good luck. It also promotes good eyesight and inspires wisdom.*

Lotus *This brings good luck, and is also used in India as an amulet to protect against illness and accidents. The flower represents Lakshmi, the goddess of beauty and fortune. The Egyptians saw the lotus as an emblem of the sun, and believed that it promoted clarity of thought and wisdom.*

Peacock *The feathers are said to bring bad luck as they are supposed to represent the evil eye. However, the bird itself is lucky and represents the triumph over death of everlasting life.*

Rabbit's foot *With its associations of fertility and speed, this lucky charm boosts your fortunes.*

Scarab *This ancient Egyptian talisman is a symbol of creation and resurrection, and brings physical, spiritual and mental health. It also acts as a protection from evil influences on the journey from the physical to the spirit planes.*

Seal of Solomon *Also known as the Star of David. It symbolizes the fire of the male and the water of the female merging in harmony. The crossed triangles also represent air and earth. The seal has six points, with an invisible seventh representing spiritual transformation, reflected within the inner eye of the magician, seer, priest or priestess.*

Spider *A talisman of success in business and money matters, spiders were placed inside a nutshell in medieval times, and worn around the neck to protect the wearer from illness.*

Teeth *In China a tiger's tooth is regarded as a precious talisman for people who gamble or speculate. In Russia imitation teeth are used as amulets to protect children from evil influences and diseases.*

Tortoise *The symbol of the earth, this protects against spells and various evil spirits.*

White heather *This Celtic talisman has the power to bring true love to the wearer.*

Wishbone *This familiar talisman brings you good luck and enables you to realize your dreams.*

Meeting your guardian angel

The moment you were born, you automatically acquired a powerful source of psychic protection – your guardian angel. Many psychics believe that the same protective being accompanies you through many lifetimes, seeing you safely through each stage of your soul's journey towards spiritual enlightenment.

On a day-to-day basis, your guardian angel watches over you at all times, and acts as an "invisible mender", constantly repairing and healing subtle areas of damage within your aura. This loving spiritual presence also protects you while you sleep, and wards off negative forces.

You may not even be aware that you have a guardian angel until something happens to trigger you into psychic contact – usually at a moment of emotional crisis. When this happens, the experience is unforgettable; it is the deep, intuitive recognition of unconditional love.

It could also be the first step in learning how to communicate with your guardian angel on a positive basis. However, this requires intelligent collaboration from you; your angel will certainly guide, heal and protect you, but that does not mean that you can avoid taking responsibility for your own actions.

Communication guidelines

Acknowledge the presence of your angel by your welcoming words and behaviour.

Choose a regular time to communicate with your guardian angel – many people do this at night before going to sleep.

Always ask for help in clear, simple terms.

If you are troubled with bad dreams or negative feelings, ask your guardian angel to protect you.

Remain open to messages from your angel at all times, especially if you sense that you are being warned of danger.

Don't be reckless with your personal safety – your guardian angel is there to protect you, but can't override your free will.

INVOKING YOUR GUARDIAN ANGEL

1 *Focus on your breathing until you become fully relaxed, as described on page 181.*

2 *Breathing gently into the heart centre, quietly ask your guardian angel to come close and make itself known to you.*

3 *Allow the angel to surround you with its healing energy, and feel yourself enfolded within gently caressing wings.*

4 *Let yourself relax completely into this warmth, and ask for any help that you may need.*

5 *Quietly absorb the responsive energy until you are completely satisfied. Although the angel does not require thanks, you'll feel a compelling need to express your gratitude.*

6 *Return to your regular state of physical awareness, and carry the sense of unconditional love with you into the rest of your day.*

Higher consciousness

7

The mystic way

Mysticism – whereby the individual aims to achieve direct intuitive experience of the divine – exists both within all major religions and outside in the form of personal spiritual practices. It is not an easy spiritual pathway; the mystic must first discover his or her "real" self in order to make direct contact with the Godhead – the ultimate, eternal, source of love.

If you want to become a mystic, you have to work at dissolving all the personality traits that obscure this true self. These are the complicated "veils of illusion", "masks", or "cloaks" that you use to conceal your inner identity, and they can all get in the way of achieving pure spiritual communication.

The best way to overcome this barrier is through honesty and regular meditation (see page 181); this will help you to confront who you really are; a true knowledge of your real self is often regarded as the highest form of intuition. Meditation may not bring you total enlightenment, but it can give you an authentic inner directive – and offers you a more fulfilling way to focus your existence. Being more focused helps you to get in touch with the universal forces of the cosmos. When this happens, you will find sublime peace from experiencing the mystical unity of all life; you'll realize that everything is inextricably linked, and that you are a single, living drop in the limitless ocean of creation. This hints at a wonderful truth shining through all living things, and inspires a unique sense of love and wonder.

Are you a natural mystic?

Give the following questions careful thought, then check those to which you have an affirmative response. At the end, add up how many you checked.

❑ Do you sometimes "know" exactly what to do?

❑ Are you actively involved in psychic self-development?

❑ Do you seek the truth?

❑ Have you ever felt that all human beings are connected in some way?

❑ Even at times of great material success, or after winning a much sought-after goal, do you sense that this is not all there is to life?

❑ Can you stand up for what you believe in, even if it goes against everyone else?

- ❏ Are you able to take a different direction to the rest of your group/family/peers, if it feels right for you?
- ❏ At times of great crisis or chaos, are you able to see beyond immediate events to some greater illumination?
- ❏ Do you always carry out what you promise, even when you don't feel like doing it?
- ❏ Do you make extra efforts to do tasks that others feel are unnecessary?
- ❏ Do you have an inclusive love of other human beings?
- ❏ Do you love yourself?
- ❏ Can you pick yourself up after disappointments, whatever they are, and carry on regardless?
- ❏ Are you very happy to be in your own company?
- ❏ Can you sense spiritual aspirations in others?

Assessment

❏ 2–3
Even if you only checked 2 or 3 questions, you already have some mystical traits.

❏ 4–10
You are walking towards a spiritual destination, even if you are not aware of it at this moment in time.

❏ 11–15
You are consciously on the road towards mystical union with the ultimate truth and spiritual illumination.

What is your karma?

Roughly understood as fate, karma is something we can affect. The law of karma says that every thought and feeling that you direct onto others, at any time, will react on you in equal measure. Our karma evolves through many past lives, but also operates in the here and now – at every second of your existence. You are the sum total of all your experiences over all lifetimes, and this is reflected in your life today. This means that you are completely responsible for your actions, and that you can choose to change your karma for the better at any moment during your life.

Your soul is your true essence and each incarnation gives it a chance to experience, learn and grow within a different physical body. In this way, you can perceive the karmic laws of cause and effect over several lifetimes, circumstances and situations. Karma is all-pervasive and powerful, yet it is also fair and compassionate; you can't escape its relentless lessons, but it is a force that attracts exactly what you need for your soul to progress.

So, whatever is happening in your life, good or bad, consider how each event relates to your karmic destiny: from this viewpoint, it is impossible to be in the wrong place at the wrong time.

Instant retribution

One day, after driving around for ages, I spotted a vacant parking space and drove ahead a little to give myself room to reverse back into it. Then, out of nowhere, another car slipped into my space. I got really mad, and directed a volley of unpleasant thoughts onto the driver with some force. I immediately realized that I had sent out very destructive energy, and tried to retrieve it as best I could.

The next day, as I was parking in another part of town, a car drew up alongside me; the driver yelled and shouted, claiming that I had stolen his place. He was in a terrible rage, and even threatened to drive into my car. I was scared and perplexed, as I had not seen him waiting. People gathered around, and I got out of my car to call his bluff; eventually he drove away, leaving me very shaken. Suddenly, I recognized that this violent energy was the very same one that I had expressed the previous day.

A KARMIC SEARCH

Use this exploratory
visualization to identify
your karmic path.

1 *Focus your breathing as described*
on page 181, until you feel completely
relaxed. Now open yourself to any
images and sensations that have
always had a particular meaning for
you. For instance, you may have an
instinctive love for a language, place,
building or landscape.

2 *Or, you may have unusually strong*
aversions; for no evident reason, you
may find that you react violently to an
animal, a uniform, a colour or odour.
This may be connected with the cause
of your last death – especially if you're
abnormally terrified of fire or knives.

3 *Allow these images to float into your*
mind without trying to rationalize
them. This will allow you to reconnect
with the deepest areas of your life
naturally and intuitively.

4 *Gradually, you'll make the creative*
link with your essential self – the core
identity that threads its way through
time. You may suddenly recognize an
image originating from eons past that
is eerily familiar to you at this very
moment. You are seeing yourself,
travelling along your karmic path.

Channelling spiritual messages

People who act as channels for spiritual information from the highest sources of knowledge practice a specialized form of mediumship. Regular mediums (see page 300) communicate with discarnate spirits – the souls of those who have died and inhabit the astral plane – whereas channellers deliver information from more impersonal contacts. These include spirits who have completed their round of earthly incarnations, the higher spirit guides and the Ascended Masters, who have journeyed beyond the soul.

Channelling can bring profound rewards; it is both a means of access to cosmic information and a

gateway that takes you into other dimensions. However, to achieve meaningful results, the integrity of your motivation is paramount. Your aim is to align yourself with the most authentic, trusted and benign sources: this takes intelligence, clarity of thought and dedicated work on self-awareness and healing.

Before you attempt the channelling exercise described on page 329, you should answer the questionnaire below to discover whether you are ready to proceed.

Are you ready to channel?

If you respond "yes" to a question, check the box next to it. Add up the checks and note your score.

What is your motive for wanting to bring through channelled material?

❏ **a** To obtain inspirational knowledge.
❏ **b** To expand your own awareness.
❏ **c** So others will respect you or pay more attention to you.

Describe your physical constitution:

❏ **a** You are rarely ill.
❏ **b** You commonly suffer from colds and other minor illnesses.
❏ **c** You often visit doctors, healers or pharmacies.

What sort of reading material do you favour?

❏ **a** Sensational stories.
❏ **b** Information covering a wide variety of topics.
❏ **c** Escapist romantic novels.

How much time are you prepared to spend on developing yourself as a clear channel?

❏ **a** When you feel like it.
❏ **b** However many years it may take.
❏ **c** Maybe once a week for an hour or two.

Are you someone who is:

❏ **a** Fearless.
❏ **b** Rarely frightened about anything.
❏ **c** Always watchful, expecting bad things to happen.

Assessment

❏ **3–5 c's**

You would be much better suited to some other form of psychic or healing work.

❏ **3–5 a's**

You seem to have some unrealistic ideas about yourself and you need to engage in more self discovery and healing before becoming involved in channelling.

❏ **3–5 b's**

You show great promise and could develop your channelling abilities very nicely, with dedication and purpose.

In recent years channelling has been widely used, but the quality of the messages varies enormously. Some warn of alarming changes to our planet, often in sensationalized, frightening terms. Other revelations have a core of authentic insight that are encouraging radical shifts in spiritual awareness. Always retain a discerning attitude to this information.

If you decide to try channelling, you should realize that this involves entering a focused state. As you may not remember the content of what has been directed through you, ask a trusted friend to tape or write down the messages that you receive.

Channelled information

When channelling comes into actuality through the spoken word, it permeates through the mind of all humanity and creates an energy of realization. Although this spiritual journey is never easy, the rewards are great.

"He may travel sometimes in the dark, and the illusion of darkness is very real. He may travel sometimes in a light so dazzling and bewildering that he can scarcely see the way ahead. He may know what it is to falter on the path and to drop under the fatigue of service and of strife, be temporarily distracted and wander down the bypaths of ambition, or self-interest and of material enchantment. But the lapse will be but brief. Nothing in heaven or hell, on earth or elsewhere can prevent the progress of the man who has awakened to the illusion, who has glimpsed the reality, beyond the glamour of the astral plane."

Alice Bailey, *A Treatise on White Magic*

ALIGNMENT TO LIGHT

1 *To prepare yourself for channelling, avoid eating a heavy meal beforehand, and allow at least two hours before you begin this procedure.*

2 *Follow the meditation exercise on page 181, and take plenty of time to achieve a deeply relaxed state.*

3 *Focus your energy into your heart centre. Hold it there, breathing regularly and deeply for at least three breaths.*

4 *Visualize a giant, diamond crystal poised above your head, and invoke the highest sources of divine spiritual consciousness.*

5 *Watch and acknowledge pure energy pouring into the crystal. Feel and hear the frequency of light vibrating through it.*

6 *At this point you may feel a responsive humming sound building up inside you – sing this sound out into the space around you.*

7 *Visualize the light being split into rainbow colours, and radiating from the crystal directly into your higher centres. Absorb these rays.*

8 *Let your mind become completely open and free – and don't think. Allow words to come into your mind, and speak them out loud without listening to what you are saying. This takes some practice, but you will learn to assess whether it is an authentic message.*

9 *When your channelling link has ended, return to your normal state. Make sure that you concentrate on your feet, and feel a strong root of energy linking them to the earth.*

10 *After completing this exercise, go for a walk and eat a solid meal with a hot drink.*

Index

A

Affirmations for
    well-being 192
Aids to mediation 183–4
Air (element) 237
Amulets 316–17
Angel(s) 306–9
    arch- 308
    guardian 306, 318–19
Angelic meditation 309
Animals, psychic 232
Archetypes 222
Ascended Masters 326
Assagioli, Roberto 17, 19,
    90
Assumptions 78–9
Astral
    attunement 113
    body 230
    channelling 115
    travel 230
    world 300
Astrology 236
Astronomical influences
    38
Aura 99–100, 186, 200
    discovering your 201
    exercises 101,106–7
    layers of 204
    photograph of 200
    plants 216
    portrait 204
    strong 314

B

Base chakra 58–9, 187,
    205, 272
Behaviourism 74
Biases 78–9
Birth chart 237
Black aura 202
Blue
    aura 202
    chakra 205
    healing with 288
Body language 36–7
Breathing 40–41
    butterfly 267
    in colour energy 189
    in the light 181
    in meditation 183
Brow chakra 68–9, 187,
    205, 273
Brown aura 203
Butterfly breathing
    267

C

Cabbala 260
Candle-gazing 176
Chakras 30–31, 32–3,
    186–9, 200, 204,
    272–3
    exercises 57; see also
        under individual
        chakras
    balancing 189
    singing to 275
    visualization of 275
Channeller(s) 175, 326
Channelling exercise 329
Chart, colour 277
Chemical sensing 34–5
Clairsentience 216
Clairvoyant 248
Collective unconscious
    222
Colour(s)
    of the aura 202
    of the chakras 30–31,
        186–9, 205
    chart 277
    healing with 276,
        278–9, 280–95
    states of mind and 32

C

Conflicts
    "Cutting the ties" 82–3
    transforming 86–7
Courage, affirmation for
    192
Crown chakra 70–71, 187,
    205, 272
Crystal(s)
    charging 271
    cleansing 270
    healing 270–71

D

Directed thought 190–93
Distant healing 264
Divine
    guidance 304
    will 190
Divining rod 256–7
Dowsing 256–9
    for water 257
Dream(s) 224–31
    diary 224
    directing 229
    interpretation 225, 226
    lucid 229
    temples 224

E

Earth (element) 236
Electro-sensing 33–4
Empath(y) 174, 264
Employment,
    affirmation for 192
Energy
    etheric 188
    good use of 88
    inanimate objects
        214–15
    plants 216
    reading an object's 215
    types of 28, 30–31, 33
ESP *see* Telepathy
Etheric energy 188
Exercises
    acknowledge who you
        are 90
    angelic meditation 309
    ask divine guidance
        304
    astral travel 230
    aura check 201
    aura portrait 204
    balancing chakras 189
    biases 79

breathing into the
    heart 47
butterfly breathing 267
channelling 329
connecting with the
    breath 46
connecting to the
    chakras 57
cutting the ties 83
directing your dreams
    229
dowsing for water 257
exploring your aura
201
finding lost objects 259
group force 196
healing circle of
    colour 279
healing with a crystal
    271
healing a plant 268
healing powers 265
hearing 178
imaginary journey 222
inner child 48
inner guide 49
invoking your
    guardian angel 319

King Arthur's table 92
making a divining rod
    256
meditation 45–7
observing yourself 80
perception shifting 198
powering your crystal
    271
programme your
    pendulum 259
psychic focus 199
psychic sight 176
pyschokinetic 195
radiant colour therapy
    279
reading an object's
    energies 215
receiving spirit
    messages 303
receiving unseen
    images 210
relaxation 181
remote viewing 213
sacred space 298
seeing the aura 51
sending arrows of
    communication 107
sensing energy 50

sensing energy of
    plants 216
shamanism 298
sing to your chakras
    275
smell 178
sting like a bee 267
talk to your angel 309
taste 179
thought energy 195
touch 179
transform conflict 87
understanding energy
    use 89
using a scrying tool
249
visualizing the aura
    106

F

Fate line 253
Fire (element) 236
Five senses 176
Flowers
    language of 217
    meanings of 218–19
Four forces 74–5
Freudian therapy 75

G

Gardening, psychic 269
Gestalt psychology 94
Ghost, freeing a 310
Gold aura 203
Green
    aura 202
    chakra 205
    healing with 286
Grey aura 203
Group
    force 196
    guidelines for working
        in a 101
Guardian angel 306,
    318–19
    invoking 319

H

Hand shape 252–3
Happiness, affirmation
    for 192
Hardy, Alister 14
Head line 253
Healing
    your aura 315
    with colour 276, 276–9,
        280–95
    crystals 270–73
    energies 264, 266

psychic 264
self- 266
    with sound 274
Health, affirmation for
    192
Hearing 178
Heart
    chakra 64–5, 186–9,
        205, 273
    line 253
    opening your 120–21
Hexagrams 238–41
Higher consciousness
    experiences with
        128–37
"Higher self" 19, 60
Humanistic psychology
    75

I

I Ching 238–41
Images
    in dreams 213
    receiving unseen 210
Imaginary journey 222
Imaging the aura 200
Indigo
    aura 203
    chakra 205
    healing with 290
Inner force 76

Interpretation of dreams
    225, 226
Intuition 18, 20, 98–9,
    172
Intuitive perception,
    levels of 55

J

Journal, psychic 168
Jung, Carl 19, 94, 222

K

Karma 324
Karmic will 190
Kilner, Dr Walter 200
Kirlian photography 51,
    106, 200
Koan 182
Kundalini energy 54

L

Layers of the aura 204
Life line 253
Light
    chakras and 30–31
    in meditation 183
Love, affirmation for 192
Lucid dreaming 228–9
Lunar cycle 39

M

Maharishi Mahesh Yogi
    184
Mandala 185
Mantra, for meditation
    183
Mascots 316
Maslow, Abraham 19, 21
Meditation 44–7, 180–85,
    322
    angelic 309
    and music 274
    exercises 45–7
Medium(s) 112–14, 175,
    300, 326
Moon-gazing exercise 177
Moving objects 196
Music and meditation
    183, 274
Mystical journey 123–4
Mysticism 121–2, 322
Myths 222

N

Names, analyzing 261
New age movement 23
Numbers of destiny 260
Numerology 260

O

Objects, energy from 214
Observing yourself 80
Odin 254
Orange
  aura 203
  chakra 205
  healing with 282
Ouija board 301

P

Pain, dealing with 126–7
Palms, reading 252–3
Pendulum, using 258–9
Perception shifting
  exercise 198
Pets, psychic 232
Pheromones 34–5
Pineal gland 35
Pink aura 202
PK see psychokinesis
Plants
  energy of 216
  healing your 268–9
Poltergeist 310
Positive thought 192–3
Prana 265, 266
Pranic energy 186
Precognition 220–21
Prejudices 78–9

Prosperity, affirmation
  for 192
Psychic
  energy 104–5
  focus 199
  healing 264
  journal 168
  protection 116–17
  training 102–4
  types of 174
Psychology 74–5
Psychometry 214–15
Pyschokinesis 194
Psychosynthesis17

R

REM sleep 224
Reading
  object's energy 215
  palms 252–3
  runes 254–5
  tea leaves 250–51
Receiving
  images 210
  spirit messages 303–5
Red
  aura 202
  chakra 205
  healing with 280
Relaxation, exercise for
  181

Religion 13
Remote viewing 212–13
Runes, reading 254–5

S

Sacral chakra 60–61, 187,
  205, 273
Sacred space 298
Scent see chemical sensing
Scrying 248–9
Self, looking at 74
Self-healing 266
Self identification 90–91
Senses 176
Shaman(s) 175, 264,
  298–9
Shankar, Ravi 274
Sight 176
Silver aura 203
Sixth sense 173
  see also Intuition
Skilful will 190
Sleep, REM 224
Smell 177
Solar plexus chakra
  62–3, 187–9, 205, 272
Sound, healing with 274
Spirit guide 302, 303–5
Spiritual development 12
  therapy as part of 21
Spiritual education 24

Spiritual psychology 17
Spiritual self-awareness 19
Spirituality 13–15
  contemporary 16
  science and 28–30
Strong will 190
Subtle energies 50
Success, affirmation for
  192
Swann, Ingo 212
Synchronicity, visions and
  124–5

T

TM *see* Transcendental
  Meditation
Talismans 316
Tarot
  cards 108–9, 242
  Celtic Cross spread 247
  major arcana 244–5
  reading 242
  self and, revealed 140–61
  simple spread 243
Taste 179
Tea leaves, reading 250–51
Telepathy 208, 210–11
Third-eye vision 199
Thought
  energy 195
  directed 190–92

Throat chakra 66–7,
  187–9, 205, 272
Touch 179
Transcendental
  Meditation 184
Transference 80–81
Transpersonal psychology 17,
  18, 45, 75, 76, 77
Trevelyan, Sir George 23

U

Ultraviolet light 31, 33
Unfoldment 75, 76, 77

V

Violet
  aura 203
  chakra 205
  healing with 292
Vision, third-eye 199
Visions and synchronicity
  124–5
Visualization 48–9, 106, 223,
  229, 230
  of chakras 275
  of colours 279
  exercise 188
  karmic path 325
  self-healing 267

W

Water (element) 237
Water, dowsing for 257
White
  aura 203
  healing with 294
Will, four types of 190

Y

Yellow
  aura 203
  chakra 205
  healing with 284
Yin and yang 238

Z

Zener telepathy test 208,
  210
Zener, Karl 208
Zodiac, signs 236–7

Acknowledgments

Author acknowledgments

In writing this book I have tried to put a seemingly nebulous subject into a format that can be easily understood. I hope I have opened the doors for the reader's further research. I have given some background authorities and scientific ideas; most importantly I have quoted real-life experiences to illustrate some of the many processes that one can encounter in spiritual self-development. In the last chapter I use archetypes to bring alive a story of development. This story is fiction, however the characters' experiences are ones that I have encountered in my work time and time again. I hope you find it readable and it helps you understand that your spiritual processes are unique to you and yet you are not alone on your journey.

Many grateful thanks to all below who have helped this work. Tony Chiva for his King Arthur meditation, and friendship. Angelika Khan for proofreading and support. Terry Larter for his King Arthur meditation. Henry Lincoln for providing me with wonderful quotes. Freda Northam, my 95-year-old next door neighbour for her fantastic mind and wisdom. Alex Soskin for helping me brainstorm. Damien Soskin for his encouragement and Rupert Soskin for writing Chapter 2.

Insight and Intuition courses and personal consultations available. Also individual personal training for overseas students. Contact: Website: www.insightandintuition.com Email:insight.intuition@blueyonder.co.uk.

Carroll & Brown would like to thank:
Illustrations Rupert Soskin for his illustrations throughout part 1, and Jürgen Ziewe for his illustrations on pages 188–9, 192–3, 231, 298–9, 303, 318–19
Text credit page 328 A. Bailey, A Treatise on White Magic (Lucius Press)
Picture Researcher Sandra Schneider
Indexer Madeline Weston

Picture credits and references

Picture credits

Tarot cards on pages **108–9** and **140–61** courtesy of
Lo Scarabeo www.loscarabeo.com;
Illustration on page **83** by Tim Ashton/Début Art; page **167** Getty Images; page **173** (left) Jules Selmes; page **185** AUM, digital image by Judith Cornell Ph.D., award-winning author of *Mandala: Luminous Symbols for Healing*, www.mandala-universe.com; page **190** (left) Telegraph Colour Library, (second left) Art Wolfe/SPL; page **198** Museo Dali, Figueras, Spain/Index/Bridgeman Art Library ©Salvador Dali, Gala-Salvador Dali Foundation,DACS, London 2001; page **200** Manfred Kage/Science Photo Library; page **233** Sue Baker/Science Photo Library; page **244** The Charles Walker Collection; page **245** The Charles Walker Collection; page **271** Elgin and Hall, customer helpline 01677 450100 www.elgin.co.uk; page **301** Getty Images; page **305** (second left) Jules Selmes; page **307** Profile by Odilon Redon 1840–1916, Christies/Bridgeman Art Library; page **328–9** David Parker/Science Photo Library

References

Assagioli, R. Psychosynthesis, Penguin Books, London 1980.

Avila, T. Interior Castle, Image Books, London 1989.

Bloom, W. The New Age, Rider Books, London 1991.

Brennan, B.A. Hands of Light: a Guide to Healing Through the Human Energy Fields, Bantam Books, USA 1988.

Elkins, D. Beyond Religion: A Personal Program for Building a Spiritual Life Outside the Walls of Traditional Religion, Quest Books, USA 1998.

Hardy, A. The Spiritual Nature of Man, Clarendon Press, Oxford 1979.

Heelas, P. The New Age Movement, Blackwell Publishers, Oxford 1996.

Heron, J. The Facilitators Handbook, Kogan Page, London 1989.

Judith, A. Wheels of Life: A User's Guide to the Chakra System, Llewellyn Publications, USA 1990.

Jung. C. G. Collected Works, Routlege Kegan Paul, London 1960.

Leadbeater, C. W. The Chakras, Theosophical Publishing, USA 1996.

Lyons, J.W. "The Mechanism of Dowsing: A Conceptual Model", York University 2003.

Maslow, A. Towards a Psychology of Being, John Wiley, Chichester 1999.

Miller, H. The Definitive Wee Book on Dowsing, Penwith Press, Cornwall 2002.

Rogers, C. Freedom to Learn, Macmillan College Publishing Press, USA 1994.

Rowan, J. The Transpersonal, Routledge, London 1993.

Sogyal Rinpoche The Tibetan Book of Living and Dying, Random House, London 1992.

Soskin, J. "Insight and Intuition", College of Psychic Studies, London 1996.

Soskin, J. "Psycho-spiritual Studies as Part of a Learning Programme", Transpersonal Psychology Review, Vol. 2 No 1, 2003.

Tart, C. Open Mind, Discriminating Mind; Reflections on Human Possibilities, Harper Row, London 1989.

Tosey, P. "Energies: A Perspective on Organizations and Change", School of Educational Studies, University of Surrey 1996.

Trevelyan G. Exploration into God, Gateway Books, Bath 1991.

Wilber, K. Integral Psychology: Consciousness, Spirit, Psychology, Therapy, Shambhala, London 2000.